Advance Praise fo

MW01671516

"John Cox's new book *The Newsom Nightmare* is as frightening as *A Nightmare on Elm Street*. Cox chronicles how Newsom's stream of leftist policies have wrecked California's once vibrant economy and turned iconic cities like San Francisco into unlivable bastions of crime, homelessness, high taxes, poverty and despair. Now Democrats want Newsom to run for president and do to America what he has done to the once-Golden State. God forbid."

–Stephen Moore, Economist and Author,
Serves as a Distinguished Fellow in Economics
at The Heritage Foundation and is a Co-Founder
of The Committee to Unleash Prosperity.

"One of the few things on which Red and Blue America can agree is that our political system is broken, but most political reformers tend to come from the Democratic party and its allies. Now comes respected conservative leader John Cox to join the debate and to offer his fascinating prescription for making our system work the way the founders intended. Whether you voted for Gavin Newsom or against him, you should be part of this conversation about how the people deserve to have a greater voice in our politics and government."

–Dan Schnur, Teaches Political Communications at USC,
Pepperdine, and UC-Berkeley, Former National Communications
Director for the 2000 Presidential Campaign of US Senator
John McCain—Another Conservative Reformer

THE NEWSOM NIGHTMARE

The California Catastrophe and How to Reform Our Broken System

JOHN H. COX

Post Hill PRESS

A POST HILL PRESS BOOK
ISBN: 979-8-88845-112-0
ISBN (eBook): 979-8-88845-113-7

The Newsom Nightmare:
The California Catastrophe and How to Reform Our Broken System

Cover design by Jim Villaflores

Post Hill Press
New York • Nashville
posthillpress.com

Published in the United States of America
1 2 3 4 5 6 7 8 9 10

I dedicate this book to my mother and my ancestors on her side who braved all manner of difficulty to come to America, believing, as I do, that it is the greatest nation in the history of the world. Not because of its culture or sports or entertainment but because it is a place where average people can achieve their dreams. I dedicate this book as well to my wonderful wife and four daughters who have demonstrated their love for their father and their country.

CONTENTS

PREFACE

THE NATURE OF THE PROBLEM ALONG WITH A PROPOSED SOLUTION

As you read this book, you'll see that the many problems facing my adoptive state, California, in large measure impact the greater United States. That's no accident as Californians figure prominently in the national government seated in Washington, D.C. As of this writing, the Speaker of the House, the vice president, the secretary of Health and Human Services, and myriad other officials and elected representatives, all with significant power, got their start and learned their craft in the Golden State.

What is that craft? It's the eternal basis of politics—influence peddling. From time immemorial, the essence of political power, from first recorded history, has been about small groups trying to control larger groups of people for their own purposes—money, riches, power, sex. Motivations differ, but the history of the world is about some person or small group working to control others for their own benefit.

Various cities in ancient Greece sought democratic systems to diffuse power and empower people. Even they failed, empowering small groups of elites and nobles. Through kings, emperors and despots, humans have experienced the pain of small groups with influence ruling them.

The United States was formed in the 18th century as a rebellion against elite rule. Our system of checks and balances was formed by men—yes, they were exclusively men—who opposed corrupted leadership and lack of representation and were determined to do something about it. They created a government that they hoped would be immune from influence peddling and arbitrary action—a more perfect union of the people, by the people and for the people.

We come to the 21st century and our perfect union has survived but is struggling with a breakdown of democratic power sharing with the people our founders nobly envisioned. Today we are saddled with a political system controlled more by money and media than by the people.

Too often, power is obtained and wielded through celebrity and connections more than good character, knowledge, compassion, and integrity. This situation produced a Hobson's choice in the last presidential election, where the choice was between a billionaire former reality TV star who communicated insults and complaints via Twitter against an aging and fast-declining career politician who had occupied various federal offices for almost half a century.

At the same time, the Senate and House are primarily populated by politicians (both on the Right and Left) more skilled in fundraising and log rolling than in crafting policy and communicating thoughtfully and clearly with their constituents. Their main talents rise in playing off interest groups and wealthy people and corporations against one another for campaign contributions and other support. They're also expertly trained in currying favor with the media—which is now clearly divided on the Right and Left—and which holds considerable sway over our elections. This is not only true of our national houses but is true of most state legislative bodies as well, especially large states like California.

What's been the reaction of the voters to this state of affairs? Apathy, cynicism, and disgust are the most common descriptives used. People vote in presidential races but if you look at state and local races, the turnout numbers are pitiful. California just had a primary election where less than 25 percent of voters turned out; among "no party preference" voters, the number was less than 20 percent. The recent turnout for the general election is was one of the lowest in decades.

Worse is voter knowledge. Relatively few people know who the members of the Supreme Court are, let alone their local representatives. Most have never met their elected representatives or know nothing about their backgrounds or character.

Every election season, voters—the few who pay attention—are treated to a steady diet of advertising that is fairly geared to slogans or punch lines when they aren't directed at outright smears or negative messages of some form or fashion. This barrage doesn't help as people watching this are even more turned off and cynical. They don't believe the positive spin and the negatives repel them. They also don't trust their representatives. They know they are nothing more than professional fundraisers or are rich elites trying to buy public office for their own aggrandizement.

We don't get the best and the brightest to run for public office. Few successful people want to subject themselves to the constant media barrage or the need to spend most of their time on the phone begging for money. Running for any office involves constant pleading for dollars along with currying favor with media that hold the keys to free publicity and name recognition. Now, with recent focus on the tax returns of the former president, they have to worry about intense scrutiny of their most personal financial data and experience going back decades. Most successful people with any private life say, "Thanks, but no thanks" to such a pursuit.

The good news in all this is that there is a way to change the system for the better so that we get a government that performs what we ask of it in a competent and truthful manner. It involves changing our system ever so slightly but with huge implications so that political campaigns aren't about money or media but about person to person or door-to-door campaigning and individual persuasion. Character and leadership would once again dictate success in the political arena. As such, this isn't just going to be a book about problems and complaints. I'm going to suggest solutions to the problems I highlight.

The problems we face aren't there by accident. They result mostly from some person or group benefiting from a problem. The key to solving these problems is to fashion solutions that reflect good practice and policy, forged by intelligent and well-thought-out tradeoffs that have the effect of helping the vast majority of our people rather than favoring a narrow interest or group.

I'm going to describe the background of why I ran for governor: to help cure the many ills mismanagement of California has brought, as well as an effort to reform its electoral system through small districts, called Hear the People, that I believe will help correct these ills.

Some will read this book as a criticism targeted at Gavin Newsom as the leader of the state and the cause of the mismanagement of the state, but understand that I am using my state's governor as just one major exemplar of the problem and he is certainly not the only one. I live in California and studied the issues for years before I started the race for Governor. As such I developed a keen insight into why California is in the condition it is. Like too many of our states, California is essentially run by special interest groups for their own benefit and Newsom is the leader of that band with a dominant media cheerleading him on.

There is little indication that Newsom believes changing our system should be a high priority. He did write a book, *Citizenville*, not too long ago, about a digital revolution transforming government. He may, in fact, appreciate the fact that small districts, with local representatives connected through our modern interactive technology, is a much better system to remove the corruptive power of money, media, and special interest groups. It would be wonderful if he and his followers would accept the challenge to change the status quo—and embrace the reforms I propose in this book.

You will see how special interest control in California is accelerating the descent of California such that it is virtually unaffordable and unlivable unless you are very wealthy. The special interests benefit from that descent and use their collective power to maintain it. As the leader of state government, Newsom could have pressed for reforms but has been noticeably absent. Thus, California's problems have gotten worse under his leadership. The scariest part is that with a compliant local and national media—which he curates by focusing on highly contentious "social" issues—Newsom may emerge as a candidate for president of the United States in 2024. This "nightmare" needs to be avoided. Other states such as Illinois and Michigan have governors who follow this technique on the Left as there are others on the Right—Florida and Texas among them—that also use the system to their own ends. However, Newsom is the most prominent and skillful at this craft, which has made our largest and wealthiest state also our country's most dysfunctional. This book explains how our present electoral structure fosters this gross mismanagement, takes us through the effort to recall the Governor, and lays out positive, nonpartisan solutions.

Most of all, this book clearly lays out a solution to the pay-to-play political culture that fosters this "California Catastrophe." It's all about changing the way our campaigns are run to emphasize small districts that allow person to person campaigns that don't require money or media and that foster voter involvement and accountability. This requires a rethinking of how we elect our leaders. I think even Mr. Newsom would believe it is a long overdue reform that would not only lessen the power of money and media but also bring about more voter involvement. I will detail how we can make that happen in a way that works for us, not against us. Success usually faces daunting challenges. But it can be achieved. It just takes strength of purpose, discipline, and leadership.

Let's get to work.

PART 1

RECALL AND REFORM

CHAPTER 1

ASK NOT WHAT YOU CAN DO FOR YOUR DONORS

On a September afternoon in 2015, I stood looking up at the dome of the California State Capitol building in Sacramento. In front of me, spread across the capitol's steps, were one-hundred and twenty cardboard cutouts, each one a life-sized photographic representation of a member of the California State Legislature. They were exact recreations, with one key difference. Each member's clothing was adorned with logos of the corporations and special-interest groups that had given them money. Emblems of donors like Chevron and AT&T, and unions such as the California Teachers Association, covered their blazers and pantsuits neck to cuff.

As I surveyed my work, a middle-aged woman noticed the strange scene and did a double take. Then I saw her crack a smile. "You actually have to do this," she shouted as she crossed the street.

"That's the idea," I replied. I had recently turned sixty years old, but I felt as excited as I had been as a nine-year-old kid, entertaining my mother by reciting JFK's "Ask not what your country can do for you—ask what you can do for your country" speech across the dinner table.

What *was* I doing for my country? That day's demonstration was part of an initiative I was spearheading called California Is Not For Sale. It was a proposed ballot measure requiring legislators to wear the logos of their top donors emblazoned on their clothing whenever they walked onto the senate or assembly floor. For months, I had been trying to stir up the passions of voters by showing them that their elected leaders more closely resembled logo-laden NASCAR drivers than public servants and trying to collect the 350,000 signatures needed to get the initiative on the ballot. This was an idea I borrowed from a couple of well-known comedians who had posited it for laughs.

Though the initiative was meant to be shocking and humorous, I was deadly serious about the reason behind it. America is a democratic republic. We elect people to represent us and make decisions on our behalf. But our elected leaders too often act as agents for elite donors who control big tech, big labor unions, and deep-pocketed lobbying organizations. A never-ending flow of money from corporations and special-interest groups has turned politicians into professional fundraisers. They must constantly spend time and energy raising money, which distracts from their job of passing legislation and makes them unduly beholden to donors.

California Is Not For Sale sparked a storm of news coverage in outlets such as *Fox* and the *Huffington Post*. "If you came down from Mars and you looked at our electoral system, you'd say to yourself, 'How dumb is this?'" I told the *Washington Times* that November. "You've got a system under which people who want something from government fund the campaigns of the people who make the decisions." Despite a groundswell of public support and getting 250,000 signatures, my initiative fell 100,000 names short of qualifying.

I was disappointed but not surprised, a feeling familiar to anyone who has tried their hand in the political arena. I had seen the power of money in politics firsthand when I ran for Congress in Illinois in 2000. During that race, my opponents depended upon special-interest money to run their campaigns and relied on their campaign workers to reach voters. Unions had operated phone banks, organized get-out-the-vote drives, and collected and solicited ballots, primarily on behalf of Democrats, who went out of their way to cater to the desires of the unions and their bosses. Republicans worked with businesses and religious groups who did the same. I realized that the dysfunction in U.S. Congress was directly traceable to campaign funders' power over politicians.

When I ran for president seven years later, I again saw how the media determined who succeeded and who didn't. I campaigned all over Iowa, New Hampshire, and South Carolina, getting pretty far with grassroots Republicans. At one point, fifty-five of the ninety-nine Iowa GOP county chairs supported me. Yet the media refused to cover me. They would not let me into the televised debates because I was not sufficiently well-known nationally. My opponents, exclusively well-known politicians familiar to the media, got into the debates and therefore got the name recognition which got them the funding from special-interest groups and large corporations and they perpetuated a broken system. Thus, I faced the classic tautology—I couldn't get name recognition afforded by the debates because I wasn't well-known enough to qualify for the debates.

But I learned something vital during my 2007 presidential bid while campaigning in New Hampshire. New Hampshire has only about a million people, but they have four hundred members in their House of Representatives. They have microdistricts, and each House member only represents a few thousand people, so no candidate must spend much money to stand for office. Legislative candidates can walk door-to-door and meet their voters. They were elected on their ideas and character, not through television ads or mass mailers. You avoid becoming beholden to funders or lobbyists when you don't have to raise money to get elected. That gives an elected official the freedom to put the people first, not the puppet masters.

After 2008, I got out of politics for three years. During that time, I witnessed the prevalence of money in politics getting worse. In 2010, a Supreme Court ruling in *Citizens United v. Federal Election Commission* essentially removed limits on corporations—and unions—from contributing to elections. Any entity, including super PACs, could now run ads without limitation. While I agreed with the decision on a constitutional basis, the practical result further entrenched political influence toward wealthy donors and corporations. Election spending ballooned to ridiculous proportions. Ordinary people were left on the sidelines, divorced from democracy.

I watched people from all ends of the political spectrum propose solutions. I spoke with a Harvard professor named Larry Lessig, who wanted to ban *all* contributions and rely solely on public finance. Another solution proposed by the Left was ranked-choice voting, which allows voters to rank candidates in order of preference and is now in use in Alaska, New York City, and some other places. If no candidate gets the majority of the vote, the candidate with the least support is eliminated, and the process continues until a candidate wins more than half of the vote. Yet none of these plans truly addressed the elephant in the room—the cost and power of mass media. Each of these so-called solutions kept in place the large-scale campaigns that cost a lot and enable the media to essentially pick and choose which candidates to cover and give them a leg up. As I saw it, the *only* way to fix the problem was to bring the campaigns to a small enough level where they are accountable, personal, and one-on-one. But I remained on the sidelines, turning the problem over in my mind.

Then I moved to California in 2011. I was gobsmacked by the pay-to-play nature of politics in Sacramento. And I saw how California's size enables lobbyists to control power, enabling their priorities to supercede good policy. California had enacted term limits in the '90s. It not only failed but made the problem worse as special-interest groups had no objection to buying a new set of politicians every twelve years. In fact, they likely favored this as politicians would be termed out before they could muster the political savvy and strength to stand up to the special-interest groups. A state like California with forty million people has only forty state senators and eighty assembly members. Each senator represents a million people. That is more people than in a congressional district. Assembly districts are half as big, but each assemblyman or assemblywoman is responsible for 500,000 people. Campaigns in districts that large require a huge media effort, empowering the media and campaign funders.

I thought there had to be a way to have our leaders elected based on something other than media influence and money. How could we inject people with character, experience, passion, and empathy into the political system? These factors should qualify our leaders—not how much cash their donors can spend or how cozy they are with the media! I remembered my experience in New Hampshire, where I met the state's microdistrict representatives on the campaign trail, in libraries, and Rotary Clubs. By and large, they were solid Americans. They were local restaurant owners, retired executives, and mothers who had once been lawyers but left the workforce to raise a family—salt-of-the-earth people. None of them bought television or radio ads. They got elected by going door-to-door, attending town hall meetings, and persuading voters one by one.

I asked myself: *if this could work in a small state like New Hampshire, could it work with a larger state like California or even the federal government?* I gathered a team of lawyers, political professionals, and professors from both sides of the aisle and fleshed out the idea. We call it Hear the People. The basic concept was to subdivide California's huge districts into one hundred much smaller districts, each with its own neighborhood legislator. Those one hundred people wouldn't go to Sacramento. They would meet in their community and select *one* of those one hundred people to go to Sacramento. Thus, you'd still get forty senators and eighty assemblymembers in Sacramento. But they would be elected by, and accountable to, the ninety-nine neighborhood representatives who remain back home in their districts.

This plan would remove the corrupting influence of special-interest money from politics. By shrinking the size of legislative districts down to the neighborhood level, any individual could run for Congress, senate, or assembly with a budget of just a few hundred dollars. Campaigns would be about personal contact, not mass media. We drafted an initiative and had a study commissioned on the idea by the Institute for Politics at Claremont McKenna College. This favorable study found that our plan would result in better legislation because the people could formulate policy, not what pleased a special-interest group.

I was tremendously excited. Hear the People would take a hammer to the elites, media, campaign funders, and influence peddlers. Ordinary people could run and have a fighting chance. Money wouldn't be needed. Battles would play out on voters' doorsteps or in town hall meetings, not on cable TV representing one side or the other. Candidates wouldn't use angry TV and radio ads and vicious mailers.

Hear the People would increase political competition because it would be easy to run for office in a tiny district. Competition drives innovation and change. Greater political competition means more competition and innovation in all other avenues of life, like education, healthcare, housing, business, banking, communications, the internet, and energy.

The key to obtaining accountability is through competition. Opposition groups in large districts use their funding to stop reforms they don't want or interrupt their power structure or profit stream. For example, the teachers' unions fight tooth and nail against school choice or any attempt at school reform or improvement. Deep-pocketed trial lawyers stop any tort reform. Oil companies obstruct the reform of tax incentives for drilling. Big pharma is greedy for government contracts that bring in billions and uses its financial might to get those deals. Environmental lobbyists want more regulations and higher energy prices. There's no free lunch. All these players want something for the money they contribute: power. Hear the People severely curtails but doesn't eliminate the ability of these groups to help elect people and influence policy; they just had to do it the old-fashioned way—make a persuasive and compelling argument.

For the next five years, from 2011 to 2016, I spent my own money to get this initiative on the ballot. We made progress, and Californians seemed genuinely excited about the plan. But our grassroots efforts kept falling short of the number of signatures needed to qualify for the ballot. So, in 2017, I came up with a new plan. I'd attack the issue from two angles: 1. hire a professional signature collection firm, and 2. promote Hear the People in conjunction with a run for governor. If my NASCAR-inspired initiative had been my tongue-in-cheek way to bring awareness to this issue, a gubernatorial run would be a serious effort to publicize it. A governor's race would attract media attention, and I could expose this idea to the masses. I truly wanted to be governor to address the mismanagement that springs from the special-interest corruption in Sacramento and if I was to be successful in addressing it, I would need a legislature that would work with me, not the special-interest groups.

I hit the campaign trail, giving speeches about Hear the People at stops all across California. The response was heartening—people were sick of the swamp in Sacramento and told me that if this initiative passed, they would run for office. They would be accountable to their neighbors. They would be the change they wanted to see in their communities. But, in February 2018, we again came up short, this time by only 25,000 signatures. While the measure didn't make it to the ballot, I felt I had started a statewide conversation about getting money out of politics and putting power back in the hands of ordinary Americans.

Then, in June 2018, I surprised everyone, winning enough votes to beat out my Democratic rival Antonio Villaraigosa to make the top two in the general election. Now I had to face Newsom in November, going up against the entrenched powers that *really* run California. By some estimates, Newsom raised over $100 million for the general election, compared to my $11 million. He also had a compliant and supportive media that gave him a pass in failing to debate me.

I thought that with an open governor's seat and the many problems facing California—homelessness, cost of living, crime, shortages of energy and water, wildfires, and other issues—there would be a lot of people who would want to embrace the idea that change was needed and a businessman would be the best leader to address the solutions needed. California is home to more billionaires than any place on earth—surely many of them would step up to help—but they were apparently cowed by the national politics of the moment as well as fear of the unknown—and they kept their wallets firmly in the pockets, not helping my campaign.

During my hopelessly underfunded campaign, I tried to caution voters that electing Gavin Newsom to replace Jerry Brown as chief executive of the nation's most populated state and its largest economy would put us all in for rough sledding. Brown was a political warhorse. While liberal, he understood the limits of government and worked to apply his liberal principles pragmatically. Brown was a fiscal conservative compared to the current crop of left-wing Democrats, who consciously stiff-armed Brown once he left office. He tried to hold back the interest groups that corrupt Sacramento. He was close to eighty years old and held no ambitions to advance politically.

Newsom is a different beast; his political aspirations are centered on gaining the White House. Newsom overwhelmed me with his superior money and name recognition. I couldn't overcome his tsunami of ads. But when I reflect on that time, my thoughts are not consumed by my defeat in the general election. Instead, I think back to my work to advance Hear the People.

This book aims to introduce Hear the People into the national conversation as a small district restructuring in the way we elect Congress. We call it "Hear the People." It's an idea—a "big solution" that has the power to transform our democracy, impacting almost every issue that faces us as a state or nation.

I view California as a microcosm of America—I'm sure you've read the saying, "As goes California, so goes the rest of the nation." There's a good deal of truth to it. Right now, that's happening in the wrong direction—the "Californication" of the nation is a topic I'll dive into throughout this book. But if we can use this small district system to put power back in the hands of the people in the Golden State, it has the potential to spread across the country.

Why I Care—My Background

Losing elections is frustrating, but it's never deterred me from trying to improve our broken political system. I could lose one hundred elections, and I'd still be trying to upset the status quo and spearhead initiatives like Hear the People. Public service is my calling.

I get that from my mother, Priscilla Pick, a public school teacher born in 1921. As a young boy without a father figure, I looked up to my mother. Because she adored John F. Kennedy, I learned a lot about him. By age nine, I could imitate his Boston accent perfectly. Over time, JFK's call to each of us to "Ask yourself not what your country can do for you can offer but what ask you can do for your country" embedded itself in my brain.

My maternal family's roots were in Poland in the old Russian Empire. One of my early ancestors was a deserter from the czar's army. The czar used peasants like cattle, putting them in *his* armies to carry out *his* wars, which were about fighting for power and control. He and his aristocrats didn't give a damn about the masses—and many of our current leaders echo that sentiment.

My mother's family entered America through Ellis Island. My maternal grandfather, Albert Pick, moved to Chicago to open a hardware store on the south side. My uncle also had a small hardware store in Chicago, which he operated until about twenty years ago. It was situated on the south side, in a low-income neighborhood. As a small business owner, he could compete and make a living. Today, many small businesses do not have that opportunity.

In 1940, my mom ventured out west to the University of California at Berkeley for her undergraduate degree. There began my connection to California. In 1940, college tuition at UC Berkeley was nearly free for residents, and tuition for nonresidents was $75 per year (about $1,500 today). Getting a higher education was possible for my working-class mom. Today at Berkeley, out-of-state tuition is $44,007. Graduates labor under enormous debt and often never catch up. As we'll later discuss, administrative costs and interest group influence have driven up costs. My mother earned two master's degrees—in Spanish literature and library science.

After my older brother was born in San Jose and she had to divorce his alcoholic father, my mother moved back to Chicago to be with her family, where she met my biological father, Albert Kaplan. My father took no responsibility for me, urging her to "Get rid of the problem." At the time, my mother was young and confused, unmarried, and already had a two-year-old. She admitted that had abortion been legal, she probably *would* have aborted me. She kept me, primarily because the law protected me. To some degree, this reality became the genesis of my lifelong aversion to abortion and my dedication to taking responsibility—as a man and a human being.

I adored my mother because she could have given me away, but she kept me. She married my biological father to have a father on my birth certificate. They divorced soon after my birth. I never heard from or saw him again. He never supported my mother or me. Since my father declined responsibility for me, I was determined to be a responsible person in my own life. Society requires men to step up as a father.

My mom remarried and took a job as a public school teacher in Chicago. She was an excellent teacher, but no housekeeper. By age ten, I had to cook, clean, and do laundry. I'd be the first to admit I didn't enjoy childhood. But it taught me responsibility.

My mother was political, owing to her days at Berkeley, and a dedicated Democrat. She loved the idealism that John F. Kennedy inspired. That love carried over to Bobby Kennedy, who continued his brother's mission. I will forever remember being seated in front of the television on June 5, 1968, watching the California primary celebration for Bobby, broadcast from the Ambassador Hotel in Los Angeles. It was midnight in Chicago, and I was not yet thirteen when I witnessed his assassination in real time. It was indelibly etched in my mind.

Another early childhood memory was helping my mother at school and seeing her harrowing experiences dealing with the Chicago public school system's bureaucracy and corruption. She would come home during my preteen and teen years crying about the principals' incompetence and arbitrary behavior. She would explain that many of these "leaders" were political appointees or had political sponsors based on relationships with key politicians. I would see the results going to school with my mom to help her tutor her students in reading. I was five to eight years younger than them, yet I was way ahead in reading skills. This taught me how political influence could undermine public education at an early age.

I worked hard in school, getting through high school and college with honors, where I majored in accounting. After college, I got a job at the accounting firm Coopers & Lybrand, where I worked during the day while attending law school at night at IIT/Kent College of Law in downtown Chicago. I graduated at the top of my law school class while working sixty to seventy hours a week at my accounting firm. It was hard work, but I led the tax department in overtime hours, getting to work at 5:30 in the morning and leaving at 6:00 at night to go to law school for three hours. I started to lean Republican when I worked at Coopers, doing tax returns for people in the 70 percent tax bracket. With tax rates so high, there was a disincentive to take risks. If you made a profit, you kept only the 30 percent the government didn't take. I felt we would increase investments and spur innovation if rates were lower. Folks building businesses would take more risks, knowing they would keep more of their profits.

After obtaining my juris doctorate in law, I quit Coopers & Lybrand and grabbed an opportunity to work for the law firm Devoe, Shadur & Krupp. I also got married and started a family. Devoe, Shadur & Krupp was a liberal Democratic law firm, but my views continued to change as Ronald Reagan ascended the political ladder. Reagan presented a plan to reduce tax rates to revive the economy and motivate entrepreneurs to put their money at risk. My confidence in reducing taxes converted me into a Reagan Republican. Reagan's economic and social ideas sat well with me. I embraced him and registered as a Republican. We could certainly use another Ronald Reagan to lead us out of the mess we're in today. Moving to the Republican party was a significant change. My family was *all* Democrats. I didn't know any Republicans for a long time.

After a year with the law firm, I decided to take a chance. I still had many tax return clients who stuck with me over the years, so I launched my own firm in 1981. I rented an office in Skokie, Illinois, and hung up my shingle. I was a tax attorney, doing estate plans, corporate work, and occasionally handled a little litigation. Owning my own business felt like carving out my slice of the American Dream. It was accessible to me because, back then, corporate taxes were significantly lower. Today, California has a high corporate income tax rate that discourages entrepreneurs while feeding the bureaucracy.

Yet, as happens, life throws you unexpected curveballs. Around May, 1995, I came home from playing golf one early Saturday morning, and my wife was on the floor of our bathroom, crying and telling me that she didn't love me anymore. Her words struck me like a bullet between the eyes. We were both turning forty and had been married for eighteen years. Our daughters were young, only eight, ten, and twelve. I thought I was a good husband and father, involved with my children and the community, and now it all seemed for naught. I gritted my teeth and worked through the pain. After we finalized the divorce, I rented a house in Wilmette, a suburb close to my kids. I continue to be an essential part of my children's lives. I like to think it made a difference in their eyes while presenting them with a role model for their future family responsibilities.

Then I met Sarah Hall on a blind date. She was a fundraiser who had worked for Children's Memorial Hospital and then for a Chicago charity called Urban Gateways. We had many shared interests, not least of which was politics. She remembered seeing one of my ads when I ran for Congress in 2000. It was an ad about abortion and how it leaves a hole. The ad showed me pushing one of my daughters on a swing and watching her disappear. It made an impression on Sarah. We decided to marry a few months after our first date. It was a whirlwind courtship and one of the best times in my life. We have a daughter, Julianne, who is now a teenager.

In 2011, I moved my family to California. I chose San Diego, specifically Rancho Santa Fe. My mother had retired to Fresno in 1980, and it felt like our American story had come full circle. California had so much I wanted for myself and my family: beaches, mountains, and deserts. But the state's sad state of political affairs troubled me. After everything I had gone through in my life, from sitting in my mother's classroom as a boy to running for Senate, I couldn't sit idly by watching my new home wither on the vine. And so, I began a period of vigorous political activism that started with my idea for Hear the People and culminated in my run for governor in 2018.

After the 2018 gubernatorial election, I thought about what I should do next. I desperately wanted another chance to bring the political ideals I had spent a lifetime cultivating back into the public arena. Then, in the dark days of a global pandemic, the rumblings of a recall supplied my chance.

CHAPTER 2

THE RECALL

In his farewell address in 1796, President Washington warned against concentrating power into the hands of unscrupulous politicians within one political party. He stated:

> ...They [political parties] are likely in the course of time and things, to become potent engines, by which cunning, ambitious, and unprincipled men will be enabled to subvert the power of the people and to usurp for themselves the reins of government, destroying afterwards the very engines which have lifted them to unjust dominion.

Washington was prescient. It holds true today in California. For almost three decades, one party has held power in California. Democrats outnumber Republicans by nearly two to one in registration. About 30 percent are independently registered to parties other than the two major ones or are "no party preference" voters. The last Republican presidential candidate who carried California was George H. W. Bush in 1988. No sitting Democratic governor has lost reelection since Ronald Reagan beat Pat Brown in 1966.

Thriving with one-party hegemony, Democrats have solidified and expanded their grip on power through well-funded and well-organized power seekers. The key insiders include public-sector unions, trial lawyers, and extremist environmental groups. All this has led California down a dangerous path toward expansive, incompetent government and, lately, as the Democratic party swings further to the Left, toward a form of socialism that the late Communist leader, Leon Trotsky, espoused through his ideas of a "permanent revolution" of the proletariat against capitalism and those he deemed to be elites. If you delve into what these individuals believe, their vision is frightening and runs counter to the values upon which this great nation was founded.

Is that an overstatement? Think back to how the state tried to quash our freedoms during the COVID-19 pandemic. Remember Sacramento's rules for celebrating the holidays? Remember no singing? Was your small business shuttered for months on end while Walmart and Costco remained open? Were your children in Zoom school at your kitchen table while you worked from home, pulling your hair out and praying for schools to reopen their doors? In contrast, a patronizing governor's children thrived in expensive elite private schools that had the resources to conduct in-classroom education.

Having a single-party supermajority govern every branch of government throws the checks and balances crucial to representative democracy off kilter. It renders democracy impotent. Politicians operate with impunity. They no longer are accountable. Influence peddling, pay-to-play activities, and corruption thrive in Sacramento. Our elected leaders are failing us.

That was the message that I tried to get across in my campaign for governor during the 2021 recall election. To tell that story, I have to tell the whole story of the recall.

After he was elected in 2018, Gavin Newsom vindicated our fears by catering to special-interest pressure groups. He ended the death penalty in

California, a move liberal groups had long clamored for, even though voter initiatives affirmed voters' desire to retain the death penalty. Indeed, voters made it clear they wanted to accelerate the execution process, which endless appeals had bogged down. Caving in to the teachers' unions, he supported legislation that would make it more expensive and difficult to establish and maintain competitive charter schools.

He fell behind schedule on his pet project, the bullet train. Then he wavered on support. First, he said he said he would end this waste of money. Then he capitulated to union pressure and a possible claim from the federal government for a refund of its advances toward its construction and reversed himself. In the meantime, housing costs soared, homelessness worsened, crime began to spiral out of control, traffic was snarled, and he failed even to suggest a solution to the state's long-running challenges posed by shortages of water and electricity and the threat of dangerous wildfires.

By February of 2020, Californians were fed up. They wanted change. They had tired of backroom deals that enriched lobbyists, donors, and billionaires. Sacramento's love affair with progressive cancel-culture, left-wing ideology sickened them.

Two citizens decided to do something about it. In February 2020, Orrin Heatlie, a former Yolo County sheriff's deputy, and Mike Netter of Rebuild California filed a petition to recall Gavin Newsom. They began their collecting signatures with $1,000 in seed money. Heatlie told the *Desert Sun*, "I'm participating in something that is monumental and historic, and it's something that, you know, this country was founded on," he said. "We're bringing government back to represent the people."

The prepandemic petition defined a credible rationale for recalling Newsom. "Laws he endorsed favor foreign nationals, in our country illegally, over that of our own citizens. People in this state suffer the highest taxes in the nation, the highest homelessness rates, and the lowest quality of life as a result," it stated. "He has imposed sanctuary state status and fails to enforce immigration laws. He unilaterally overruled the will of the people regarding the death penalty. He seeks to impose additional burdens on our state by the following; removing the protections of Proposition 13, rationing our water use, increasing taxes and restricting parental rights."

The pandemic shutdown that Newsom initiated worsened the situation. Newsom's executive orders shuttered small restaurants. Churches were forbidden to conduct services. Children were forced to attend school from home computers, essentially shutting out many children who lacked that capability. Newsom declared a state of emergency—which continues to this day—and abused it to promulgate new rules. The politicians picked winners and losers in the economy. They identified some businesses and activities as "essential," while leaving others behind. Newsom entered into major contracts with medical equipment suppliers without accountability or review.

Gavin Newsom's abuse of power fueled the recall effort.

The grassroots efforts relied on volunteers to collect signatures. They used social media and conservative news outlets to spread their message. But gathering the almost one and a half million signatures needed to qualify a recall proved challenging due to COVID restrictions and closures. Heatlie and Netter faced an uphill climb. The last successful petition to recall the governor came in 2003 when voters recalled Governor Gray Davis. Arnold Schwarzenegger, California's last Republican governor, replaced Davis. Since 2003, California's changing demographics have turned the state a deeper blue, further impeding the recall effort.

At the same time, news was breaking about a novel coronavirus spreading from China to Europe and the United States. The first documented case in the U.S. was detected in Washington state on January 21, 2020. Five days later, health officials identified the third case in an Orange County man who had traveled to Wuhan, China. This was the first known case of COVID-19 in California.

On March 13, the same day President Donald Trump declared a national state of emergency, most of California's nearly eleven thousand public schools suspended in-person instruction for two weeks. Almost six million public school students began online instruction, commonly known as Zoom school. The school closures were slated to last for two weeks. On March 19, 2020, Governor Newsom issued a statewide shelter in place order, closing down the state. He ordered residents to stay at home except for essential business or risk a $1,000 fine or six months imprisonment. Essential businesses were permitted to remain open, but the governor shuttered all businesses he deemed not essential, as well as churches. By the end of March, Newsom had closed schools for the remainder of the school year.

While the pandemic gained steam, trouble was brewing at the state Employment Development Division (EDD). The massive business closures due to the governor's decree cost 2.4 million people their jobs in April. Statewide unemployment would reach a record high of 16.3 percent, with some hard-hit areas like Los Angeles topping out at over 20 percent. Millions of Californians filed for unemployment. It was time for Sacramento to step up.

On March 17, 2020, as the state closed down and unemployment skyrocketed, the EDD closed its doors and turned off its phones. When the agency put up a new website to deal with claims, it was quickly overrun. The EDD was kind enough to post a helpful sign: "We are having problems. Please check back later." Problems indeed. In 2020, 99 percent of calls to the agency went unanswered. Assemblymember Jim Patterson, R-Fresno, told the *Sacramento Bee*, "The one thing that remains true with all these backlogs is an undercurrent of incompetency. EDD has hurt a lot of good people who have yet to be paid what they are owed."

Fraud surfaced as a problem at the agency. Forty-five thousand prison inmates, including some on death row, collected an estimated $1 billion in fraudulent claims. Let me say that again. Incarcerated criminals copped an estimated $1 billion in fraudulent claims. No wonder taxes in this state keep going up, up, and away. One claim was filed in the name of convicted killer Scott Peterson, who murdered his wife Laci and their unborn child. Law enforcement officials believe organized crime rings saw an opportunity to use unemployment insurance money to fund human trafficking, drug rings, and gun smuggling.

One woman collected $21,000 under the name and social security number of Senator Dianne Feinstein. An "unemployed actor" who had just celebrated her first birthday collected $167 a week in fraudulent checks. Fontrell Antonio Baines, a rapper who performs as Nuke Bizzle, bilked the agency for $1.2 million and bragged about it on YouTube.

Few people know that the EDD had a fraud detection system that was working well from 2013 to 2016. Then old-school politicians decided the $2 million price tag was too high. They refused to purchase the software for the following year. Many experts believe that the system would have prevented billions of dollars in fraud. The federal government had also developed a system to check Social Security numbers against prison inmates. But, ever mindful of illegal immigrants with fake numbers, California politicians refused to participate in this system. Their action opened up the unemployment insurance system to prisoner fraud.

While unemployed and increasingly desperate Californians needed Gavin Newsom to fix an urgent problem, the governor busied himself releasing prisoners from jail to protect them from the coronavirus. Many questioned why he was prioritizing convicted criminals over unemployed Californians.

Newsom waited until his governor's seat got hot before taking action. Democrats understood the meltdown at the EDD made the governor vulnerable to recall. Newsom created a task force to look into problems at the besieged agency. Later, the same day that California's secretary of state declared that enough signatures had been collected to force a recall election, Newsom's unemployment task force announced a string of arrests and a series of investigations into fraudulent claims.

The EDD proceeded to freeze the accounts of 350,000 legitimate claimants who had filed because of Sacramento's stay-at-home edicts and business closures. If your account was randomly frozen, the wait time to get a claim reviewed averaged twenty-six weeks. How can an unemployed parent wait six months to pay rent and buy food for their family? In March 2021, the beleaguered agency faced a backlog of over one million cases.

Before the pandemic, the EDD was running a $3 billion surplus. The agency is now in the red to the tune of $48 billion. The unemployment insurance debacle was the most significant fraud scandal in the history of any state, estimated in October 2021 to be around $20 billion. That's five times the budget of California's second-most populous city, San Jose, and nearly double Los Angeles's $11.2 billion 2021 budget. Twenty billion dollars wasted (not spent) works out to over $500 for every man, woman, and child in the entire state of California that government waste and mismanagement flushed down the toilet.

EDD's failure to provide the most basic service during the crisis was a failure of our state government to help its citizens in their time of greatest need. It highlights the dangers a one-party system poses. When there is no competition, no one feels the need to perform or meet expectations. A one-party system is not accountable because there is no viable alternative. California has become a one-party state. EDD's failure marks the ineptitude and inefficiency of this single-party rule.

As weekly COVID-19 cases and deaths decreased during the first weeks of May, Sacramento began a phased reopening. But in the second half of the month, culminating on Memorial Day weekend, California started to see record-high numbers of new cases and deaths. Confirmed cases, hospitalizations, and deaths continued to climb. Newsom ordered most "nonessential" businesses to close again on July 13, 2020.

During the spring and summer of 2020, Black Lives Matter (BLM) and other so-called social justice protests swept across the state and country, sparked by the death of George Floyd. The mass protests left many Californians wondering why Sacramento politicians supported mass gatherings of BLM protesters, but not those citizens who exercised their First Amendment rights when they protested government lockdowns and business closures. Even when BLM protests turned violent, state government stood on the sidelines. Our law enforcement leaders declined to support their officers, who too often found themselves wrongly scapegoated for isolated incidents of police violence. They praised Black Lives Matter, even though it turned out its leaders were diverting funds for personal advantage. It was one more case of Sacramento picking winners and losers. Our leaders put protestors ahead of police officers. Newsom and the extreme Left asserted their power to advance ideas that supported their leftist agenda while quashing dissenting views.

The decade-long Democratic domination of the executive and legislative branches meant our elected representatives no longer had to look across the aisle to build bridges to reach common ground. Democrats packed our courts with liberal judges, so the judicial system rarely overturned misguided legislation. The California Democratic Party has moved farther and farther to the Left in its quest to mollify a political minority of activists and solidify its power. We need a healthy Republican Party to force Democrats toward the political center.

Democrats have framed differences of opinion as an assault on morality and our way of life. They painted the other side as a threat to California's values. They made politics toxic and polarized society along ideological lines. Is it any wonder fighting broke out in the streets? Or suddenly, gangs saw no risk in launching assaults on retailers with uncontrolled looting and pillaging?

While the streets simmered in the heat of a violent summer, California electricity companies ordered the first rolling blackouts in twenty years, beginning on August 14, 2020. Residents ordered to stay at home suffered through a prolonged heat wave without electricity. California didn't generate enough electricity to meet demand. People paid the price of years of ill-advised energy policies and the undue influence of extremist environmentalists. Perhaps the biggest mistake was closing power plants—decisions fueled by politics, not sound energy policy.

While Californians sweltered, waiting for the EDD to process unemployment claims, for schools to resume, and for Governor Newsom to reopen the economy, 367 fires ravaged the state. The smoky haze that blanketed vast swaths of California was a constant reminder of Sacramento's failed fire mitigation policies.

As the fires raged in August and into September of 2020, so did the virus. The California Teachers Association (CTA) and local teachers' unions used their political influence to keep schools closed. Parents were outraged. Other states took protective measures and opened at the beginning of the school year, but not California. It became clear that schools would not reopen due to CTA lobbying and pressure, subjecting millions of public schoolchildren to months of substandard distance learning.

Democrats preach about the gaps between rich and poor. They know a bit about that. Their leaders are as guilty as anyone. Newsom's children were receiving in-person instruction at their private school. Conveniently, private schools, where the ruling liberal elite educates their children, were exempt from the rules that denied public schoolchildren the same access. An outraged populace was turning against the governor and Sacramento. Protests over arbitrary and draconian COVID restrictions and closures grew and intensified. The recall movement gained momentum.

Against this backdrop, Heatlie and Netter came to see me. They convinced me their effort could bear fruit and begged me to help jumpstart the recall. In September, I donated $50,000 to help pay for their legal counsel to gain an extension of time to gather the required one and a half million signatures. On September 22, 2020, nail salons reopened while schools and churches remained closed.

Things brightened in October. Counties moved up or down a complicated colored tier system based on multiple factors. In October, cases, hospitalizations, and deaths began to decrease. Businesses in some counties began a phased reopening. The recall petition was stuck in first gear while the governor's aggressive mitigation policy seemed to pay dividends. Then came the infamous French Laundry incident.

Newsom attended a fundraising dinner on November 6, 2020, for his close friend and lobbyist Jason Kinney at The French Laundry, an exclusive restaurant in the Napa Valley that ranks among the world's most expensive. It's a place you need to make a reservation six months to a year ahead of time. Newsom and his wife dined with top lobbyists from the California Medical Association (CMA). Twelve diners from six different households sat maskless and feasted on $350-per-person nine-course dinners. That's not counting the $12,000 tab for the wine.

Newsom and his fat-cat lobbyist cronies were breaking the pandemic safety rules and guidelines they had mandated and touted. The CMA had funded an ad touting the benefits of wearing masks. Yet two of their top executives felt they were above the rules and ignored their own messaging.

Discovered and outed, Newsom claimed, "It was an outdoor restaurant." Published photos exposed the governor's statement as a lie. Newsom apologized, stating, "The spirit of what I'm preaching all the time was contradicted." It was far more than the "spirit" of what he preached that he violated. He violated the public trust. Only a month before, the governor's office tweeted, "Going out to eat with members of your household this weekend? Don't forget to keep your mask on in between bites."

The French Laundry incident undermined Newsom's credibility and revealed him to be the out-of-touch elitist whom I and many others already knew about. Flouting his own regulations, dining at a three-star Michelin restaurant while record numbers of Californians were suffering food insecurity, was a bad optic.

The uproar was national and damning. Rarely had one incident so brilliantly captured—and exposed—the shortcomings of a governor's hypocritical leadership. Social media erupted. Media outlets had a field day. More important, Newsom's rich-boy antics fueled the recall fire. It was game on.

Volunteers started gathered signatures by the thousands. Veteran political consultants Anne Dunsmore and Tom Del Beccaro joined forces with the recall proponents by forming an organization called Rescue California. The name's significance was not lost on political types who remember that the effort to recall Gray Davis in 2003 had the same title. When these two Republican heavyweights got involved with the recall effort, gathering the required signatures became a real possibility. Dunsmore was a top-level GOP fundraiser in California, and donations poured in. Del Beccaro had a savvy media presence and was the former chairman of the California Republican Party. These top-tier players added political gravitas, organizational expertise, and financial prowess to the recall effort.

Newsom began feeling the heat. Early November saw a 32 percent spike in hospitalizations and a 30 percent increase in Intensive Care Unit (ICU) admissions. New cases increased to over ten thousand per day, a number not seen since August. Bowing to pressure from liberals, Newsom ordered almost all nonessential businesses to close again on November 16. He also issued a universal mask mandate that required residents to wear a mask outdoors and indoors, despite no scientific evidence that the virus was transmitted outdoors.

The hated mask would become a symbol of government overreach. Californians have endured more pain and have lost more freedoms than residents of states like Florida and Texas where governors banned mask mandates. The leaders of those states understood that individual citizens are fully capable of making informed decisions about the best way to protect themselves and their families.

The deadline to gather the 1,495,709 signatures needed for the recall was November 17, 2020. The petition had less than half of the signatures required to put the matter before the voters. Heatlie and Netter had filed a request for an extension in the California superior court. The rationale was that volunteers gathering petition signatures typically canvass at shopping malls and other community gathering places shuttered by the pandemic. The superior court of California granted an extension that gave organizers until March 17, 2021, to collect the required number of signatures.

The petition deadline extension, the renewed COVID closures and mandates, and the French Laundry incident galvanized supporters. Money began to flow into California from national and state sources. Then, on November 21, Newsom mandated a 10 p.m. to 5 a.m. curfew. The scientific logic behind that decision baffled Californians. The governor was taking away civil liberties at will without sharing the science behind his actions. The curfew did not curb the spread of the virus. COVID numbers continued to hit record highs. On December 3, Newsom ordered stay-at-home edicts for all regions with less than 15 percent ICU capacity. By Christmas, all regions were at 100 percent ICU capacity. At the end of December, Newsom extended the lockdown indefinitely.

On December 14, 2020, the state chairwoman of the Republican Party, Jessica Millan Patterson, endorsed the recall, imploring Californians to "Make sure your voice is heard, sign the petition today." National Republican figures like Mike Huckabee and Newt Gingrich got on board. By the first of the year, it became clear that the effort would collect enough signatures by the March 2011 to force a recall. In the end, over two million Californians signed the petition.

In February 2021, I entered the race as a Republican candidate to replace Newsom. Newsom was not going to solve the problems of this state. I was a political outsider, had residual name recognition from opposing Newsom in the 2018 race, was untarnished by the corruption in Sacramento and well positioned to solve tough problems. I thought my experience as a businessman would be invaluable in restoring our state to its former glory. I thought I could win.

CHAPTER 3

SPECIAL (INTEREST) ELECTION

Gavin Newsom and I had taken very different paths in life. I didn't enjoy the privileged upbringing of the governor. Like most Californians, I had to earn my own way. I started with nothing. I never received a government contract or scholarship. I was accountable for every dollar I borrowed, every decision I made. Nancy Pelosi is not *my* aunt. The billionaire Gettys were not *my* benefactors.

The early ads I ran highlighted the differences between the governor and myself. The theme was beauty and the beast. With his gelled hair and perfect teeth, Newsom was the beauty. I was the beast. To that end, I campaigned with a Kodiak bear named Tag, clearly designed to grab the attention of voters distracted by all the national issues and dealing with the pandemic. I ran some beauty-and-the-beast commercials with Tag in which I promised to be as aggressive as a bear to fix California. I would not kowtow to donors, special-interest groups, and public-sector employee unions. Government would no longer be for sale in the capital. My administration would be a genuinely representative democracy. The good people of California would have a governor who represented them and who would work tirelessly to improve their lives.

The liberal press, eager to focus on the sensational over the substantive, seized on the bear. Animal rights activists were apoplectic about using a bear in my campaign. I can assure you, Tag was lovingly cared for, and my campaign followed all state and local rules and regulations. It strikes me as disingenuous that so many people would care more about a bear that was obviously well cared for than for the estimated 130,000 homeless people living in squalid conditions across the state. The beast strategy was a double-edged sword. It garnered the attention we had hoped for, but it took the focus away from my plans to solve the problems being faced by Californians.

At the same time I was entering the race in February, Chamath Palihapitiya, the billionaire Silicon Valley tech venture capitalist and former Facebook executive who had previously supported Elizabeth Warren's presidential bid, donated $100,000 to the recall campaign. Palihapitiya, the president of Social Capital, hinted that he might challenge Newsom and began exploring a run for the governor's seat. His website touted eliminating the state income tax, promoting school vouchers, and improving the business climate in California as key components of his platform.

"I think Gavin Newson has done a terrible job," Palihapitiya told CNBC. "People are leaving in droves. Crime is really high. Our education outcomes are the worst of any state, our taxes are the highest of any state, our air quality is the worst of any state."

Palihapitiya's decision to turn his back on Newsom was a sign of the governor's vulnerability. With its enormous technological and financial clout, Silicon Valley had always been reliably democratic and pro-Newsom. Jennifer Kerns, a former spokesperson for the California Republican Party, said, "The fact that the Silicon Valley guys are wading into this recall is a game-changer. They have been gun shy about getting into political fights here in California…but now that they're doing so, tells me Gavin is in a lot of trouble."

The left let out a huge uproar. Liberals sensed that if Silicon Valley turned against Newsom, the balance might shift toward the pro-recall forces. Palihapitiya owns 10 percent of the Golden State Warriors basketball team. They play in a stadium owned by the public, and the other owners of the Warriors are politically connected in Sacramento. Steve Kerr, their coach, is well Left of center. A lot of the players like Steph Curry are also very liberal. That Palihapitiya, one of the Warriors' owners, announced that he would run for governor sent shockwaves through the Democratic establishment. It must have taken extreme pressure from Newsom's camp to persuade Palihapitiya to pull his hat out of the ring.

Soon after, John Kruger, an Orange County Republican donor, contributed $500,000 to the recall. Kruger objected to Newsom prohibiting indoor religious services. The political operatives in Sacramento tried to paint the contribution as "dark money." A complaint was filed with the state attorney general's office and Fair Political Practices Commission. Speaking for Rescue California, Dunsmore portrayed the complaint as a partisan effort to suppress donations. She stated: "The big message to me is that they are taking us seriously now."

During the pandemic, the churches were one of the first targets of the state government. When Newsom shuttered churches, synagogues, and mosques, collection plates could no longer be passed around, choking off the financial support churches needed to survive. Operating via Zoom and the internet proved a challenge. It did not have the same community feeling that people loved about their church. Sacramento should have leaned on religious groups to support those in need during the pandemic. Instead, religious communities were impotent to help their community.

I spoke to a church group in Murrieta that defied the ban on in-person services. I reminded them that the Constitution enshrined our first amendment rights of religion. People who attended the church were perfectly willing to socially distance themselves and wear a mask. But the church was central to their spiritual and social lives. It didn't seem fair that churches were closed while marijuana dispensaries remained open. These folks were willing to play by the rules and follow COVID protocols to attend in-person services.

I went to Godspeak Calvary Chapel in Thousand Oaks, California while on the campaign trail. Rob McCoy had famously stood up against restrictions that targeted religious gatherings. McCoy was the mayor, then on the city council of Thousand Oaks, an affluent suburb north of Los Angeles. In April 2020, he had resigned from the city council and opened the doors of his church for Palm Sunday services. At first, the church followed all the rules established for other essential businesses. But when Newsom supported BLM protestors who were ignoring the very rules his church was so fastidiously following, McCoy had had enough. He would not permit Sacramento to play politics with his faith any longer. He opened the church fully: no masks, no social distancing, no limitations on the size of the gathering. McCoy thundered from the pulpit, "The king of California is not greater than the King of all creation."

Indeed, Newsom is not. Californians let the governor know that on March 17, 2021, when over two million signatures calling for his recall were submitted to the secretary of state, easily surpassing the one-and-a-half-million threshold needed to force a recall election.

Soon, Newsom's poll numbers started tanking. One poll in July projected Newsom to lose the recall election. What did he do? Governor Newsom unveiled his California Comeback Plan, which rehashed the same left-wing themes and policies: inequality, increasing opportunity, and a useless, regulation-heavy approach to fighting climate change.

Newsom was banking on financial giveaways to shore up his base. A torrent of federal money, along with record tax receipts from a resurgent stock market and gains in Silicon Valley companies, flowed to him. Newsom allocated $7.2 billion to pay off outstanding rent and utility bills and $300 million to wipe out traffic and parking tickets. Perhaps the most controversial provision extended state benefits and Medicaid to illegal immigrants. Many Californians questioned why the governor was prioritizing illegal immigrants over California citizens.

Money played a crucial role. Newsom's political machine raised $70.9 million while the pro-recall forces could muster only $13.9 million. Organized labor contributed 45 percent of the antirecall fundraising total. Healthcare unions donated $3.5 million, building trade unions $2.6 million, tribal governments $2.2 million, prison guards $1.8 million, and the

CTA $1.8 million. The Democratic Governors Association contributed $5.5 million, doubtless worried that a Newsom defeat spelled trouble for Democratic governors across the nation.

One of the best moments of my campaign was getting involved with a group called Let Them Play California. I had watched with interest as this loose coalition of thousands of high school coaches, medical professionals, student-athletes, and parents implored the governor to permit student athletes to resume playing the sports they love. The Facebook group had grown to over fifty thousand members. Cofounder Brad Hensley said, "Athletes are not Democrats or Republicans. All we want to do is play."

A growing chorus of healthcare experts, doctors, and mental health professionals provided studies and anecdotal evidence that the damage to students' health outweighed the risk of contracting the virus. Fifty-seven physicians penned a letter to Gavin Newsom imploring him to allow a safe return to high school sports. The consequences of closing down programs had devastating effects outside the lines of the empty fields across high school campuses. Over 80 percent of coaches reported increased dropout rates, teen pregnancies, and incarcerations, particularly with vulnerable students in inner-city schools.

Two San Diego high schoolers joined Let Them Play and filed a lawsuit claiming forty-seven states had resumed high school sports. They pointed out there was no evidence linking participation in sports with increased transmission of the virus. The state realized it had no science to support its position. California settled the case in March 2021 and allowed students to return to organized high school sports. It was a big win for kids, parents, democracy, and common sense. Sadly, the rest of the election did not end up so positive.

Let's look at how events in the recall election unfolded.

The legal process governing the recall was complicated. It was a product of efforts by the Democrats to lengthen the process, to give them time to let emotions cool while their political operations kicked into high gear. However, in this case, the Democrats decided that an early election gave them an advantage because Newsom had his fundraising juggernaut in full gear while prorecall forces were still trying to mount a grassroots effort. They moved the date up to have the election as soon as possible, September 14. The Democrats wanted to maximize their fundraising dominance and avoid having unfavorable conditions such as water and electricity shortages along with wildfires—which had plagued the state during September 2020—reappearing and reminding voters of Newsom's mismanagement.

Once Sacramento set the election date, a Republican named Larry Elder entered the race. Elder was a conservative radio show host and was a Fox News contributor as well. He was also a well-known endorser of products hawked on endless ads on the network. The self-proclaimed "Sage of South Central" had significant name recognition from his years on radio in Los Angeles and his national radio show on Salem Broadcasting. He was an early supporter of former president Donald Trump, even proclaiming that his candidacy was a "gift from God." Many political activists saw Elder as the right figure to stoke the national debate in our nation's largest state. Sure enough, Salem Broadcasting, Fox News, and the *Wall Street Journal* (which has common ownership with Fox), decided it was a great idea to get Larry a much bigger audience. It played well with Fox viewers and gave the network a new star to generate revenue.

I knew Elder was a formidable opponent. My priority was to defeat Newsom by highlighting his failures. But as soon as Elder got in the race, Fox News shut out all the other candidates. Fox focused on Elder and put him on their broadcasts.

Elder not only had Fox News but also the *Wall Street Journal* trumpeting his candidacy. A lot of conservatives liked the idea of a Black conservative as a spokesman for their cause. And frankly, that's great. I was on Larry's show. I like the fact that Larry's a Black conservative who would regularly point out the Left's hypocrisy, particularly as it relates to issues of race. He called out Black liberals who encourage African Americans to give their votes to a Democratic party that takes them for granted and gives them lousy schools, lousy housing, and lousy healthcare.

The *Journal* published two flattering pieces about a Black conservative possibly becoming the next governor, which generated tremendous interest in California. It supercharged Elder's fundraising. All of a sudden, he was raising millions of dollars.

But Elder's candidacy also fanned the flames of the national debate about former president Trump. Elder attacked the media as the former president had done. He also challenged elections officials in the same fashion as President Trump. It allowed Newsom to make Elder, along with the former president, the face of the recall and shift the debate from Newsom's failures to demonizing an opponent as a proxy for former president Trump in a state that had overwhelmingly voted against Trump in 2020 by five million votes.

Gavin Newsom made no bones in framing the recall as a Republican coup driven by Trump supporters and right-wing ideologues. He wrote, "And let's call it what it is: it's a partisan, Republican recall—backed by the [Republican National Committee], anti-mask and anti-vax extremists, and pro-Trump forces who want to overturn the last election and have opposed much of what we have done to fight the pandemic."

The "Stop the Republican Recall" campaign enlisted an army of ninety labor and community groups to staff phone banks. Newsom raised over $70 million, more than all the Republican candidates combined. His campaign flooded the airwaves with ads connecting Elder to former president Trump. It bears stressing. Whatever you think of Trump as president, he is political poison in California.

Elder became the face of the recall, and Newsom demonized him. Elder didn't have credibility as an executive. People viewed Larry as a conservative ideologue based on his years as a broadcaster. He appealed to voters who wanted to continue the ideological war and Trump's battle with the media. Many viewed him as a Far-Right purveyor of conservative ideology. Our polling showed that my appeal was to people who thought that a businessperson would help improve the daily lives of Californians by decreasing the cost of living, supporting small businesses, and cleaning up the streets of homelessness and crime.

But Larry Elder made it all about battles: conservatives versus the media and the ideology of Right versus Left. That juiced his name recognition and fundraising, particularly among conservatives. The national news media and Fox savored an election framed as a war. Trumpers and left-wingers turned the recall into a national media circus. A Marxist California professor and BLM leader, Melina Abdullah, called Elder "a Black face on White supremacy." The *Los Angeles Times* echoed the "Black face of White supremacy" in its controversial headline. The liberal news media mounted a full-court press to stymie Elder's momentum and preclude a Republican victory.

In early July, before Larry's entry, the focus of the recall campaign was on Newsom's failures. I was leading among the replacement candidates and Newsom was fifty-fifty to be recalled. But most voters hadn't focused on replacements yet. Polls were showing Newsom more vulnerable on the substantive issues. One major poll showed him losing the recall by a slim margin. That alarmed the interests dependent on the governor keeping his job. Elder was a welcome gift to them. He turned the recall into an ideological war.

A lot of Trump conservatives relished an ideological war with Newsom. I understand that. To them, Gavin Newsom exemplifies a failed ideology. Newsom doubled down as conservative media played up the Elder effort. Newsom painted the recall as a safety issue by playing on Californian's fear of COVID-19. He argued that we were safer with his aggressive handling of the pandemic. By contrast, he claimed that voting for a Republican would put Californians at risk.

Larry Elder insisted on promoting his opposition to the mandates instead of talking about what we could do to encourage people to get vaccinated. This misstep played into the Democratic narrative. Newsom portrayed Larry as an antivaxxer, which mischaracterized his position. Newsom painted all Republican challengers as antivaxxers, which we were not. In every instance, we encouraged people to get vaccinated. Larry and I were both vaccinated. We just opposed mandating vaccinations for all Californians as unnecessary (natural immunity was being ignored) and infringing on freedom of personal autonomy.

The Democrats successfully transformed the vaccine mandate into a political issue. In their view, you were killing somebody else if you did not go along with the mandate. Republican candidates were wrongly accused of being antivaxxers who wanted to kill Californians. Netflix founder Reed Hastings funded an ad that claimed it was a matter of life and death that Newsom defeat Elder. The Hollywood establishment flexed its muscle to coerce people to vote no on the recall.

The recall campaign became a classic fight of Left versus Right ideology. The news outlets, both liberal and conservative, were gleeful. Ideological and culture wars generate more clicks and ad revenue than talking about important issues. Newsom exploited that. He manipulated the debate away from electricity, water, housing, cost of living, crime, and homelessness—the issues I was talking about—and made it all about ideology and the former president. They were able to paint Larry Elder as Trump 2.0 in California. The Democrats repeated the mantra "Trump" and "Republican takeover." People got scared and voted for Newsom.

Meanwhile, I published extensive reports and studies on my website, addressing California's myriad of problems with exact solutions on how to fix them. As you'll read in this book, I proposed an overhaul of our housing regulations, solutions to homelessness involving treatment, an air corps to fight wildfires, school choice to improve education, diversification of our water and energy resources, road improvements, budgetary solutions, and many more ideas to turn around the country's most expensive and mismanaged state.

I knew California voters were looking for something different. They wanted someone to lead California who would improve their lives by solving problems. I had a lifetime of fixing problems and delivering results for my investors and clients, but that was almost totally overlooked. The bear campaign my consultants pushed likely helped the media as they focused on that symbol rather than the substantive points I was making. Elder's inflammatory rhetoric stoked his fundraising but didn't help make a case for recalling the governor. Many voters were worried that an Elder victory would keep the focus on ideological wars and not on fixing the issues in our state.

As September 14 drew near, Democrats pulled out the big guns calculated to mobilize a Democrat base. Former president Obama starred in an ad supporting Newsom. Vice President Harris and Senator Elizabeth Warren (D-Mass.) campaigned for the governor in California. On the eve of the election, President Biden touched down in Long Beach. Biden rallied the crowd at Long Beach City College. "I got to run against the real Donald Trump," he said. "Well, this year, the leading Republican running for governor is the closest thing to a Trump clone that I've ever seen."

Election night, as we all know, was anticlimactic. The final tally was not close: No: 61.9 percent, Yes: 38.1 percent. The Democrats capitalized on their two-to-one voter registration advantage, their get-out-the-vote prowess powered by an army of loyal union volunteers, and the deep desire of the ruling party to maintain its stranglehold on power in Sacramento. The Democrats flooded the airwaves and drowned out the prorecall message. In the end, the recall became more about money and ideology than solving the state's many real-life problems.

But behind the final numbers, there were some cracks in Newsom's armor. More counties voted to recall the governor than cast "no" ballots. Newsom carried the most populous counties where his left-wing policies and free giveaways played well. He lost in the Central Valley and more rural areas of the state. The Central Valley and rural portions of our state remain underrepresented. The sheer numbers of voters along the coast dilute their voices. This has been a successful Democratic strategy here and across the nation. It drives their open border and proimmigrant policies. If you build a utopian Socialist state that showers illegal immigrants with benefits and cash prizes, they will come—and vote Democratic.

There is a lesson. When a government free from checks and balances oversteps its boundaries, the people will raise their voices in protest. Two activists began a movement that put the powerful Democratic Party in California on pins and needles, unsure of its grip on power for the first time in over a decade. I doubt the tone-deaf politicians in Sacramento heard the message, but millions of fed-up Californians did. A representative government must serve all its citizens, not just the majority. Nearly five million Californians stood up for what they believed in and voted for a truly representative democracy for California.

Though Newsom is still in power, I view the recall as a beginning, not an ending. All the issues California faces are still in play—and they'll likely continue to get worse under his leadership. He won't do what is needed to change because the interest groups he needs for his future political ambitions want the status quo to continue. They benefit from it. There's a reason the state has the problems it has. Special-interest groups profit from it, and nothing will change until leadership changes. Leadership will only change when the system that elects them changes as well.

California is in crisis. Preventable wildfires ravage the hills and reduce homes to smoking embers. The tax rates would make a Socialist blush. When adjusted for the cost of living, the poverty rate is the worst in the nation. California accounts for 12 percent of the U.S. population and yet has a quarter of the nation's homeless population. Our state economy is the fifth largest globally, larger than Great Britain by most measures. But if you factor in our unfunded pension and healthcare liabilities, we are broke, not in surplus as our governor maintains. He has just signed a $308 billion budget, more than double what it was when he took office and still claims a $100 billion surplus from our high taxes and federal largesse—a surplus which pales next to an estimated $1 trillion actual deficit in future pension and healthcare obligations to state workers.

We have shortages of energy and water, fueled by extreme climate politics; our regulations and business licensing deny opportunity to the folks who need it the most. Our business climate is regularly voted one of the worst in the nation, as is our once-vaunted education system. At the same time, to distract from these issues, Newsom is stoking the culture wars, taking advantage of recent Supreme Court opinions to cast this state as the leader in fighting battles on abortion and guns, while 75 percent or more of the state struggles to pay high gasoline prices, try to afford sky-high rents, and purchase ever more expensive food for their families.

It wasn't always this way. What glittered was gold in California. There's a saying, "As goes California, so goes the rest of the nation." In many ways, the Golden State still leads this nation. It sets the tone. It defines the national direction. It incubates exciting talent and fresh, innovative ideas and thinking. But it can also work the opposite way: other states can see the power grab in California and replicate those bad actions.

There is hope on the horizon. The recent results in Virginia and New Jersey indicate that the political effect of blaming the former president may not succeed. This is particularly true where there is a contest between a businessperson intent on solving problems and a craven career politician representing the failed policies that have led to dysfunction. We can see that with Glenn Youngkin's gubernatorial victory in Virginia. It's not about a moderate winning; it's more about electing a businessperson who focuses on achieving success and goals—in his case, his focus on improving education and giving more power to parents than union bosses proved a winning argument. Terry McAuliffe, a poster child, like Newsom, for craven political power and feeding special-interest groups, kept trying to make the election about Donald Trump as well as the hot-button social issues. That strategy failed miserably. Voters wanted problems fixed, and they elected an experienced businessperson with a proven record of success to do it.

I wrote this book to examine all of these issues through the eyes of real Californians. I spoke to dozens of them. You'll read their stories and mine. I wrote this book to point out that there are real solutions to our problems; we can fix these issues if we focus on what works and stop fighting over ideology. I wrote this book to put forth and explain a change—Hear the People—to our election system that while some may portray as radical, is a rather simple change that will put the people back in charge and take power from the donors and funders who control our political leadership today. I'm hoping that you will work with us to make things right again.

I know that, together, we can turn this political swampland into the rich, fertile ground it was always meant to be.

PART 2

SAVING CALIFORNIA AND THE COUNTRY FROM GAVIN NEWSOM

CHAPTER 4

WHO IS GAVIN NEWSOM?

Gavin Newsom stepped out of his state-issued black SUV to join the crowd of marchers crossing the Tower Bridge in Sacramento, hand in hand with his rich, beautiful wife and their four beautiful children. It was a typical photo op for the telegenic politician—evocative of a march that could have been part of a Barack Obama/Bobby Kennedy milieu. The march itself was organized as part of Newsom's second inaugural "celebration" and was ostensibly all about "protecting democracy" from those that would erode it by asserting problems with election procedures. Under this theory, so-called "election deniers" are a threat to democracy because the dared to challenge the all-mail ballot rules and other changes wrought by the pandemic response of politicians like Newsom.

As soon as the photos had been taken by a fawning press corps kept suitably at a distance from the well-coiffed chief executive of the state of California, Newsom exited the march to another waiting SUV to be whisked to the stage where he would deliver his speech, filled with well-calibrated soaring rhetoric about the freedoms he has protected in his home state. One of those freedoms—freedom of the press—was not part of this consideration as the press, much to its chagrin, was kept at great distance and not allowed to sully the proceedings with inconvenient questions about living conditions in this once very livable state.

Thus, the voting public, which had barely noticed that there was a gubernatorial election in 2022, was deprived of any real discussion of the soaring cost of living, the shortage of housing, the blight of homelessness, the shortages of water and electricity, the cascading impact of wildfires or the epidemic of crime. These and myriad other problems were washed away by the governor's partisan attacks on Republicans, on the insurgents at the Capitol, and of course, red-state governors who would be his prime opponents if—or when—he runs for president.

It's that overarching ambition that is at the root of Gavin Newsom. It's something passed down in his blood; his grandfather William Alfred Newsom II was a businessman and confidant of Edmund "Pat" Brown, the governor of California who succeeded Earl Warren in 1958. William II, as we'll call him, ran Brown's campaign for district attorney, which vaulted him into the governor's mansion. This elder Newsom knew his way around Sacramento and with his own son, William Newsom III, known as Bill, was able to call in his chits with the governor and cajole him into passing along to them the rights to develop a new ski mountain, Squaw Valley (since renamed Palisades Tahoe in a woke cleansing of a derogatory term).

Alas, the partnership between the governor and his chief benefactor, William II, was torn asunder by, what else? A dispute over money, as the elder Newsom wanted to build a convention center associated with the resort, a move that was opposed by some in the governor's administration. This brought about a wrenching division and a promise from Newsom to seek political retribution against Governor Brown, which may or may not have contributed to the election of Ronald Reagan in 1966, spoiling the governor's effort for a preterm limits run of three terms.

Fast-forward to the early '70s, when Governor Pat Brown's son—a young former seminary student nicknamed Jerry (he was Edmund Jr.) became the governor for two terms. This healed the family rift between the Browns and Newsoms, culminating in Jerry Brown appointing Bill Newsom (Gavin's father) to a judgeship. It was also during this time frame that Bill Newsom's sister married a young businessman by the name of Ron Pelosi, the brother of Paul Pelosi, who as most of us know by now, ended up marrying Nancy D'Alessandro, the daughter of Baltimore's machine politician mayor. Nancy Pelosi, as we now know her, has become one of the most powerful politicians in history as congresswoman from San Francisco and Speaker of the House.

The family power connections don't end there. One element necessary to this entire picture is the grease of big money. That comes in the form of the Getty family.

J. Paul Getty became the richest man in the world in the '60s, the first billionaire in the world at the time. He was famously eccentric, marrying five times and once refusing to pay a ransom for the release of his kidnapped grandson. He ultimately did pay that ransom, which was famously delivered by one Bill Newsom.

J. Paul Getty was the scion of an oil-drilling family formed in the early 20th century gold rush for the new resource that would power the future of our transportation network. His father moved out to Oklahoma and traded oil and gas leases, ultimately leaving the business to his son, J. Paul. Growing the business by a huge amount, including an incredibly lucrative concession from the Saudi royal family, J. Paul moved the center of his personal life and the business to California. At his death in 1976, he was by far the wealthiest man in the world and left the business in the control of his son Gordon, but subject to the terms of trusts J. Paul had set up with his mother, Sarah, in the '30s. What played out was a lot of litigation and attorney fees, and when the smoke cleared in 1985, Gordon was in control of billions and ready to make his mark on the world.

Along the way of his life in California, William II had gotten to know the Getty family and had taken young Gordon under his wing, so to speak, saving him from a dysfunctional family. That connection continued to Bill Newsom (Newsom III), who befriended Gordon Getty, ultimately managing his billions. Bill's son Gavin, the future governor, was returned the favor by Gordon Getty when Bill divorced Gavin's mom, Tessa. Gavin was essentially adopted by Gordon and grew up with a best friend by the name of Billy Getty, Gordon's son, and a notorious player, well known in the Bay Area.

It was this Getty connection that greased young Gavin's rise in the political world of San Francisco. Having already been put into business by Gordon Getty with Plumpjack Winery and Restaurant Corp. (Plumpjack was the name of an opera authored by budding composer Gordon Getty) which interestingly had its first site in a hotel in Squaw Valley, Gavin set out to make his mark in the world of politics by running for San Francisco County supervisor.

Gordon used his connections in politics and business to aid his young protégé. He introduced him to the socialites he knew in San Francisco elite circles and let it be known that helping the young scion was a good way to get in his good graces for future contributions to this or that needy charity or political campaign. One hand washes the other, as it were.

Gavin was appointed to a commission by then mayor Willie Brown, himself a beneficiary of Gordon Getty's largesse. From there, it was an appointment to a vacant position on the board of supervisors of San Francisco County, a post from which incumbency, along with Willie Brown's support along with the Getty connection, made reelection a virtual surety. As a supervisor, Newsom actually won plaudits from business groups. He advocated improvements to local transportation as well as a program to put the homeless through drug treatment programs instead of just giving them cash. He advocated for business interests, which sometimes put him at odds with labor leaders.

That effort as supervisor fueled his run for mayor in 2003. Again, having Gordon Getty, Willie Brown, and Nancy Pelosi in your corner was a big help. Along with that came the mayoral election in 2003, when Newsom was elected mayor at the ripe old age of thirty-six, the youngest mayor in San Francisco history. He was reelected, again with the help of the socialites of San Francisco funding his campaign, with 72 percent of the vote.

It was as mayor that Newsom saw the opportunity to exploit a "wedge" issue. Gay and lesbian couples in San Francisco had been denied wedding licenses from the city. Newsom, seeing the opportunity granting those licenses would mean to both the city as well as the state and national press, went ahead and defied precedent and a judge's order to issue those licenses. This action won him almost universal press adoration, but the licenses were annulled by a court as a violation of state law. He subsequently cut ads to urge a disapproval of Proposition 8, a ballot initiative to end same-sex marriage in California. Even though Newsom's effort failed—the proposition passed—he ultimately was successful as the courts threw out the proposition and ultimately the Supreme Court weighed in to institute same-sex marriage nationwide.

Newsom's mayoralty was not without controversy, as he was caught in a sex scandal in 2007, having had an adulterous relationship with the wife of his campaign manager and top aide as mayor. The aide resigned—he had a close relationship with Newsom prior to this—and Newsom survived, winning reelection easily.

After some initial forays into a possible governor's race in 2010 to succeed Arnold Schwarzenegger, who had been elected governor in the wild 2003 recall and had survived reelection in 2006, Newsom thought the better of it and let Jerry Brown take the mantle of savior of the Democratic party and the state. Instead, he pulled back on his ambition—he was still pretty young at forty-two—and decided to bide his time in an apprentice position of sorts as Brown's lieutenant governor.

Eight uninteresting and pretty boring years later, Newsom decided to run for governor, as was widely expected given his well-known reputation for ambition. On the Democratic side, he faced three challengers, the most formidable being the former mayor of Los Angeles, Antonio Villaraigosa. I participated in a number of debates with these two well-known Democrats, and believe me when I tell you that the ego-driven clashes between these two were classics. Newsom only deigned to appear for a few of these debates, skipping many more. When he did appear, he would come in late and breeze past the other candidates, barely acknowledging that there were other candidates vying for the job.

I remember one notable exchange between Newsom and Villaraigosa having to do with who made more money while they were in office. This was a classic, because both of these politicians had their own story of inside investments—Newsom accused the L.A. mayor of making money from consulting; Villaraigosa shot back something about all the money on silver contracts Newsom had made while in public office as well the special deals given his wine and restaurant company. Both of these powerful Democrats could be accused of being the pot calling the kettle black—that's not intended to be a racial term; it's about being hypocritical, which is frankly a qualifier for their posts.

At the end of the day, Villaraigosa failed to make the top-two runoff election; I surprised the country by getting almost twice as many votes as the former mayor of L.A. Part of it was the campaign I ran to Republican voters; part of it was an endorsement by then President Trump negotiated through Minority Leader Kevin McCarthy; still another part were television ads run by the Newsom campaign—which was flush in campaign cash from the connections Newsom had built up—which detailed how I was too conservative for California but had the effect of introducing me to many Californians that hadn't yet paid attention.

The idea of running those ads that were seemingly against me was part of a cynical gambit by Newsom to raise my name recognition and assure that I would make the top two instead of the former mayor of L.A. This was the first use of a gambit that has been used by politicians since to select their favored opponents in a general election to assure victory. Villaraigosa was considered a more formidable general election candidate against Newsom given the blue tilt of the state; he might have won a head-to-head contest. We'll never know if that would have happened but given the lead in fundraising Newsom had along with the historical voting record of the Bay Area versus Los Angeles, I suspect Newsom would have still won the race if Villaraigosa had made the top two.

In any event, my making the top two was a surprise—both the *Wall Street Journal* and the *New York Times*—newspapers on the opposite ends of the political spectrum—put me on the front page of their editions on the day after the primary. A framed copy of the *Wall Street Journal* front page signed by President Trump, hangs in my office today, reminding me of short-lived victory.

I raised $11 million in the general election campaign and didn't have to put any of my own funds to work—I spent $6 million in the primary, raising about $1 million from donors. Still, I was dwarfed by the special-interest avalanche generated by Newsom. Not only did he raise a significant sum for this campaign, but his cronies put together political action committees (PACS), which multiplied the amounts he was able to spend to win the race.

Teachers, nurses, prison guards—myriad employee unions were the chief funders of Newsom's campaign and got great deals from him after the election. Add in a lot of other interest groups, from realtors to doctors to energy interests—they all wanted to be a part of the winning team and make sure they had the governor's ear after the election. I know that's how politics works in America in the 21st century—to the victor go the spoils, along with a lot of influence generated by interest groups who make contributions in order to get their place at the power table.

As I'll detail many times in the course of this book, this is what is wrong with our political system. To put it bluntly, we have the dumbest, most corrupt system you could imagine. Think about it—people or groups that want something from government fund the campaigns of the people we elect to make decisions on whether they get that action from government. It could be a law they're trying to pass; it could be a raise or a pension increase; it could be a law to punish a competitor or to assure a shortage of some good or service. Whatever it may be, these interest groups use their funding of politicians' campaigns to make sure their consideration is put above the average voter's.

Newsom is and has always been an expert at playing this ridiculous and corrupt system. It's not just that he hands out benefits to those that send him campaign money or fund PACS to support him. It's also that he makes sure policies are geared to what these groups want.

As you will read in this book, California is one of the most expensive states in the union to live in. That's not an accident of geography; that's well planned. The regulations that drive up the cost of housing are advocated for by groups that benefit from them, be it environmental groups that argue for them and then brag to donors—and potential donors—that they've achieved something for the donations given them. Same for the lack of water or energy—groups that advocate for protection of fish or want to eliminate fossil fuels use their funding to make sure regulations don't allow construction of reservoirs or allow oil companies to obtain drilling permits. Advocates for the homeless want government largesse—the homeless industrial complex, it's called—to address the problem but only in the way they want—with government-funded expensive housing first instead of addiction or mental health treatment.

The biggest group impacting government policy is the teachers' unions. They are often called the third branch of government in Sacramento—apparently supplanting the judicial branch. California—with the full support of the teachers' unions (read that as millions of dollars in ads) passed a proposition a number of years ago requiring that 50 percent of state spending has to go to education. California now spends over $100 billion a year on education, yet the results are some of the worst in the nation, placing forty-ninth or so, right around Mississippi, which spends a fraction of what California spends.

Newsom is not only an expert at raising money—he's also an expert at divisive issues and playing them for all that they're worth. Abortion is one of the most divisive in the country. Is Newsom interested in forging compromise that both sides can live with? Not a chance. When the Supreme Court weighed in on reversing *Roe v. Wade*, a decision criticized by many constitutional lawyers, including late justice Ruth Bader Ginsburg (who liked the result but often said it was not a well-reasoned opinion), Newsom not only didn't seek compromises: he stepped up the heat, turning California into the abortion capital of the country, even using taxpayer dollars—including much from many taxpayers who personally abhor abortion—to fly women to California to dispose of their infant unborn children.

I would submit that championing a cause—such as making sure your constituents who want an abortion can get one, if that's how you feel—is one thing. But turning your state into a magnet for women around the country to come here and get taxpayer-paid abortions is not serving your constituents; it's grandstanding on a national scale.

It's that way on many other issues—particularly the ones that energize the left wing of the Democratic Party. That's no mistake either. Newsom is definitely going to run for president at some point; his courtship of the Left is directed at that effort. The Left is the controlling arm of the presidential primaries. He knows it.

Every time there is a shooting that horrifies Americans, Newsom is right there to decry gun ownership. Nary a word about mental health or ending the media sensationalism surrounding these events that incentivize the next shooter.

California has some of the most restrictive gun control policies in the nation; it hasn't exactly made this state a utopia of safety. Did Newsom call for enhanced mental health treatment? Did Newsom call for ending the sensationalism of violence in our popular media or decry a morbid fascination with death? Did Newsom call for the media to stop publicizing the names and backgrounds of the perpetrators? Let's face it: most of these mass shooters want to go out with a blaze of glory from the massive press attention. No. Instead he proposes more gun control laws that these perpetrators didn't care about to begin with.

The same holds for environmental laws in California, many of which help drive up the cost of living and otherwise make living here less than ideal. We have shortages of water and energy—even though their costs are outrageously high, precisely due to the environmental extremism that powers politicians like Newsom.

While Californians are paying through the nose for energy and water, not to mention gasoline, China and India are literally spewing clouds of particulates into the world's atmosphere, polluting more than the rest of the world combined. It's actually worse than this. Natural gas is a fossil fuel that does burn cleaner than either coal or oil. China doesn't have great reserves of natural gas, so it buys expensive coal, mostly from Australia and other places, and builds coal-fired electricity plants to feed its insatiable need for energy. If we were able to develop our ample natural gas reserves—we burn off millions of cubic feet each day uselessly—we would produce enough to lower the price significantly—this would make it competitive to freeze and ship it to China and India. In so doing, natural gas could compete effectively with higher-cost dirty fuels like coal and oil and lower the pollution and the temperature of the earth. However, since natural gas is a fossil fuel and environmental groups that raise millions scaring people need to use their money to ply politicians in the U.S. and particularly California, this doesn't happen. China and India go on their merry way, polluting the world and Californians pay the price in higher gasoline, energy, and water prices.

The latest—and maybe greatest—diversionary tactic of Newsom and his leftist legislature is reparations. No one can deny the injustice of slavery. Our country has already admitted this horrendous treatment of our brethren and spent literally trillions—the Great Society is only one of the many efforts we have made as a nation to correct the ills of this despicable practice.

That's apparently not enough for the Far Left. Now, in a massive display of divisiveness, it is proposing reparations that would literally bankrupt the state. Having failed to speak up when this disaster was being debated in his legislature and allowing an "exploratory" committee to hold hearings, Newsom has opened a pandora's box of reparations that has him painted into a corner. Either way he goes creates a problem given the enormous sums needed for reparations. Newsom may have been sanguine when he reported a $100 billion surplus in advance of the recall, but that "surplus" is gone—if it ever existed at all and the state faces a fiscal reckoning of deficits even without massive spending for reparations.

All the while, homelessness continues; housing keeps getting more expensive; energy production is ignored; education keeps being weakened; and the exodus from California continues. A future bill from reparations will surely accelerate the exodus. Yet Gavin Newsom's special-interest backers double down, pledging millions more to keep his legislative agenda and the status quo the same while Californians endure the mismanagement and the exodus continues.

That's our system. Policy corrupted by campaign contributions. The media used as a tool by these same politicians. In fact, the media has become one of the most powerful interest groups there is. That's true whether it's Left or Right. The so-called mainstream media—ABC, CBS, NBC, along with major newspapers like the *New York Times* and *Los Angeles Times*—are decidedly Left of center in their bias and control news access to their watchers and readers. Same with Fox News on the Right. The gatekeepers in the media—the producers and agents—control who gets on and who gets a message out. They, in turn, make millions from the ads placed by those same candidates who use the media fame they get to raise their profile and raise millions, which promptly gets spent on ads, enriching that same media. A corrupt circle of money that distorts our policy, turns off the electorate, and threatens our country's future.

As I said, a dumb and corrupt system. Those that want something from government fund the advertising that elects the leadership engaged to make those decisions. This has to change. And Gavin Newsom is at the center of it and one of the best manipulators of the system. He cannot be empowered to accelerate it on a national basis.

Why Gavin Newsom Should Never Be President

Leadership matters, and Newsom's type of leadership is the opposite of what we need.

I believe the United States is the greatest country in the history of the world and our leadership matters to the future of the world.

That's not meant to be pejorative toward other countries or egotistical. It's spoken in a spirit of thanksgiving that our country, warts and all, has stood for freedom and opportunity for peoples all over the world. I don't think it is too much an exaggeration, particularly given the past one hundred years, which have seen not only remarkable progress in human living standards but also two World Wars and the deployment of advanced weaponry with the potential to destroy the world.

As such, it is important for America to succeed. Time and again, we have come to the aid of countries the world over. Should we not succeed, that ability to help would be limited. That would be a loss for the world.

It's important to our success that we have a strong economy and defense; equally important is strong leadership to make sure we do the right things to build the strength of our country. We've seen throughout history how a lack of strong/principled leadership has had a deleterious effect on a country's future as much or more as the presence of strong leadership has helped a country surmount major challenges. At the turn of the 20th century, Argentina was one of the strongest and most successful countries in the world. By the middle of that century, as the Peronistas ran that country in massive debt that led to bankruptcy, Argentina was a basket case.

It's happened more recently in Cuba and Venezuela. In both cases, charismatic leaders looking to consolidate absolute power have led their countries downhill. Both of those countries, once wealthy and successful, are now backward countries where human rights are abused and opportunities for young people are almost nonexistent. Both of those countries have had a "brain drain" of their best and brightest; they have also experienced massive migration away from them, which has endangered neighbors and other countries in the region.

It's often worked the other way in times when countries have been challenged. Who can doubt that Great Britain and the United States benefitted from the strong leadership of Winston Churchill and Dwight Eisenhower? Ronald Reagan almost single-handedly led to the end of the

Cold War, freeing so many Eastern Europeans from the grip of the Soviet Union. Leadership matters greatly.

That brings us to California and the possibility that Gavin Newsom will potentially run for the U.S. presidency. Widely considered by supporters to be articulate and handsome, Newsom is the epitome of a leader handpicked by the powerful and connected as well as someone who seeks power for its own sake. As I've laid out earlier in this chapter, he is the scion of a family whose connections he has used to both accumulate power and riches for himself and his cronies. Along the way, he has consistently exploited divisive issues while ignoring or in fact making many basic management issues much worse.

At times, he has seemed to want to reform the system. He did write a book, *Citizenville*, that proposed a digital revolution for government services. While the book talked a lot about connecting people to government to get its help, it didn't involve any meaningful reform of a political system long captured by special interests. On those kinds of reforms, Newsom has been noticeably absent, although I hold out hope that his penchant for "big hairy audacious goals"—a quote he uses often—may lead him to embrace and support a reform like Hear the People that empowers citizens and removes the power of special interests.

As with most politicians, he is expert at manipulating the media while keeping them at arm's length. He has used his position to accumulate enormous stores of campaign cash, which he has then used to his best advantage. This extends to increasing his national profile. He went so far as in the most recent reelection campaign to purchase billboards in other states to poke at governors who would be future opponents. Most recently, he moved $10 million from his campaign accounts to a national effort to support candidates in red and swing states that would be important to a future presidential election.

All during his governorship, Newsom has stayed relatively silent on the operational problems of California, preferring to speak out on hot-button issues like abortion, guns, and immigration. He's not exhibited an overriding concern to compromise or search for solutions on those issues, preferring to fan the flames of divisiveness, focusing his attention on the issues most calculated to energize the extreme Left of his party, which he knows will hold sway in the presidential primaries. At the same time, a compliant media, which pretty much agrees with most of what he says, goes along with him and highlights his most extreme statements, which also generate lots of clicks and eyeballs.

It's continued into 2023. Despite the fact that California has the highest cost of living and the highest gasoline prices, Newsom has pushed through a new commission to impose penalties on oil companies that make "too much" profit. Rather than lower gasoline taxes or encourage more production to lower prices, which would use markets to lower prices, Newsom is going to use the heavy hand of government to judge which companies are making too much money. These fines are only going to make gasoline more expensive and drive producers to other states.

He's doing it with pharmaceuticals too. Rather than break down barriers to competition in the insulin market, he's putting the state of California into the insulin production business. A state that spends billions on education while having lower test scores than most of the nation, a state that can't get you through the DMV in less than a couple of hours, a state that spends billions on the homeless while watching their numbers soar, a state that lost billions on fraudulent unemployment claims during the pandemic—this is a state that Newsom wants to put into the pharmaceutical business.

There is no end to the expansion of government in California. We now have a state bank. Our pension and healthcare systems for retirees are huge and grossly underfunded and badly managed. Our state budget, under $100 billion in 2010 when Jerry Brown took over, is now well over $300 billion just thirteen years later despite very small population growth and very light inflation except for the past two years. After inflation, the per capita spending in California has doubled in the past twelve years, with population growth of about 10 percent. This is especially egregious when you consider that most of the state's spending is on labor and advances in computing technology have resulted in massive administrative savings on labor in the private sector over the past decade. That technology revolution hasn't yet had much of an impact in what most acknowledge is the leading tech state in the country.

As I detail very carefully in later chapters, California is the poster child for government mismanagement and inefficiency. If you are very rich, you enjoy the state and its many blessings—its wonderful weather and natural beauty, its cultural diversity, its gateway to the Far East. However, if you aren't rich, you likely struggle to make ends meet; you probably watch as your children have to move away to pursue an affordable life; you suffer with increasing homelessness on our streets, uncontrolled crime and wildfires that threaten your life and property; your children have to endure an educational system stuffed with administrators and where poor teachers can't be replaced. On top of this, you pay the highest taxes in the country while enduring shortages of housing, water, energy, and an affordable lifestyle.

This doesn't have to be the case. The problems can be solved. This state has the resources and brainpower to overcome our challenges. What we need is leadership dedicated to searching for answers that involve harnessing the good work of many and the freedom to pursue that good work. As Ronald Reagan said often, government isn't the solution to our problems; government is the problem. Large and incompetent government is the problem in California and we don't want it to spread over the entire country.

At the same time, our nation is in a political crisis of sorts right now. Due to the explosion of social media as well as the overpowering impact of fundraising on our political system, our political differences have been magnified. This has resulted in "cancel culture"—a shutdown of free speech. Often, it has resulted in violence as the demonstrations after George Floyd's death and the January 6 Capitol riot showed.

Gavin Newsom lives off these differences. His entire political career has been about exacerbating these differences and using them for political gain. We don't need our divisions to be opened up even more. We need leadership right now that seeks solutions instead of firing up emotions. In a time of turmoil, not only in America but in the world, we need someone in office who will work to put out the flames, not fan them. A huge national debt, a war in Europe, an ambitious, huge force in China—these challenges must be met with cool heads and steely resolve. Newsom has not demonstrated either of these characteristics. He's a child of power who seeks more—any way he can get it. That's leadership we need to shun, not embrace in a very dangerous world.

That's why it's essential that Gavin Newsom not bring his mismanagement to the White House.

CHAPTER 5

THE GREAT EXODUS

Jorge Martinez loves the large backyard of his home in Phoenix, Arizona. As we spoke over Zoom on a February day in 2021, he panned his laptop camera over his shoulder, showing the nature preserve that runs wild in his neighborhood. Mountains rise over a jogging trail. It is a quiet place where his children can ride their bikes and play without a care.

Martinez was born in Mexico in 1975. As a young boy, he bounced around between the Michoacán countryside, Mexico City, and California. His father would cross the border into America and do odd jobs like washing dishes in the old Amfac Hotel in Los Angeles. When Jorge was seven, his family legally moved to the U.S. for good.

Martinez told me, "I started school in the U.S. in second grade at Jefferson Elementary School in the city of Lennox." Lennox, California, is a working-class city that lies on the eastern boundary of Los Angeles International Airport. Tourists leaving the airport on the elevated 105 freeway look down on Lennox on their way to somewhere else. *Two* freeways, the 105 and the 405, form the western and southern boundaries of the city. It's the kind of place where people put bars over their windows and don't walk alone at night.

Martinez was a good kid who wanted a better life. He graduated from Hawthorne High School and pondered his next step. "I wanted to get out of Lennox. A lot of gang violence. Too many near misses. Not because I was doing anything illegal. I was just at the wrong place at the wrong time." Gang violence is common in Lennox. The violent crime rate is 61 percent above the national average.

Martinez related one particularly harrowing story. "I had graduated high school. I wanted to get out of California real badly because of all the gangs. So I signed up for a trade school in Arizona. I had learned drafting from my freshman year through my senior year in high school. I was in the top three in my class. I signed up for the school, and they accepted me, so I went away."

Martinez came back to visit his parents for the holidays in November of 1995. He was driving in a car at night with three friends. Continuing his story as the Arizona sun shines down on him, he says, "My friend George was driving, and we were heading westbound on 104th Street near Inglewood Avenue. I was behind the driver, and my friend David was right next to me. My friend Gus was in the front passenger seat. We saw a gold GMC truck roll by at a fast speed, going northbound on Inglewood Blvd. The driver stopped at a dead stop and put the truck into reverse until he was right next to us. The passenger of the truck pulled out a gun and started shooting at George. BANG! One, two, three. I turned to look at the passenger who fired the shots. I got a clear look at the person. He saw me move in the backseat and pointed the gun at me. I saw the fire coming out of the muzzle. He unloaded his weapon at me. It was surreal. There was this loud buzzing in my ears, and time had frozen. I looked down and saw blood all over my hands."

Miraculously, Martinez was not hit. "I don't know; maybe it was divine intervention or whatever you call it." The blood was coming from George, the driver, shot in the abdomen and legs. George tried to drive the car toward the hospital but passed out and crashed into a parked tow truck.

The neighbors who came out of their houses began asking the teens, "Where you from?"—slang for "What gang are you in?" Sensing more trouble, Martinez took the wheel and drove his friend to the hospital. Two days later, Martinez left California for his trade school in Arizona. "I was going to school to get educated so I could get out of Lennox; that was the goal. My dad always told me that with hard work and education, you could get yourself out of here—which turned out to be true."

Martinez graduated with a degree in architecture. He moved to the west side of Los Angeles, disregarding the high cost of rent in exchange for safety. He took up surfing and lived the beach life, eventually settling in Redondo Beach. He got married, had two sons, and worked his way up to become the facilities manager of Com Dev USA, an aerospace company in El Segundo.

By 2007 Martinez had saved $120,000 and started looking to buy a home. He remembers, "I was doing great at my job. I had a great career making just over one hundred thousand dollars, but five hundred thousand for a three-bedroom, one-bath? It just didn't make any sense. I would have to live to pay off my house, and I wouldn't get to enjoy my California lifestyle. Go surfing, go camping, all the great places California has to offer like Yosemite. I wanted to stay here because that's where my roots are, that's where I grew up." Martinez's decision was all too familiar in California: stay and be house poor or move out of California.

While the house hunting dragged on, Honeywell bought Com Dev in 2018 and decided to shut down the plant. His boss came up to Martinez and told him to apply for open positions in Arizona. "Jorge, you're very talented—stay with Honeywell. Look at the value in Phoenix. There's opportunity everywhere."

When Martinez and his wife started looking at the houses for sale, they could not believe what they found. In a tone any Californian knows all too well, he told me, "$340,000 could get us a two-story house with five bedrooms and three baths, a backyard, out by the countryside where I want to be. This is too tempting."

Martinez worried about uprooting his family. "I was not going to do it until I had buy-in from everybody. My kids grew up in Redondo; all they know is the beach. The good life. A nice healthy lifestyle. No gangs. No shootings. No nothing. That's something I always wanted for my kids—the ability to go outside and ride their bike, go to the beach, go wherever they wanted in the neighborhood—without getting bothered." His wife, Victoria, was all in. He knew his school-aged boys would be a tougher sell.

Martinez heard of a job opportunity at another aerospace company that would allow him to stay in California. But he and his wife could not find a house in a safe neighborhood the family could afford. The Martinezes could stay in Redondo Beach and continue to pay $2,000 a month for a 950-square-foot two-bedroom apartment or move out of the state he loved. "This is the place where I want to grow old and die, man. It just killed me." He grew sanguine and said, "Maybe the universe had something else in store for me. Financially it just didn't make any sense for me to stay here."

In 2019, after receiving the go-ahead from his sons, the family left California and moved to Phoenix. "It was our dream house: hardwood floors, beautiful kitchen, four bedrooms, three baths—just everything we always wanted," he said. He pulls off his red and black baseball cap adorned with the state flag of Arizona and runs his hand over his head. "I don't know. Is this home? I guess it is because we have a house and my family is here. But would I love to go back to California? Hell yeah, I would." He paused and added wistfully, "It kind of sucks, but here I am."

In the end, his family's decision to leave California was the only choice that made sense. "Arizona's been good to me. I was paying $2,000 for rent in California, and I'm paying $2,000 for my mortgage here." He spoke about his emotions on May 28, 2019, the day he closed on his new three thousand-square-foot home. "It was just the greatest day, something that was only a dream in California."

For an hour, we talked about the high cost of living in California. He paid $350 to register his 2007 Ford F-150 in California. In Arizona, it cost him $80. He went on, "I thought, man, this is great. In California, you pay fifty dollars for a smog check. Here you pay fifteen bucks. If I wanted to take my family out for a meal in Riviera Village in Redondo Beach, I would spend roughly one hundred fifty. Here it's seventy-five bucks for a nice little dinner." He spends over one dollar a gallon less for gas than I do in San Diego. He earns the same amount of money but reckons that living there costs about 15 percent less overall.

As we wrapped up our conversation, I asked him if he had any parting thoughts on leaving California.

He paused and replied, "How do you put a price on roots, on the family? How does a three-bedroom, one-bath house in an OK neighborhood cost seven hundred thousand dollars? I understand how the market works and all that, but it just makes no sense to me. I have my roots in California. I'd stay there the rest of my life if I could, but..." His voice trailed off. "I just don't get it—the state of California. I mean, I'm a Democrat and all that, but something has to change."

Martinez counts himself as one of the lucky ones. He got out of Lennox, got an education, and lives the American Dream, if not the California Dream. He wonders about those he left behind, "What happens to all those families that can't afford a home? I got an education, right? But what about all those people in low-income neighborhoods? How are they going to be able to afford a home? How are they going to be able to put down roots?"

The answer is that they likely won't. California leads the nation in people moving out of state. According to Newsweek, 661,026 people left California in 2018. More than seven million people born in California have left the state for good. When Jorge Martinez moved to the Phoenix area, he was in good company. In total, 396,728 people born in California now reside in greater Phoenix. In total, six hundred forty thousand former Californians live in Arizona. More than seven hundred fifty thousand California-born residents have left the Golden State to relocate to Texas, the number-one destination for Californians fleeing the skyrocketing cost of living.

This ongoing departure does not bode well for California's economy. According to IRS data, for 1992–2018, California lost $73.52 billion in adjusted gross income (AGI) as measured on personal income tax returns. Texas gained $53.5 billion in AGI, and Arizona gained $42.7 billion. These figures represent people like the Martinez family, who support local businesses, buy cars, pay taxes, and enrich their state. Their children will put down roots and flourish in places with a lower cost of living. Generational wealth is created elsewhere, and California loses in both the short and long run.

Sixty-two percent of Californians believe California's best days are behind it, according to the 2019 Edelman Trust Barometer. Seventy-two percent rate the cost and availability of housing as a severe issue. Fifty-three percent—over half of all Californians—are considering leaving California because of the high cost of living.

Jorge Martinez's story is the new California story: driven out of the state he loves by crime and the high cost of living. What sensible person wouldn't consider moving out of state when you will pay $2,000 a month for a two-bedroom apartment *and* worry if your children will be safe walking home from school?

Do you feel safer than you did ten years ago? Neither do most Californians. Jorge Martinez feels safer in Arizona; I can tell you that. The streets are safer and cleaner without masses of desperate people living in makeshift shelters, shacks, or tents under and around freeway overpasses.

Crime Climbs in California

Crime is out of control in California, and people are afraid. The 2020 Safest Cities Survey found 58 percent of Californians worry about crime *every day*. That is 26 percent higher than the national average. Seventy percent of Californians are highly concerned about someone breaking into their home, and 38 percent have experienced a property crime in the last year. As a result, Californians have a higher percentage of home security systems than any other state. We are living in fear.

People need to feel safe in their homes, their communities, and their state. Psychologist Abraham Maslow talks about this concept in his seminal theory of a "hierarchy of needs." He placed safety right below food and water in importance and above love and friendship. In a modern version of our fight-or-flight instinct, people are fleeing California in record numbers.

It is easy to blame society for crime and our urban problems. But first, we must look at ourselves. Personal responsibility is one of the foundational pillars on which our society rests. Each one of us must be held accountable for our actions. Lately, our collective mindset has shifted toward a victim mentality. Ronald Reagan took a stand against the abdication of responsibility when he said, "Every time a law is broken, we must reject the idea that society is guilty rather than the lawbreaker. It is time to restore the American precept that each individual is accountable for his actions."

California is in the middle of an unprecedented crime wave. Sacramento's soft stance on crime has given criminal gangs carte blanche to steal without the threat of criminal prosecution. Proposition 47 made it a misdemeanor to steal under $950 worth of merchandise. The only consequence is a ticket, which is hardly a deterrent to hardened street thugs. Organized groups of thieves are ransacking stores, and the police are powerless to stop it.

Without the threat of jail time, criminals have become brazen. A mob of eighty thieves cleared out a Nordstrom department store in November 2021 and fled the scene with between $100,000 and $200,000 worth of merchandise. Smash-and-grab robberies are plaguing large cities like Los Angeles and San Francisco and small towns like Torrance and Beverly Hills. Thieves have even broken into Gavin Newsom's business three times this year. On one November Friday night, gangs of criminals robbed six high-end stores like Louis Vuitton and multiple cannabis dispensaries in the Union Square shopping district in San Francisco. These robberies hurt companies' bottom lines and traumatize workers and customers. The Walgreens at 15th and Geary in San Francisco recently decided to lock up its freezers holding pizza and ice cream because they were being looted daily by shoplifters!

The Los Angeles district attorney, George Gascón, is an ally of Gavin Newsom and was the subject of a recall attempt in 2022(his fellow soft-on-crime DA in San Francisco was just recalled in June 2022). Gascón cowrote Proposition 47. Not only did Prop 47 make robbery a misdemeanor, but Gascón refuses to prosecute misdemeanors in Los Angeles County. Police officers complain that the thieves are often released before an officer can finish their report. Former L.A. County Sheriff Alex Villaneuva had been particularly critical of Gascón's refusal to hold criminals accountable. Villanueva said, "So, you're doubling down on a really bad idea [Prop 47], and now we're seeing the consequences of it."

Gascón responded by insulting the sheriff. "My dad used to say that when you wrestle with a pig, you both get muddy, and the pig likes it." With words like that from the DA, it's no wonder criminals feel emboldened.

Gascón's criminals-first mentality has angered peace officers, business owners, and victim-rights groups. Even Gascón's deputy district attorneys have turned on him. The Association of Deputy District Attorneys filed a lawsuit alleging Gascón is ignoring laws meant to protect the public. A Los Angeles superior court judge agreed and sided with the plaintiffs.

Gascón issued a statement calling the criminal justice system "a dated institution steeped in systemic racism." Gascón defended his policies despite the recent crime waves spreading like wildfire across L.A. County and the rest of the state. He went on to state, "We can no longer afford—morally, socially or economically—to justify tough-on-crime policies..." Tell that to the store owners and customers who are being terrorized by criminal gangs, Mr. District Attorney. It is time to put law-abiding citizens first and stop coddling criminals.

Criminal justice reform measures are endangering public safety. The bleeding hearts in Sacramento have prioritized the rights of criminals over citizens. The governor shifted blame to mayors who "need to step up" before boarding a jet to vacation with his family in Mexico. His lenient laws and soft-on-crime policies are like a virus spreading through California.

Business owners are losing money they don't have after repeated COVID shutdowns. Shoppers are scared to go to the mall. Police are frustrated because misguided legislation and liberal judges have handcuffed them and given the criminals the upper hand. Crime is out of control due to ten years of Democratic dominance and a political culture that prioritizes criminals and ignores the rights and needs of law-abiding citizens.

Just recently, a Riverside County sheriff's deputy was gunned down by a criminal who had been released by a compliant judge. This deputy, Isaiah Cordero, was just thirty-two years old and was gunned down by a criminal who had previous convictions for armed robbery and a myriad of other crimes. Under the "three strikes" law, he should have been in prison forever, but the judge in L.A. County let him out on bail from yet another crime. This criminal was ultimately gunned down by police after a long chase but the damage was done and a family lost a dedicated son and public servant.

We all acknowledge that crime is a complex problem that cannot be solved by simply throwing more people in jail. We need to take a balanced approach that incorporates mental health and drug treatment for those that genuinely need help. We should develop more partnerships with faith-based and nonprofit community organizations to give people the support they need to turn things around and lead productive lives. Local groups know their communities better than Sacramento does. They can distribute resources more fairly and efficiently. A holistic approach that incorporates education, mental health services, drug treatment programs, and job training will help end the generational cycle of incarceration. I also believe in restorative justice to bring together victims and offenders in a dialogue designed to reduce recidivism—the offender's commission of more crimes in the future. Understanding the hurt done to the victim is an essential part of the rehabilitation process.

At the same time, we have to recognize that there are some people who do not want to conform to society's laws. These people must be separated from society so that those who want to flourish in our society and obey the laws can do so without fear. If someone commits a crime, they may express remorse and be rehabilitated, but if that happens continually, we must decide as a society that the protection of the vast majority of us who obey the laws warrants our protection and we need judges and law enforcement professionals, as well as political leaders, to recognize this fact.

High-quality education and the economic benefits it imparts are the surest way to decrease crime systemically. Providing parents in lower socioeconomic neighborhoods the opportunity to find better schools for their children improves their chances of living a happy, productive life and becoming good citizens. Every child deserves an equal opportunity, and the choice of a good education is essential to that opportunity. We owe it to our law-abiding citizens who live in crime-ridden neighborhoods and don't have the education, the resources, or the chance to leave. If you don't have a choice to move, you need better school choices even more. That's why scholarships or vouchers for low-income and middle-class children are a key aspect of any comprehensive effort to combat crime.

There has been a *cultural* exodus from California as well. In the summer of 2020, comedian Joe Rogan, who has one of the most popular podcasts globally, with over 190 million weekly downloads, packed up his studio and left for Austin. Many other comedians and content creators followed him to Texas, where Rogan opened his own comedy club. He has created jobs elsewhere for dozens, if not hundreds, of creative Californians.

In September 2020, a few months after Rogan's move, political commentator Ben Shapiro, probably the most influential voice at reaching young conservatives, announced that he and his media company, *The Daily Wire*, would be relocating from Los Angeles to Nashville. "We're leaving because all the benefits of California have steadily eroded and then suddenly collapsed," he wrote in a *Fox News* op-ed. "Meanwhile, all the costs of California have steadily increased and then suddenly skyrocketed. I want my kids to grow up safe. I want them to grow up in a community with a future, with more freedom and safety than I experienced growing up. California makes that impossible. So, goodbye, Golden State. Thanks for the memories."

Add to this Joe Lonsdale, a young venture capitalist who was one of the early employees of PayPal and a Silicon Valley giant. Lonsdale moved to Texas and penned an op-ed in the *Wall Street Journal*, criticizing the quality of life in his home state of California. His piece, ironically titled "California, Love it and Leave it," discusses his long history in the state of his birth, attending Stanford University and starting a venture capital firm in the Bay Area. He says that the gross mismanagement of the state, including public safety, electricity, housing, homelessness, education, roads, and more, has made it unlivable for him and his family and his employees.

It hurts our state to have all of these talented people walking out the door. Imagine if we had overregulated Hollywood during its Golden Age! We certainly wouldn't have had the great entertainment industry we have enjoyed in California. This migration will continue until the situation becomes more tenable for business owners and job creators.

It's not just citizens, entertainers, and entrepreneurs leaving California. Businesses are fleeing the Golden State in droves. Recently Oracle, Hewlett Packard, and Charles Schwab have joined Toyota, Nestlé, and other major corporate employers in calling it quits in California. In the coming months, they are sure to be joined by others, along with tens of thousands of individuals who have likewise given up on the Golden State. Late last year, it was announced that California has lost one of its congressional seats in the last census due to its declining population, barely avoiding a loss of a second seat as many had expected. Quite a comedown the California Dream that had seen decades of uninterrupted growth and prosperity in years past.

Why are so many people and businesses leaving California? Other states offer businesses incentives to relocate. The Texas Enterprise Fund is a program that incentivizes corporate relocation. The Lone Star State gave Toyota $40 million to come to the Lone Star State. That works out to about $10,000 per job. That may sound like a lot of money, but Texas will get that ten grand paid back many times over when employees pay sales taxes, spend their money supporting Texas businesses, and raise children who will live and work there. All that money stays in Texas.

Carl's Jr. is a California success story. In 1941, Carl Karcher borrowed $311, using his Plymouth as collateral. He purchased a hot dog cart and set up business on a Los Angeles Street corner. Fifteen years later, he opened the first of many Carl's Jr. restaurants. Today there are 677 locations in California. Sadly, there will never be another Carl's Jr. built in California. It can take two years to complete the regulatory process required to open a new location in our state. In Texas, it takes two weeks. Carl's Jr. pays $200,000 more per location in California than Texas due to red tape. Recently, Carl's Jr. packed up its corporate offices and left for Tennessee. In a *Wall Street Journal* op-ed, Andy Puzder, then the chief executive officer of Carl's Jr.'s parent company, called California "the most business-unfriendly state we operate in." The cost of doing business in California is driving companies and jobs out of state.

California is losing the last vestiges of its once mighty automobile industry. For decades, California's car culture, highly educated workforce, and cutting-edge technology incentivized automobile makers to establish headquarters and production plants in California. Not anymore. Mitsubishi Motors announced in 2019 that it was leaving Cypress for Nashville, Tennessee. Nissan left Gardena for a new home in Tennessee in 2006. Along with thousands of middle-class jobs, these car companies fled to states with no income tax, lower cost of living, better schools, and fewer government regulations.

For Many, the Final Straw

Tesla is the latest in a long line of companies freeing themselves from the burden of California's regulations. After a row with government regulators about COVID-19 precautions at his Fremont factory in June 2020, Elon Musk tweeted, "Frankly, this is the final straw. Tesla will now move its HQ and future programs to Texas/Nevada immediately. If we even retain Fremont manufacturing activity, it will be on how Tesla is treated in the future. Tesla is the last carmaker left in CA."

Toyota left Torrance for Plano, Texas, in 2017. Chuck Dannis, a real estate professor at SMU, cites housing costs as the main reason Toyota relocated to Texas. In the Dallas area, homes cost four times the median income. In Torrance, a house is seven times the median income. The median home price in Torrance is about $300,000 more expensive than a similar home in north Texas. The cost per square foot for a house in Torrance is triple that of a home in the north Dallas suburbs. Toyota researched and found that employees were willing to move elsewhere to live the American Dream and buy their own homes.

Jim Lentz, CEO of Toyota North America, told *Automotive News*, "California is a great place to be, but it's costly, and the commute times are rough." To him, Texas was a better choice. "I think life is a little bit easier for people here. As a result, I think the work-life balance is much better. If you live in Southern California and you're driving two or two and a half hours each way, you're leaving at 5 a.m., and you're getting home at 8 or 9—that kind of wears on you." When asked if he would do anything differently, he replied, "Yes, we should have done it ten years earlier."

The population of Texas is growing, while California's population is shrinking. In the last ten years, 700,000 Californians have immigrated to Texas. Why are so many Californians choosing the Lone Star Republic over the Bear Flag Republic? Stanford University and the University of Texas released a joint study in September 2021 on that very question. They found the number-one reason was the cost of living, particularly taxes and housing.

Californians pay the highest state income taxes in the nation, while Texans pay no state income tax. Californians who move to Texas add over 9 percent to their take-home pay, even more if you are in a higher tax bracket. You could use that money to save for your children's college or toward a down payment for a home.

Speaking of down payments, the average down payment in California will run you about $137,000. In Texas, that figure is $49,500. The prohibitive cost is a significant obstacle preventing Californians from buying a home. To realize their dream and save enough money for a down payment, the typical California resident would need to set aside $2,283 a month for five years. In Texas, you would need to save $825 a month. No matter where they live, most people cannot afford to save over $2,000 a month to put a down payment on a home.

California is hemorrhaging our best and brightest. I've spoken to college students who graduate with marketable degrees but significant student debt. They simply cannot afford to save enough money to buy a home in California. The prohibitive cost of housing is a significant reason why so many people are fleeing California. New grads choose to begin their careers in states like Texas and Tennessee, where homeownership is more than just a dream. The average home in Texas costs about $436,000 less than the average home in California. In fact, most homes in Texas cost less than $200,000. Contrast that with California, where most homes cost over $500,000. Parents across this beautiful state are fed up with high housing prices driving their children out of California.

Our leaders in Sacramento are causing our housing crisis in California. California is forty-ninth out of fifty states in new housing units per capita. Environmental regulations and frivolous lawsuits stop new projects from being greenlit or bog projects down in the courts until they become economically unfeasible. People keep moving farther and farther away from their jobs because they can't afford to rent or buy a home, which leads to longer commutes, increased traffic, more pollution, and a diminished quality of life.

To add insult to your daily commute, we have the highest gas tax in the nation. All in, counting cap and trade and other environment related charges, Californians pay 97 cents in taxes on every gallon of gasoline. The national average is twenty-five cents. Sacramento siphons off more than twenty dollars in taxes every time you fill up your tank. Texans pay twenty cents per gallon of gas in state taxes. In Arizona, the state tax adds nineteen cents to every gallon. That translates into a savings of about seven dollars per fill-up. California's sky-high vehicle license fees and the highest gasoline taxes in the nation are some of the reasons why so many families can't make ends meet anymore. The most urgent need is to repeal the new vehicle license and gas tax increases.

Spectrum Location Solutions, a business relocation firm, says 18,000 companies left California between 2008 and 2019. And we're not only talking here about giant corporations. The Small Business and Entrepreneurship Council ranked California forty-ninth out of fifty states in the small business policy index. Small businesses are vital to economic growth. They generate jobs and power California's economy. Small businesses simply cannot shoulder the burden of regulations created by bureaucrats who know nothing about them or their business.

Silicon Valley is an epicenter of innovation, a place where cutting-edge ideas incubate and grow. Yet, when new start-ups succeed and expand, they leave the Golden State for greener pastures. The success stories are well-known: Oracle, Cisco, Hewlett Packard—and they are all leaving California. Even established giants like Google, Intel, and eBay are expanding in other states, leaving California and its regulations behind. Our middle class is fleeing the state. The bleeding needs to stop.

You don't make those research and development investments if your tax rates are much higher than the rest of the world. Sacramento uses business tax revenue to create more bureaucracy and more regulations. That's a win-win for special-interest groups, lobbyists, and public employee unions. That is why I endorse corporate tax cuts. Corporations will use that capital to make better products, generate income, and create good-paying jobs. It's a win-win for everyone.

California has two significant problems in retaining businesses and their employees. First, Sacramento is failing to protect public safety. Everyone I talk to says the same thing: they feel less safe than they did ten years ago. They are afraid to walk the streets or go to the grocery store. Secondly, the government needs to promote a more business-friendly environment. High taxes, excessive regulations, powerful public employee unions, frivolous lawsuits, and a burdensome environmental review process drive businesses out of our state.

The best way to facilitate and foster economic development is by creating a regulatory climate that protects the public interest while providing a robust environment in which businesses can thrive. In this duty, the public sector is failing. We must look to the private sector and free-market solutions to retain California companies, the jobs they create, and the Californians they employ.

Much of this is caused by the special-interest political control in Sacramento. Public sector unions love more regulations as that requires more employees to administer which generate higher dues they can use to support politicians who give them higher wages and benefits. How's that for a vicious circle?Other lobbying groups like environmentalists also benefit from more regulations that they can point to in acquiring more donations to fund their operations. Trial lawyers benefit from the thicket of regulations as well as the litigation that ensues; they funnel more and more of that largesse to politicians who then enact more rules and liability statutes that enrich them even more. More vicious circles of pain for consumers and non-political actors. These groups can do all of this because of a system where their money elects their political handmaidens. All of this points to more and more evidence that the election system in this state must change for these conditions to change.

California is failing cities like Lennox, companies like Toyota, and citizens like Jorge Martinez. The American Dream is no longer attainable for most Californians, so they leave to find it elsewhere. We must improve public safety, lower housing costs, reduce taxes and fees, and retain businesses—or the great exodus will continue.

CHAPTER 6

MERITOCRACY: FREE MARKETS, FREE PEOPLE

Lowell High School is the oldest high school west of the Mississippi. It ranks among the best high schools in the nation. Lowell's unassuming campus is in the Sunset District of San Francisco. Lowell High School bears another important distinction from which we can learn lessons. It was the last academic merit-based high school in California.

In January 2021, in an act of academic perversity, the San Francisco Board of Education cast quality to the winds and eliminated the merit-based admissions policy at Lowell. The board replaced it with a random lottery. Predictably (unless you were serving on the board and living in La-La Land), parents cried foul. The Lowell community outcry produced lawsuits, anger, and accusations of racism from both sides.

Lee Cheng and I talked over the phone in April 2020 about the controversy. Cheng is an attorney and a Lowell High School graduate. He is a founding member of the Asian American Legal Foundation, a nonprofit organization based in San Francisco. Its mission is to protect and promote the civil rights of Asian Americans. They believe Americans of all races and ethnicities have the right to be treated as individuals and live free from discrimination. We had a wide-ranging discussion about meritocracy.

Meritocracy as Opportunity for All

I asked Cheng what made Lowell special. "It's the students," he replied without hesitation. "Lowell stood out because it had a selective admission policy that admitted students on merit." Lowell families place a premium on hard work, rigorous discipline among students, and academic performance. "When you put a critical mass of such students together, they start to inspire each other, and they learn from each other, and they push each other. That's the experience that I had. That's the experience most Lowell students I knew had," Cheng said.

Liberal elites like to depict schools like Lowell as fortresses of white privilege. Nothing could be further from the truth. Lowell has stood as a gateway to success for generations of immigrant and less-affluent students. Many of its students qualify for free or reduced fees for lunch.

"These public, selective admission schools are not negatively elite. Their student bodies reflect hard work and sacrifice. Lowell students are not kids born with silver spoons in their mouths. They learned English, as I did, as a second language. Many of their parents were dishwashers and seamstresses living or working in Chinatown."

Cheng's parents were World War II refugees. Cheng said, "They fled China because of the Japanese invasion and then the communist revolution. My father lived in a refugee camp for three years and grew up in a government boarding school." Cheng's parents immigrated to America from Taiwan in the 1960s. His father became a librarian at San Francisco State University, where he remained for thirty-five years. His mother worked as a bookkeeper. The family stressed the importance of education. Cheng's parents allowed him to watch the *CBS Evening News* with Walter Cronkite as a reward if he completed his school work and extra homework.

When Cheng entered the eighth grade, his family moved to San Francisco from nearby Pacifica so Cheng could attend Lowell High

School. Cheng faced racist abuse at his new school. A Black student and a white student beat him up in gym class. He said, "I can tell you that when you get punched by a Black person, it doesn't feel any different than being punched by a white person. Anybody can be racist: white people, Black people, Asian people."

Those who behave like racists include the San Francisco Board of Education. When Cheng applied to Lowell, he was appalled to discover a different, more rigorous admission standard for Chinese applicants. Shockingly, the board had established unfair—let's label the behavior for what it was: bigoted—anti-Chinese quotas at high schools. These effectively barred many Chinese students from entry to elite schools. In 1994, Cheng sued the San Francisco Unified School District, asserting that the policy was discriminatory and unconstitutional.

Cheng won the battle but, in the end, may lose the war. The forces who espouse what they euphemistically call "equity" are fighting back, with the full backing of Sacramento Democrats. Somehow, they think judging a person on their merits is wrong. You can bet they look down on Dr. Martin Luther King Jr.'s declaration that we should judge a person not by the color of their skin but the content of their character. For these extreme left-wing ideologues, equity is an Orwellian word that stands the meaning of equality on its head.

Cheng said, "Destroying Lowell does no one any good. When people say they are doing it in the name of equity, it's the same kind of equity that the Soviet Union and Communist China under Mao attempted to achieve: the equity of the lowest common denominator with everybody suffering except for a handful of the elite at the top."

There is a darker side to the San Francisco Board of Education's rift with Lowell. Cheng observes: "The people on the board don't care about the children of San Francisco. Their view their elected office as a stepping stone to the board of supervisors. They are not there to optimize the education of San Francisco schoolchildren. They have taken positions that are increasingly extreme to appeal to the people and voting blocks in San Francisco that they believe can deliver local victory to them."

Cheng, other Lowell alumni, and Lowell parents believe the Board of Education is racially biased against Chinese Americans. Evidence backs up his belief. In 2016, former board vice president Alison Collins tweeted that Chinese Americans were "*house (N-word)*." The absurdity of the tweet speaks for itself. The idea that Asian Americans are "white adjacent" is laughable to anyone with a basic understanding of California history.

Cheng criticized California's left-wing movement that has shunned meritocracy. Chung says, "Studying hard has nothing to do with skin color. There's nothing wrong with being elite based on your hard work. There's nothing wrong with being elite based on your talent. That's how a society moves forward." The good news is that this policy was changed. But what about the next time it's tried? San Diego schools are caught up in a similar controversy involving elimination of testing and academic requirements for some of its schools.

Apparently, the lefties believe that no one can move forward in California until everyone else gets the chance to catch up. Every kid gets a trophy. Every kid gets an equal opportunity to get into the best high school in California. Can you imagine putting this crowd in charge of the National Football League draft? What becomes of the unfortunate players not selected in the first round?

Here's the real world. California left-wing politicians—and Governor Newsom ranks at their forefront—hope to create a society of dronelike workers trudging toward a Socialist future. Stalin and Mao would approve.

California benefits from having high-achieving schools like Lowell. Do any of these names ring a bell? Former California governor Pat Brown, the rapper Paris, Supreme Court Justice Stephen Breyer, Sly and the Family Stone member Dennis Marcellino, and famous Beat Generation writer Jack Kerouac. All Lowell graduates. And hardly privileged rich kids. Lowell has graduated three Nobel laureates. Cheng points out, "That is the dividend that society has reaped from having a school like Lowell."

Perhaps not. Meritocracy is giving way to 'equity' in California. We no longer reward hard work and initiative. The San Francisco Board of Education was giving away the crown jewel of California high schools to the winners of a lottery. All it takes is a little luck (but no hard work or talent), and you too could be a winner.

Lowell High School was not the only casualty of politicians' war on meritocracy. The SAT is fighting for its life. Extremists and liberal elites paint standardized tests as racist and a tool of white privilege. "They contribute to the inequities of our system," UC Berkeley chancellor Carol T. Christ sanctimoniously opined, talking about standardized tests in a 2019 Berkeley forum on college admissions.

In May 2020, the University of California board of regents voted unanimously to phase out the SAT and ACT in the admissions process over five years. The same year, a judge ruled that the UC system could no longer use standardized tests like the SAT and the ACT in college admissions. The judge bought into the argument that standardized tests are biased against economically disadvantaged students and people of color.

The College Board, which owns the SAT, argued that a combination of grades and test scores is the best metric to select students who are likely to succeed in college. Advocates contend that your SAT score is a valid predictor of success in college as it is objective and administered uniformly.

High school grades are susceptible to grade inflation. In addition, grades are subjective because they vary from district to district, school to school, and teacher to teacher. The College Board's research suggests that affluent schools inflate grades more than lower-income schools.

UC Riverside's data suggests that SAT scores do matter. Students with lower SAT scores had GPAs .58 points lower than their peers who scored higher. Students with lower SAT scores had higher dropout rates and lower graduation rates.

Many worry that disparities among high schools will lead to mismatches between students and universities. The College Board maintains that SAT has been shown to correlate with academic success in college and helps match students with a school where they will thrive. Still, let's not make a hasty generalization. An SAT score is just one part of the overall picture of a student. Academic institutions need to look at the whole person. But test scores remain valuable information that helps the university and the student find the best match.

"Equality." In California, special-interest groups and government officials repeat the word often enough to qualify as a religious mantra. Governor Newsom preaches about "exposing equality gaps in our society" to become "more equal," not that he has ever offered any concrete solutions to make that happen. The California Department of Education funds and staffs an "Office of Equal Opportunity." The word "equality" makes it sound like they have noble intentions. Alas, achieving actual equality isn't part of their plan. Equality is opposite to their view.

A cartoon widely shared on social media by "progressives"—a phony label to disguise the actual views of left-wingers—illustrates this mindset. The first panel is entitled "Equality." It depicts three men of differing heights trying to watch a baseball game behind a fence. The tallest can easily view the action. The man of average height can just see over the fence. The short one stares at a plank of wood. In the next panel, "Equity," the two shorter men have been given crates to stand on. Now everyone can watch the game. The message is clear: to be fair and just, we must standardize the outcome of human experience.

The problem here—and this is *always* the issue with a collectivist mindset—is that this strategy assumes all three of the people depicted in the cartoon have the same skill sets, want the same things, and are incapable of helping themselves. In a free market, these people would have the right to try to see over the fence any way they saw fit. They could work together to use the wood from their crates to build a ladder to sit on top of the fence. One could stand on another's shoulders. Or better yet, they could remove the fence entirely. The fence is the problem.

What does the fence symbolize? Those who follow a collectivist philosophy see the fence as a symbol for the barriers that society, especially capitalism, puts up to stifle opportunity. I see the fence as a symbol of the impositions big government and big business put on individuals to control their behavior.

Humans are capable of creativity, ingenuity, and charity. But to achieve, we must be free: free to start businesses, free from burdensome regulations, free to engage in healthy competition, and free to reward each other for excellence.

American society flourishes as a genuine meritocracy, unshackled by corruption and spurred by innovation. It's a society filled with rewards. Meritocracy reflects rewarding your effort, skills, and passion. It doesn't matter if the endeavor is medicine, business, charitable works, public service, or something else.

This is about more than financial reward. In a meritocracy, the reward includes respect and opportunity. Meritocracy is color-blind. This system also doesn't care what country your parents were born in, whether you are disabled, or whether you are—to return to our earlier metaphor—short or tall. It is not someone putting their thumb on the scale. It doesn't reward the children of the wealthy or corporate cronyism.

Meritocracy provides a table where everyone has a seat because everyone has something to contribute. I have something to contribute to society, as do you. Our highest purpose is arguably to identify our potential and fulfill it to the best of our ability.

Competition Kills Corruption

In an ideal world, every individual would get up every morning to innovate and create. But we don't live in a perfect world. We live in a world where humans pursue different ambitions, needs, and attitudes. In the real world, incentives motivate us to get out of bed and be productive.

Society incentivizes people through competition. In some circles, competition has become a dirty word. It shouldn't be. Competition is healthy and social and produces the best products, services, and culture. Imagine an NBA game where they didn't keep score, or if every artist was allowed to show their work at the MOMA. It would make no sense.

The cure is the free market. Competition requires a free market, and a free market exists where there is spirited competition. In a free market, you aren't subject to the whims of a bureaucrat, a career politician, or a big-business charlatan who buys someone off or benefits from a crony relationship. Free markets open up opportunities and drive abundance, quality, and affordability.

In August 2003, I debated this topic with someone you may have heard of: President Barack Obama. He wasn't the president then. He was a relatively unknown Illinois state senator and, like me, a candidate for the United States Senate in Illinois. We met at Chicago State University, his home turf, and clearly, he was an accomplished debater who exuded charisma. We debated for over an hour and a half before a raucous crowd about the fundamental differences between our philosophies—differences that are starker today.

Much of the specifics centered on education and healthcare. Obama argued that people cannot intelligently choose their schools or healthcare providers. Instead, the government must make that choice for them. He proclaimed that most people need the government to protect them against the exploitation of the free market. He felt it was better to give people fewer options than let them make the wrong choice. He wanted to give people a considerable subsidy to buy healthcare insurance without changing the system to streamline it or make it better, more efficient, and less costly.

I told him that his healthcare plan, not yet named the Affordable Care Act or "Obamacare," was wealth redistribution. He could never grasp that a vacuum in competition among healthcare insurance companies and other providers would damage the entire healthcare system. When healthcare and education are genuinely competitive, prices will lower to the point where they are affordable for the vast majority of people. Private charity or a government voucher makes up the difference at the lowest economic strata and for those most vulnerable. Happily, relatively few people would need government help. I said that if we give people the tools to learn and improve themselves, they can do what they need to do to obtain and evaluate these services—all for the greater good.

Obama called me a "Social Darwinist." Hey, if you're going to be insulted, at least I can say I was insulted by the future president of the United States.

I believe in people. I believe in them enough to let them make their own choices. I don't think that left to our own devices, we will, as a general rule, try to exploit one another. If you give people the freedom to choose, they will make choices that benefit themselves and society. Markets will adapt to that choice and work more efficiently to produce better healthcare, education, and other markets. Choice and competition deliver quality and efficiency.

Obama won the crowd of mainly liberal college students. Less than five years later, this obscure state legislator was inaugurated as president. But like many who studied Obama's ideas, reservations about the Affordable Care Act proved correct. Obamacare increased costs because a lack of competition enabled insurance companies to jack up prices. Obama bent over backward to choke off competition.

Americans suffered—the same old story. As for education, we can see for ourselves that America is losing ground worldwide. Our politician-driven education bureaucracy is creating a two-tiered system: private quality education for the elite and well-off, but substandard services for those without means.

A Fair Playing Field Threatens the Swamp

Who benefits the most from a lack of competition? I'd say it is government officials and special-interest groups that government enables: the proverbial "swamp." Many of our institutions—the postal service, the public school system, and subsidized healthcare providers—fare poorly when comparing them against their free-market alternatives. They do not offer enough incentives for people to be efficient.

Let's take another look at public schools. We have allowed our public schools to be run as political organizations. Bureaucrats indulge in political indoctrination (such as the current Critical Race Theory) and embrace mediocrity. When was the last time you looked at what they teach in school these days? It's an eye-opener. They teach the kind of left-wing concepts that the Communist leader Leon Trotsky—who was even more military than his rival Joseph Stalin—espoused as a "permanent revolution." It is no surprise that we get ineffective teachers whom unions protect and guarantee set salaries whether their students pass or fail. They are not graded based on the quality of work they do.

That approach is absurd. People who feel unappreciated for excellence will go somewhere else. I had excellent teachers in my public schools. I don't see that now. Worse, in most California public schools, you can't easily fire a lousy teacher. You're stuck with them—and our children pay the price.

Taking the Thumb off the Scale

We need to slash bureaucracy and reward achievement. California can be a golden laboratory for meritocracy. We have the resources, talent, and drive. I won't say it will be easy. The dragons will fight back. But we can win this effort if we have the will and the discipline.

They say "politics is downstream from culture." I agree. Changing the mind of the public means more than enacting legislation. Let's reawaken our political system. Let's champion meritocracy. That is how to conquer inequality and ensure that we all share a better life.

What does a better life mean? To me, it means prosperity. It means you get access to what you need to feed and clothe yourself. It means you can provide that for your children. That includes affordable homeownership or at least a comfortable roof over one's head.

That ideal has been the driving force in America for 250 years. Let's revitalize that mindset. That's the key to building a future we can be proud of and restoring something that for too long has been missing from California: hope.

CHAPTER 7

BLOATED AGENCIES CHOKE PROGRESS

In California, special-interest groups, bureaucrats, and union bosses are choking us. Ronald Reagan famously quipped, "The nine most terrifying words in the English language are, 'I'm from the government, and I'm here to help.'" Bureaucrats show breathtaking imagination in precisely one dimension: protecting their budgets and power. Helping *us* ranks low on their agendas. That's inexcusable. The California Teachers Association (CTA) is the most potent special-interest group in California, so much so, that many view it as the fourth branch of government. CTA's pressure tactics and foolish policies have sent public education into a tailspin.

I don't blame these people. They're doing what the system allows. The massive growth of the population in California empowers mass media as an essential factor in elections, another major reason to change our system. Paid advertising costs big money. These interests and groups supply that money—for a price. They get special treatment, and we pay the price. It's our fault the system allows this. Later in this book, we'll discuss in greater detail the remedy I favor—Hear the People. First, let's look at some history that sheds light on where we came from and where we are.

California once saw better days. During the 1950s and '60s, California was a national leader in learning. The nation envied its colleges and universities. Yes, it cost money. But children received a solid education that prepared them for good jobs. How things have changed. Today *US News & World Report* ranks the state twenty-second in education—just below North Dakota. We rank dead last in the teacher-to-student ratio. The average elementary school class size is twenty-nine students—hardly ideal for learning.

The CTA, however, is thriving. *City Journal*, the nation's premier urban-policy magazine, published an exposé of this scandal, "The Worst Union in America." This well-documented investigation detailed how CTA profited from a "fat bank account fed by mandatory dues that can run more than $1,000 per member." Members' dues in 2020–2021 will garner over $207 million in revenue. And get this: every penny the CTA takes in is tax-exempt.

Don't blame teachers. My mother was a dedicated teacher. She was committed to her students. I know that most teachers in California feel the same way. The devil is money and power. Union bosses ruthlessly seek and assert power. They understand that politicians control schools and budgets. Control the politicians, and you control the money.

Many teachers tell me that they dislike being evaluated by school boards or administrators, as these parties are political animals. No wonder they're upset. Would you want your performance judged by people who don't answer to those most interested in good performance?

Who is that constituency in education? Parents. Parents are the closest to their children. It's not that voters don't care. Everyone wants good schools to educate future generations. But parents are the ones standing on the front lines. They see how much their children learn and prepare for their future. Parents are the best judges of performance. Parents hold the most significant stake in having excellent schools.

That is why empowering parents is critical to improving education. Some Californians have gone a step farther, creating and organizing "parent unions" to become a force in the administration and management of the schools. I would go still further in encouraging the development of more independent charter schools and voucher programs that place funding decisions in the hands of parents. The goal is to foster competition. Only competition will assure the quality and efficiency of schools. Real competition requires consumer power that enables parents to choose among competitors. The best schools will attract the students—and the money. Competition provides strong incentives for schools to excel and penalizes those who fail to do so.

Name a leading politician, and you'll find a parent who exercised the power of school choice. When Barack Obama and Bill Clinton occupied the Oval Office, they didn't send their children to a public school in Washington, D.C. They sent their children to high-performing private schools. Gavin Newsom sent his children to an elite private school. The governor enjoys this option thanks to his wealth and position.

Does a single mother sending her children to a failing school have the same opportunities? How is it fair that some people can choose their schools while others cannot? Improving education mandates provides the power of choice to *all* parents.

The vested interests argue that school choice takes funding away from the public schools. That's nonsense. Charter schools do not alter budgets. They merely broaden the power to determine where spending occurs.

Again, don't throw rotten tomatoes at our teachers. They deserve to be honored. I want to see teachers paid like rock stars and baseball players—not necessarily making millions of dollars each year, but compensated fair and square based on their job performance.

We need a bidding war among schools for the best teachers. School choice would help the middle class and low-income families get a better education for their children. This much seems clear. We need to crack down on the role special-interest groups play in children's lives. Ask yourself: do the interests of a union trump good education?

A Little Horror Story

Bentley Little once served as a technical writer for the Southern California city of Costa Mesa. He presents a cautionary tale. An op-ed he wrote for the *Los Angeles Times*, entitled "Working for a Local Bureaucracy for Eight Years: A Horror Story," described how, after struggling as a novelist, he "put on a white shirt and tie, and sat at a desk in the bowels of City Hall writing computer instructions."

Little's experience rivaled the plots of his horror novels. He witnessed inept management and inefficiency at every turn. Little reported, "Fifty positions were eliminated during budget cuts, thirteen regular employees were gone, and no management personnel had been let go. The result? Members of the public now had to wait an inexcusable amount of time for building permits and inspections because the Development Services Department was short-handed, yet there were no vacancies among the attendees at the next city-sponsored executive retreat."

Bureaucratic ineptitude relates to what bedevils excellence in education: special-interest power. Here is a harsh fact. Incentives for bureaucrats are opposite to those in the private sector. The private sector thrives on incentives for quality and efficiency to better compete. I continually test my team to do things more efficiently with fewer people. I modernized the technology my business utilizes. Over the past twenty-five years, I have upgraded my company's computer systems three times. We have greatly expanded our business with four times as many properties while our bookkeeping department has only doubled in size. That is the benefit of technology and the efficiency it brings.

Contrast that with government bureaucracy. California hasn't upgraded most of its computers since the '70s and '80s. Some still use COBOL operating systems popular around that time. I made a huge issue in my gubernatorial campaign of 2018 about the hours-long waits at the Department of Motor Vehicles (DMV) that frustrated thousands of applicants. More aggravating, they knew that states like Florida issued their licenses in minutes.

California is now investigating massive fraud and mismanagement in its unemployment insurance agency, the EDD. This agency has an enormous backlog of potential recipients waiting for a life-saving payment. It hasn't helped that fraudsters stole as much as $20 billion using phony names and Social Security numbers. Twenty billion dollars. Imagine what we could do with that money to improve our lives. The fraud is inexcusable.

Bureaucracy discourages efficiency. More state workers mean more bureaucracy, more dues-paying government union members, more repressive union political power. And bureaucracy perpetuates itself. The more problems it can create with regulations on private business, the more it can force companies to kowtow.

Bureaucracy makes affordable housing immensely challenging. I build and manage apartment buildings for a living. I've applied for many building permits in other states, and I have talked to many builders in California and discovered that what Little says is spot-on. In California, it costs around $500,000 to build one apartment unit. And that's after you often wait as much as a dozen years for the needed approvals.

I build mainly in Indiana. There I'm approved within a few months and, on average, can develop a beautiful complex for $130,000 per unit. Why is California construction four times more expensive? The answer is that government regulations add an extra 60–80 percent to the cost to build. Municipal fees, permits, and wage rates that Sacramento imposes add up.

Little wrote: "Perhaps the single biggest problem with local governments is the arrogance of their administrators—the tendency of minor faceless bureaucrats to suffer from the big-fish-in-a-small-pond syndrome. Midlevel bureaucrats believe that they are essential people, the focus around which everything orbits. And they act accordingly."

Bureaucracy begets bad behavior—at the expense of us, the taxpayers. Not all that long ago, the *Los Angeles Times* ran a front-page story revealing that in the city of Bell, California, the city manager, Robert Rizzo, was receiving a salary of $787,637. Pretty good deal, isn't it? Well, for him but not us. This rip-off is no isolated case. Is it any wonder that Californians distrust officials?

In 2015 the "State Integrity Investigation," a data-driven assessment of state government accountability and transparency from the Center for Public Integrity and Global Integrity, gave The Golden State a score of seventy-three, or C-. Things have not improved. OpentheBooks.com, a charity that looks at government spending nationwide, reports that California is the only state in the nation that refuses to make its checkbook available for inspection. Doesn't the lack of transparency from bureaucrats concern you?

Californians pay among the highest taxes in the nation. Sacramento takes $7,482 from the average Californian in state income taxes and property taxes. The average Floridian pays $2,390 in state taxes. The good people of Tennessee pay no income tax. The average Californian pays 9.3 percent in income tax; that rate bracket starts at about $60,000 of income, which is poverty level in most of the state. We have the highest state sales tax rate. Yet California has far more tourism, agriculture, natural resources than either of those states. Plus, we have Silicon Valley and Hollywood.

Thank goodness Proposition 13 protects us from excessive property taxes. Naturally, the career politicians and labor unions keep trying to chip away at Prop 13 protections. Their latest tax attack came in 2020. Proposition 15 would have rolled back protections against property tax increases for businesses. It was defeated—but only by a small margin. The wolves will be at the door again soon. Keeping taxes from totally crushing us is a war with many battles that we will have to fight over and over, and we have to stay vigilant and strong to hold the line.

At this writing, the assembly is making another go at raising income taxes again. Voters will also be asked to raise income taxes on high earners to pay for electric vehicle chargers and wildfire prevention. Our income tax on top wage earners is already the highest in the nation. If left-wing politicians prevail, the California state tax rate for the highest wage earners will increase to 16.8 percent. When combined with federal income tax, the wealthiest Californians would pay a whopping rate of 54 percent. Taking more than half of someone's pay for taxes—especially when we receive so little for them—is outrageous.

It doesn't stop there. Sacramento left-wingers want to redistribute our wealth. Under current Assembly Bill 310, the most affluent Californians would pay a 1 percent or 1.5 percent wealth tax annually. This bill is no income tax. It is a Socialist tariff on Californians' net worth. No other state would dream of imposing such a tax. Maybe you are thinking: rich people, why feel sorry for them? Here's why. The left-wingers are vampires. Give them one bite, and they'll keep biting and sucking. This isn't the Soviet Union. The Ill-advised Socialist policies that the Communists pursued were why communism collapsed. Can we even afford the risk of letting politicians who hold such extreme views control our state government?

Raising taxes on the wealthiest does not work. A study for the National Bureau of Economic Research by the Hoover Institution at Stanford University found that increasing taxes on the rich leads to a *decline* in taxes collected from the highest earners. Instead of paying the bill, many wealthy Californians like Elon Musk and Charles Schwab have moved out of state. After the last tax increase on the highest earners in 2011, more millionaires and billionaires left the state than in previous years. Others turned to creative bookkeeping and offshore accounts to avoid the extra tax bite. Almost by definition, the rich own the factories, farms, natural resources and service businesses; when you raise their taxes, they raise prices to compensate, which increases everyone's cost of living and widens the "equality gap" between rich and poor.

The favorite refrain among left-wingers is that the rich need to pay their fair share. In California, the top 1 percent of wage earners pay 46 percent of the state's income tax. That seems pretty progressive. The radical Left loves taxing the wealthiest 1 percent because they are easy political targets. Who cares about millionaires and billionaires? Well, as it turns out—we should. Driving *up* taxes drives *down* job creation, erodes our tax base, and hurts our economy. It's not trickle-down economics; it's Econ. 101. Taxing people and businesses until "the pips squeak" causes them to flee the state, and that hurts all Californians.

Jack Frost is the president of Pro Small Biz California, a small business advocacy group. Jack is a mortgage banking and real estate businessman who feels strongly about this. He serves on the boards of the Sacramento Taxpayers Association and the Latino Professional Development Project. I spoke to Frost by phone in mid-May 2021. Frost told me, "The more that you tax, the less you get. Suppose you reduce the tax burden and the regulatory burden on small businesses. In that case, they will thrive, and the additional revenue and job creation that would come as a result would be good for the state of California."

The regulations and taxes imposed in starting a new small business create barriers to entry into the market. Frost said, "Trying to get permits is a huge problem. The time frame, the number and cost of inspections, the cost of the permits is making it very, very difficult for new businesses to get started."

Sacramento knows that small businesses are the engine of our economy. Over 90 percent of California's private-sector jobs come from small businesses. Why aren't politicians creating a small-business-friendly atmosphere? "It's real simple," Frost said. "The people that are in power don't care. Politicians don't get money from small business owners. They don't have the funds to give them campaign contributions. They don't have the money to hire lobbyists to represent them. They don't have the money to hire expensive law firms and accountants to try to figure out how they can avoid paying taxes."

Minorities own over half of all small businesses in California. If Sacramento wanted to help them, they would help small business owners. Slashing burdensome regulations and lowering taxes will help minority-owned business owners prosper and build generational wealth. Why is this not happening? The reality is sad. The political elite doesn't want to expand the middle class to include underrepresented people. They like having people of color depend on the government. Any objective observer would call that philosophy systemic racism. If we want equality, let's decrease taxes and regulations on small business owners so they can make a better life for themselves and their families.

Citizens have a day-to-day stake in their quality of life. I trust people enough to let them make their own decisions—and even to learn from their own mistakes. They deserve to be masters of their destiny. It's time we claimed that destiny.

CHAPTER 8

LEVELING THE PLAYING FIELD FOR SMALL BUSINESSES AND START-UPS

Erica Douglass called California home for over a decade. After graduating from San Jose State in 2002, she started a tech company called Whoosh Traffic, which she sold for over $1 million at age twenty-six. Erica moved close to my home in San Diego, hired employees, and tried to carve out her vision of the American Dream. She was, by any measure, the kind of person a state would be lucky to count among its citizens.

Then, in 2011, Erica fled California. On her blog, she explained her decision through an open letter to her former home. "Dear California," she wrote. "I'm leaving you. I've struggled with a notoriously business-unfriendly government—with everything from high taxes on earnings to badgering businesses to work more to comply with bureaucracy. I paid enough in California income tax in one year alone to hire another worker for my business. And you charge me $800 annually as a corporation fee when most states charge just a few dollars. California just isn't worth it. My priorities have changed. I value income freedom and flexibility more than I value living near the beach. I value having a paid-off house I can call 'home' more than I value having a half-million-dollar noose around my neck that declines in value by the day."

Erica's story frustrates me. She did everything right, she played by the rules, yet the state still wasn't able to provide her with the prosperity she had earned. Instead, it squeezed her dry.

We need entrepreneurs like Erica. They are the innovators and "can-do" folks who make things happen for everyone. They reinvest in their community and create the future. As she said: "I'd bet that I'm far more efficient at creating jobs as a small business owner than the state is, given the same amount of money." That's a bet I'd take any day. I'll always bet on people over the government.

As a business owner myself, I feel her pain. California has become too expensive for small businesses. In 2019, the Cato Institute, a think tank headquartered out of Washington, D.C., ranked California second worst nationally in business climate and second worst in regulatory burdens. Those rankings haven't shifted much over the years. California remains a perennially burdensome place to conduct business.

Erica went somewhere friendlier. In 2011 she moved her company to Austin, Texas, which imposes just a 0.75 percent franchise tax on business margins, compared to California's 8.85 percent corporate tax. Business News Daily ranked California as the third-worst state for small businesses in 2021. We can do better. Just look at some other states: Arizona's corporate tax rate is 4.9 percent; North Carolina's is 2.5 percent; Nevada collects no corporate taxes at all. Lower corporate tax rates create jobs and help small businesses grow.

Gavin Newsom used California's 2021 budget surplus to create more entitlement programs. He's still doing that even as the state runs a deficit. He would have served Californians better by lowering the corporate tax rate so small business owners could hire more workers and expand their businesses. Improving our business climate helps Californians, their communities, and our state. Lower corporate tax rates mean more jobs and more wealth for all Californians, and would likely have generated more tax revenue, avoiding the current deficits. Most small businesses in California are minority-owned. We can close the income inequality gap and open up economic opportunities to more people of color. We need to let small businesses thrive by lowering their tax burden.

Let Flowers Grow

Like Erica, florist Jim Relles is someone I view as an example of the American Dream realized. In a moving 2019 essay, Relles reflected on what it meant to serve his community through his business. "As an entrepreneur and longtime small business owner in the Sacramento community, I consider my path to be very fortunate—and perhaps inevitable," he wrote. "It's safe to say carnations, roses, and baby's breath have adorned our family tree for generations, with my father founding Relles Florist in 1946 and my brother and myself taking over the family business in 1972. That's 73 years of arranging and delivering flowers to the greater Capital community."

However, in early 2019, the state legislature passed the California Consumer Privacy Act (CCPA). The Act was supposedly Intended to safeguard consumers' digital information. In reality, the CCPA created red tape for anyone trying to market their services online. Which, in this day and age, means *every* business. Relles immediately felt the impact.

"We have a small website, we keep records of calls, we text customers, we have a leads database, and we buy digital ads. We do not collect data," he said. "But under the provisions of the CCPA, we would be considered to be collecting personal information, even when it is not linked to an individual. Even as a small business, my company would suffer from CCPA because it would diminish the value and effectiveness of the online marketing tools I'm using now. And if I hit a certain threshold for sales or customer interactions, then I have a whole set of daunting legal compliance obligations. In response, our company would be required to collect more information about consumers than we need and provide it to the consumer upon request. Relles Florist is not a big tech company. The compliance costs of such an effort, in terms of person-hours and data capture, would be hard to bear. It's a high-tech version of the same old story: small businesses will be at a competitive disadvantage in competing with larger players."

The CCPA is a prime example of how even well-intentioned regulatory efforts often end up hurting the people they want to protect.

Luckily, Relles's story has a happy ending. Even though he took a financial hit, he was able to keep his flower shop profitable because of the strong ties he had built to the Sacramento community he had served for decades. But it must have been infuriating to know that just down the road from him, in the marbled capitol building, lawmakers who knew nothing of him or his business could throw a wrench into all he had worked to create. And the CCPA only went into effect in early 2020, so its long-term consequences are not yet fully assessed.

Above all, the CCPA, which has national effects because it affects any California resident, no matter where they happen to be located, was drafted without the politicians thinking through the impact on small businesses like Relles's. Even in those rare instances when the assembly may be attempting to do the right thing, block-headed thinking produces results that hurt rather than help our people. That's avoidable and inexcusable. It's apparent they did not even think to talk to small business owners to ascertain the impact of this legislation. Although its intentions were noble, the CCPA has had disastrous unintended consequences.

Small businesses across this country suffer from overregulation, not only in California. Yes, some states, like Texas and North Carolina, are beacons for start-ups, and plenty of Californians are flocking there to set up shop. Good for them! I wish them nothing but success. But I live in California, and I want to help our people. We should all worry about those trapped by bureaucracy and bad rules that stifle rather than foster jobs and growth. Not everyone has the means to pack up and move across the country.

In May 2019, the U.S. Small Business Administration Office of Advocacy, created by Congress in 1976 as an independent voice for small businesses within the federal system, did something almost nobody in government does: it *listened* to the people it serves. Over a week, it hosted regional regulatory reform roundtables in Oklahoma City, Oklahoma; Phoenix, Arizona; and Summerlin, Nevada. It heard complaints from a broad range of small business people, from farmers to retailers. People pleaded for relief. "Forty percent of our budget goes to regulatory compliance!" one exasperated man advised the panel.

"All of these rules are burdensome and costly," said a farmer, describing his concerns with banking, trade, transportation, and environmental regulations. "Nobody wants to protect this environment more than a farmer...but all of these regulations are preventing farmers from being able to succeed."

These stories had a profound impact on me. Nobody works harder than these people. Yet the government constantly holds them back with red tape and a bureaucracy that erects barriers to success.

I fear that the recent governmental overreach during the COVID-19 crisis will continue. I worry arbitrary rules waste the time of small business people and entrepreneurs and empty their pockets. We need to stand up for their right to operate. Government needs to get out of the way so business owners can do what they do best: innovate, build community, and inject money into our homes and economy.

CHAPTER 9

MY POTATO CHIP WAR: A STUDY IN UNFAIR COMPETITION

In early 1983, my first wife Nancy and I had a high school classmate and her husband over for dinner at our townhouse. This classmate's husband worked for a Chicago snack food company called Jays Foods, Inc. Jays was owned and operated by the Japp family, headed by patriarch Leonard Japp, Sr., since 1927. Jays potato chips were wildly popular in the Midwest. Their slogan was "You can't stop eating 'em." Our guest was fascinated by the strategies I had used at my old accounting firm, Coopers & Lybrand, to save businesses money on their taxes. "My company isn't doing anything nearly that resourceful," he said. "Why don't you come in next week and talk to our VP of Finance?" I said I would love to.

The more I learned about Jays, the more I saw a shining example of the American Dream. Leonard Japp, Sr., started selling potato chips on the street. After tasting his chips, none other than Al Capone encouraged the young man to start mass-producing them. They quickly became a Chicago staple. Japp almost lost everything in the stock market crash of 1929 and the ensuing Great Depression, but he won it all back with a bet on a lucky racehorse. Later on, President Kennedy invited Mr. Japp to lead a seminar in the Soviet Union on how to mass-produce potato chips.

I was impressed by the intense emotional connection Midwesterners had to the brand. "I would pass by their factory near I-94 south," wrote a man named Mike O. about his steadfast loyalty to Jays' snack products, "and the wind would blow down plumes of white smoke with the sweet smell of freshly cooking potatoes onto the expressway."

Shortly after that dinner, I sat down with the VP of finance, Joe Whelan, a son-in-law of the founder, and met some family members, including Leonard—a charming and dynamic man. They liked my ideas, gave me a few projects, and over time trusted me with more and more legal and accounting work. I enjoyed visiting the factory in Chicago's Roseland neighborhood on 99th Street to see how their snack foods were made and packaged. One interesting fact was that no human hand touched the potato or chip from the time the potato left the field until a consumer took a chip out of a bag. Everything was automated all the way through, even the unloading of the potatoes—achieved with a truck's nearly vertical lift that spilled potatoes into the plant.

Within a few years, I was on the board of directors and was directing quite a bit of their financial activities, including its eventual sale to Borden Inc. in 1986. Before that sale, the company initiated an antitrust suit that helped crystallize my feelings about antitrust laws and how unfair competition can inflict severe damage.

From the 1950s to the '80s, Jays faced stiff, and in my opinion, unfair competition from Frito-Lay. Frito-Lay was and still is the preeminent potato chip manufacturer in the nation and a subsidiary of PepsiCo. Frito-Lay had consistently engaged in predatory pricing, illegal price discrimination, deceptive trade practices, and anticompetitive conduct. Finally, its monopolistic tactics forced Jays to sue Frito-Lay for violation of antitrust laws.

Jays claimed that it sustained a loss totaling $4,311,806.73 for fiscal years 1975–1981 because of its inability to increase prices due to Frito-Lay's anticompetitive conduct. In other words, Frito-Lay was regularly sending salespeople into grocery stores and supermarkets to undermine Jays' agreements with those stores. Frito-Lay held such a huge market share that it could price its product below market cost in certain places, knocking Jays out of business and making the pricing up for itself in other areas. It would also conspire with grocery stores to keep Jays' shelf space smaller than Frito-Lay's.

The antitrust case was a war. When I came on board in 1983, I was determined to help Jays win it. We believed that we could show the courts that Frito-Lay had engaged in a wide range of anticompetitive activities. The case went to the U.S. Supreme Court. In 1985, after Jays spent years in litigation and a fortune in legal fees, the justices decided in Frito-Lay's favor. It was a disappointing decision. We had no choice but to think of alternatives.

In 1986, shortly after the court's decision, the Japp family asked me to help sell their company to Borden, the national food giant. Borden was the largest U.S. producer of dairy and pasta. We sold the company for $30 million. I was sad to see a family business taken over by a conglomerate, but Frito-Lay had forced our hand.

When Borden bought Jays, it had the idea how to put together potato chip companies to compete with Frito-Lay. It bought regional brands such as Wise Potato Chips and tried to compete for shelf space. But Frito-Lay continued its monopolistic practices, and Borden faced many of the same problems the Japp family had faced. Within seven years, Borden had run Jays Potato Chips into the ground. By 1994, Jays was losing $17 million a year on $120 million in sales.

When we sold the company, the annual sales had been around $80 million. Borden had increased sales by 50 percent in seven years, but they were not profitable. Borden had not negotiated good deals on insurance, distribution, and marketing. A whole series of other promotions and sales initiatives were wrong. Borden's biggest mistake was that Borden had miscalculated the competition that Frito-Lay put up.

I put together a bid for the company. I recruited an executive team to turn around this landmark Chicago company. We built a plan—a bridge we called it—to turn Jays into a profitable company. Time was urgent: the company had substantial debt, and lenders were not patient.

We repurchased the company in 1994 with a big press event. The news media covered us standing in front of a wall of snacks. Once the family had reacquired Jays Potato Chips, we executed our plan. We turned a $17 million loss into a $3 million profit in one year (that's the kind of turnaround I see possible for California). I had negotiated an excellent buy-back deal for $10 million—a third of what Borden had paid for it—and had put together a skilled group to run it, including the Japp family's original bookkeeper. I hired a former client who had run the Butterball Turkey Company as the CEO while I served as CFO. Choosing him turned out to be a wrong decision. We clashed, and I sold my shares back to the company.

While attempting to run Jays profitably; we confronted other issues besides Frito-Lay. **President** Bill Clinton and Senator Bob Dole drove another nail into the Jays coffin by subsidizing ethanol to help farmers. That drove up the cost of corn, which drove up the price of corn oil. Jays chips were made with corn oil, and when the price of corn oil tripled overnight, the family business was soon hurting. I left the company in 1995, and even after my departure, Jays continued to face issues with Frito-Lay's monopolistic practices. The Japp family sued again in 2004 and was semi-victorious in this case. A federal judge ordered Frito-Lay to tear down a billboard in downtown Chicago that boasted: "Chicago prefers the taste of Lay's over Jays" and told it to stop running similar radio ads based on so-called taste tests. The judge said that the anti-Jays ad blitz was "not only unsavory but tasteless" and "motivated by greed." That greed finally sank Jays, and what was left was sold at auction in 2007. Eighty years of potato chip manufacturing in Chicago's south side came to a close.

The monopolistic practices Frito-Lay engaged in continue today in many other industries. Amazon, Facebook, Apple, Google, and other major internet players consume so much of the marketplace that they dominate anyone in their path. Richard Branson is one of the toughest, most imaginative entrepreneurs on the planet. He produced a cola that he and his team believed was superior to Coca-Cola. Coke's power and clout proved too much to take on. There's no getting around this fact: big corporations are greedy and ruthless in quashing competition.

On December 9, 2020, the *New York Times* published a bombshell story that the Federal Trade Commission and more than forty states had accused Facebook of buying up its rivals to illegally squash competition. "Separate lawsuits," the *Times* writes, "allege that Facebook's purchases, especially Instagram for $1 billion in 2012 and WhatsApp for $19 billion two years later, eliminated the competition which could have one day challenged the company's dominance." The problem is that Facebook has inexhaustible resources to pay a squadron of lawyers. It will not surprise me if it wins this case, just as Frito-Lay won its own case by throwing superior resources into litigation.

These monopolies raise a challenging question: "What should the government do?" As you know, I am not a big fan of government action to break up companies. I am a fan of creating a business climate that gives smaller companies a better opportunity to get into a market and compete on a level playing field. Big companies like regulation. They can hire more lawyers and accountants than the competition and overwhelm them. I favor a lighter touch on smaller businesses, which would give them a chance to build their businesses without excessive regulatory costs.

Many politicians herald regulations as the best way to ensure affordable and high-quality products and services. Unfortunately, the regulators benefit their interests instead of the marketplace. Regulations make getting started difficult for small businesses. We need to level the playing field. A competitive marketplace is essential for consumers as well as start-ups and family-owned small businesses.

Some regulations are necessary. They protect our rights and ensure products and workplaces are safe. But too often, big companies hire armies of accountants and lawyers to navigate through obstructive regulations, deal with bureaucrats, and fight lawsuits. We need to strike a balance to provide laws that protect the public and foster competition.

Let's look at what happened to small businesses during the pandemic. We'll use the example of a small florist. In California, the governor ordered flower shops to shut down because of COVID-19. They couldn't have customers inside of their stores. But large grocery stores were allowed to stay open, and they sold flowers too. Small stores were out of business, and the big stores had free reign to steal their business. Will they ever get it back? Maybe—a big maybe. A lot of these people will never be able to reopen.

From where will the next small florists come? With all the big grocery stores selling flowers right now, how does a new florist get started and take some of that business away? It is challenging, especially in California—where that small florist has to comply with the same level of regulation as the big grocery store. The big grocery stores argue that the small florist should abide by the regulations. However, again I point out that, unlike the little guy, the big grocery stores have deep pockets, and they leverage that advantage. There's no fair play. This has inhibited our economic growth. It started with George H. W. Bush. Bill Clinton accelerated it. George W. Bush accelerated it more, Obama even more.

Make no mistake. That is a significant factor in the inequality gap that inspires the news media and political leaders to gripe. The inability of those at the bottom to start or maintain a business is a critical factor limiting their capacity to close the gap. The way I succeeded was to have my own business, which I started with almost nothing. Granted, I was a CPA and lawyer, so navigating the thicket of dense and confusing regulations didn't bother me. However, imagine a young person without wealth or much experience having to do the same. It stacks the deck in favor of the big players.

California's leaders must examine regulation to ascertain what chokes off opportunity. We have to either exempt small businesses or make it easier to comply with regulations. The more restrictions we have and the more court cases that get filed, the more we limit small businesses from getting into the marketplace. The emphasis shouldn't be on going after big companies but on reducing regulations on small businesses and providing easier ways for small or new companies to comply. Regulations made reopening in the wake of the pandemic hard for small or midsize companies that had shut down, while Costco, Whole Foods, Amazon, and others like them prospered.

Going back to my potato chip wars, I admit the battle did not diminish my appetite for the salty snack. I still love a nice bowl of chips with my burger and an ice-cold beer. I've even gone online to buy Jays Potato Chips, which a pretzel company from Pennsylvania now owns. That's where you can find them these days—and they still taste great.

CHAPTER 10

HOW TO HOUSE AND HELP THE HOMELESS

I spoke by phone to Wallace Lee. Lee is the president of Safe Embarcadero for All, a community organization supported by neighborhood residents and businesses. In March 2019, San Francisco announced a plan to build a two hundred-person homeless shelter—also known as a Navigation Center—in the Embarcadero district. Lee said, "They just announced they were going to do it in six months. Everyone said, 'Wait a second. You can't get a pothole fixed in six months, and they're going to turn an empty lot into a homeless shelter? This is crazy.'"

The homeowners in the area were upset because the city did not consult them about the project and its potential impact on the neighborhood. Ten thousand people live within a five-block radius of the homeless shelter. A false narrative often plays out in the media that portrays housed persons as wealthy, white, and privileged. "It turned into this thing where rich people don't want to interact with homeless people," Lee told me. "There were legitimate concerns about drug use, crime, and defecation on the streets which turned into rich people are opposed to homeless people."

This center opened in December 2019 despite strong objections from neighborhood residents. Lee said, "It was terrible when it first opened. There were people in tents all over the outside, people sleeping outside." Large homeless shelters act as a magnet for the general homeless population in an area. Navigation centers often have an overflow problem. There weren't enough beds inside the facility, so the homeless slept outside the fence.

The quality of life in the neighborhood declined. Lee continued, "There were needles all over the sidewalk. Drug dealers set up across the street from the navigation center in a little park. They've got a chop shop in that park for bicycles. We've got screamers who come out onto the street and just scream at all hours of the night."

The newly elected Democratic mayor of San Francisco had to fulfill a campaign pledge to provide one thousand beds for the homeless. Her goal was noble, but that number overwhelmed the residential neighborhood. "They really didn't care about the impact on the people who were already living there or choosing the best site. They just needed as many sites as they could get to meet this goal," Lee said.

When the pandemic hit, the capacity decreased from two hundred to forty. "It was night and day," Lee said. "They've reduced the number of people going in and out. It's really calmed down a lot." The neighborhood has returned to a sense of normalcy. The residents would welcome the shelter if it continued in its more modest form." Lee continued, "The problem is this mega-shelter. It was an experiment, and the result was not good. I hope that going forward it stays smaller and never goes back to the two hundred person capacity. That would be a great solution for us. But I don't think my wish will be granted."

Homelessness is complicated. It requires careful examination and reforms in education, employment opportunities, and mental health. Treatment for mental illness and substance abuse should coincide with housing the homeless. The government should fund private organizations to provide mental health counseling and substance abuse treatment. Two examples are Father Joe's Villages in San Diego and Solutions for Change in Carlsbad. Many others, both religious and secular, provide such residential treatment. The key is holding such organizations accountable. Government agencies are notorious for coming up short. We should defund parties who fail to provide effective treatment and return people to society.

Many advocates for the homeless push the policy of 'Housing First' and decry efforts to force the homeless into mental health and addiction programs.Usually these advocates have a connection to groups or organizations that benefit from building subsidized housing or are funded by people involved in that industry. Often, they push for the purchase of motels—usually at ridiculously inflated prices—that don't have services to offer.They claim that services for mental health treatment and addiction recovery are available but without a forcing mechanism, how many do you think take advantage of this? Forcing treatment sounds harsh—advocates claim it is criminalizing illness—but what would you do for your own children?If my children were stricken in this fashion, believe me that I would force them to seek help with whatever tools I have at my disposal!

The battle against homelessness is about ensuring the safety and health of those living on the streets and how the homeless affect our health and public safety. Having an affordable roof over our heads is a human *need and it is our obligation to make sure it is available to all who need it.* Our fellow American citizens deserve an affordable, safe place to live. We also know that many assumptions about those who wind up with no roof over their heads are often way off base.

The saying, "There but for the grace of God go I," comes into play. One example of a descent into homelessness that I have followed closely illustrates how homelessness can creep up on anyone in many different ways. Shawn Pleasants's experience is unique to him but, in many ways, emblematic of the larger problem.

From the Ivy League to the Street

For most of his life, Shawn Pleasants lived the American Dream. He was the valedictorian of his high school and then went to Yale, where he majored in economics. Harvard courted him, but Pleasants thought Yale better suited his business-minded outlook.

Yale was a good choice. After graduation, Pleasants worked on Wall Street and founded a profitable business in California. He led a healthy, productive life and was a shining example for many other ambitious young African Americans from humble beginnings who valued the opportunity for a good education and were willing to work hard to fulfill their dreams.

Unfortunately, Pleasants hit a patch of rough luck. In 2019, he lost his business and couldn't find affordable housing. This phenomenon is happening with greater frequency today due to the COVID-19 crisis—even for college graduates, small business owners, and skilled workers who, historically, aren't considered high risk for homelessness. But even before the pandemic, Pleasants found himself living under a tarp near an overpass in Los Angeles, his meager belongings in milk crates and shopping carts. A street brawl permanently disfigured one of his eyes. His face, demeanor, and essence were miles away from the smiling young man who threw his cap into the air at an Ivy League School.

According to The Corporation for Supportive Housing, a think tank that searches for thoughtful solutions, Pleasants' story is common. California has the largest homeless population in the nation. Over three hundred ninety thousand California residents experience homelessness every year. One in ninety-five Californians will experience homelessness at least once a year. Over one hundred thirty-three thousand people sleep on our streets or in a shelter in California on any given night. They represent almost 21 percent of our country's total homeless population.

That's a disgrace. Driving on San Diego or Los Angeles streets these days, you see scenes that seem ripped out of a post-apocalyptic film. Addicts inject drugs in public, leaving needles on the ground in parks. Median and highway dividers transform into structures that resemble nightmarish circus tents. Even more distressing, many who roam the streets were once, like Shawn Pleasants, productive members of society.

That's why a story like Pleasants's cuts deep. How did someone who did everything right, who had much to offer society, end up in such an impossible situation? What does his story teach us about the homeless crisis that plagues Los Angeles and massive stretches of the metropolitan West Coast?

While drug use and life choices contributed to Pleasants's predicament, that's far from the whole story. According to a nonprofit California Housing Partnership Corporation study, there is a shortfall of 490,340 homes that could be affordable and available to Los Angeles County's low-income households. The cost of living is one culprit. Median rents in Los Angeles County increased by 25 percent between 2000 and 2012, while the median income declined by 9 percent. As you read this, about 39,400 men, women and children face homelessness in LA County. Shockingly, one in nine is a veteran. Los Angeles County has seven of the ten zip codes with the worst housing overcrowding in the nation and sixty-four zip codes that rank in the worst half percent for housing overcrowding.

In the state itself, at the last official count, 151,278 individuals are homeless, according to the U.S. Department of Housing and Urban Development, which reported this as "the highest number since at least 2007, and represents a nearly 17 percent uptick since 2018."

The pandemic has increased this number. Yet homelessness was a pressing challenge beforehand. Housing costs far too much in California, especially in metro areas. Californians pressured by extreme rents and property taxes cannot focus on thinking beyond day-to-day survival—before addressing other problems such as mental illness and substance abuse.

Compared to other states, California's middle class is being squeezed. Who would want to pay $3,200 a month for a one-bedroom apartment surrounded by tent cities?

Mike Dickerson, an organizer for the homeless advocacy group Known for All, told CNN in a September 2019 interview that Pleasants's riches to rags tale should surprise no one and that we should consider homelessness at least in Los Angeles a threat to every citizen. "For myself and other volunteers, what we found is people who are just people like everyone else, who have fallen into hard times, whether that's because of their issues or because their landlord evicted them or because the rent rose in a way they could no longer pay."

Dickerson doesn't think that government intervention is the answer. "I think people point to things like mental illness or drug abuse, which do exist in this population, but they aren't the primary problem," he told CNN. "The idea that we're going to force people into a facility that's probably located in a very remote area is not a solution. That's not going to connect people to jobs, to housing, to services (like) mental health and addiction treatment. And more importantly, putting thousands of people into a giant building isn't going to get them housed if there's nowhere for them to permanently live that they can afford."

Pleasants echoed that sentiment in a January 2021 interview with *The Day* newspaper. "I want people to know that anyone can become homeless. Most of the people…on the street with us now [its] because of skyrocketing housing costs. It's disheartening. "

Even though our situations are worlds apart, I relate to Pleasants, and I see his story as a dire warning. Here's a guy who worked his tail off, made many good decisions and a few bad ones, and then slipped through the cracks of society. Sure, actions have consequences—early on, my experience with my absent father cemented the importance of personal responsibility in my mind—but there's no reason for motivated, college-educated citizens to fall within a hair's breadth of being on the street. We cannot allow this standard of living to become normalized.

Housing costs must decrease. We must make building housing faster, cheaper, and easier. That is a key to motivating builders. The heavy-lift will be reforming the California Environmental Quality Act (CEQA), the most significant contributor to needlessly high housing costs. This

1970s-era statute allows virtually any interested party to file a lawsuit to stop any project on a specious environmental pretext. Granting case-by-case exceptions can be a potent political tool, which Governor Newsom has used without reforming it.

Policymakers should reduce impact fees, minimize litigation, cut mandates, and streamline regulations. The government has created nearly every factor that limits housing. The good news is that it lies within the power of elected officials to remove these barriers. This may have to wait for the implementation of Hear the People as I will detail later in Chapter 22.

Thankfully, Pleasants's story doesn't have a tragic end. A fellow Yale alum named Kim Hershman heard about his plight and rushed to the rescue. "She walked into my world, and it's never been the same for me," Pleasants said in a November 2019 interview with *Yale News*. "I think she is an angel amongst us. It's a debt I will gladly spend the rest of my life trying to repay. She did something that no one else did," Pleasants said. "Instead of just offering me things, she asked me what I wanted."

Ms. Hershman, a high-powered entertainment lawyer, quickly grew weary of the endless bureaucratic red tape that surrounded the government programs available to Pleasants. "There is no accountability," she told *Yale News*. "There's no training, and there is no timeline. It's not just throwing them someplace and then leaving them, and then they're setting up encampments in their apartment. We need to get them back to whole and healthy."

Ms. Hershman didn't rely on the government. She got Pleasants off the street and into a treatment facility and continued working with him to help him readjust to life on the "inside" until he could stand on his own two feet. "We think homeless people are one category of people, but in reality, it's just people who have lost their home," she said. "Let's get them back to their life. We're not even valuing our capital here by letting homeless people rot in the streets." I couldn't agree more.

As for Pleasants, he has some plans of his own. "I'm gonna start a small business again," he told CNN in January 2021. I hope he'll succeed.

Hotel California

You can look no further than the mayhem in the streets of Santa Monica or Venice to know the state's response to the homeless crisis has been a disaster. The homeless are not the only victims of Sacramento's failure. Residents and business owners have suffered.

I walked the famed Venice Boardwalk many times in the past twenty years. This area will never be Rodeo Drive in Beverly Hills. Venice Beach is a bastion of counterculture and eccentricity. Its quirkiness is part of its appeal, especially for tourists who snicker at California's craziness. It's not my cup of tea, but I support everyone's freedom of expression.

If you walked through Venice today, you would be appalled. Homeless people line the entire one-mile length of the commercial shopping area. They live in semipermanent tent encampments on a narrow grass strip between the shops and the beach. You do not feel safe—and you are not. Locals avoid the beach area at night: it is too dangerous. Shopkeepers close up at sunset.

I spoke with merchants that line the boardwalk. Not one wanted to be identified out of fear of retribution. One shop owner said that the merchants had tried to form an association to band together, but the homeless threatened shop owners. Intimidation is rampant. The business owners are at their wit's end.

The police rarely respond to disturbances or shoplifting calls, although perhaps the mass smash-and-grabs that have afflicted the state in 2021 may herald a shift. One proprietor told me homeless people steal from him every day, then sell his merchandise outside their tents across the boardwalk. The police refuse to intervene. Due to a 2019 lawsuit, the shopkeeper said, the police must catalog every item in a homeless person's encampment to be put into storage and returned to the homeless individual. "No cop has time for that," he said. He related that the police are frustrated as well and have told him, "Do you think we like this? All this violence and drugs, but what can we do?"

The problem goes beyond Venice. Under current California law, if a criminal steals anything less than $950, it is a misdemeanor and is treated like a traffic ticket. You can go into a store and shoplift, and as long as it doesn't exceed $950, you won't go to jail. Store owners are besieged by shoplifters who have no reason not to steal. Seventeen Walgreens have closed in San Francisco since the new law went into effect. Organized gangs came in and stole thousands of dollars of merchandise in a few minutes. Shoplifting is booming in California.

The feckless left-wing district attorneys in places like Los Angeles and San Francisco refuse to prosecute shoplifting cases. Robbery is now a no-jail-time offense. This soft-on-crime approach has motivated organized crime gangs of fifty or to steal items from Nordstrom, Best Buy, Foot Locker, Canada Goose, and other retail stores in California. The problem is more than mere property theft. Violent gangs of criminals have injured security guards and are jeopardizing the safety of shoppers. Small businesses, already hurting from repeated government shutdowns, are losing money because frightened shoppers are staying home.

The criminal justice system must quash this lawlessness. Personal violence is also a challenge. On the Venice boardwalk, disputes between homeless people escalate quickly. Fights and burning of an adversary's tent are common. Someone torched a commercial building on the boardwalk in January 2021. I talked with a clothing store owner while his second-grader did Zoom school from a dressing room converted into a classroom. He told me, "Everybody knows there's always been some homeless in Venice, but they've let them stay, and they never used to let them do that. The fact that they're staying in one place now means they feel like it's their territory—or their home."

A recent court ruling prohibits moving homeless people unless you have a bed for them. Beds are few and far between. The word has gotten out that the police will not bother you in Venice. Nonprofits come daily and deliver food and personal care products. There is a public bathroom with outdoor showers. Consequently, a "city "of homeless people has sprung up between the stores and the sand. The business owner continued, "More people have come, so it's almost like a community full of drugs and violence. Past nine o'clock, it's just lawless. Drug dealers come down here every night to sell drugs to the homeless. Locals won't come down here at night."

I asked him how it has impacted his business. "It's been terrible," he said. "More than half of the people who come into my shop comment. They say, 'Oh my goodness—the homeless. I never thought it would be like this. I feel bad for them, but, oh boy.' People are shocked. You already see it on websites. Oh, don't go to Venice because homelessness is really disgusting and dangerous. It's going to prevent people from coming."

The small business owners understand homelessness is a complex problem that calls for empathy. A proprietor told me, "It's a free country, and I know they have rights. But I have rights too. This is infringing on my rights. These people are defecating in front of my store. The beaches are filthy. You don't want to be some callous person and say, 'Just move them,' but this isn't the answer either. I know that. Would you want to bring your family down here?"

***

In April 2020, Governor Newsom announced a new initiative called Project Roomkey, which forced homeless individuals into 10,974 hotel and motel rooms and 1,133 trailers. Sacramento mandated these *private* businesses, most of them already under tremendous duress from the pandemic's impact on travel and tourism, to swap potential paying customers for people who exhibit high rates of drug use, mental health issues, and often have zero income. Let's examine how the plan panned out.

Predictably, it flopped. *LA Magazine* reported in September 2020 that L.A. had only reached one-quarter of its fifteen-thousand-room goal. There were widespread reports of theft, sexual violence, and hotel employees at the end of their wits. Things were even worse at the historic Capitol Park Hotel in downtown Sacramento. "The conditions in that hotel have been horrific. We're talking one elevator. At times there've been two toilets for

118 people," Sacramento Homeless Union president Crystal Sanchez told Fox News in a September 2020 interview. "The cost of what they're trying to charge is completely outrageous. It's a shame how much money is going into the Capitol Park Hotel renovation project, more than $58 million, to only house 134 homeless people. We could do so much better with the amount of money that they're facilitating for this to turn into housing. It's going to cost a lot more to just renovate versus just starting over."

In response, Governor Newsom doubled down. In September 2020, Newsom announced another $62 million in grants for counties to help them transition more people into permanent housing, including $35 million to pay for rental subsidies. Once again, he shoveled taxpayer money into a doomed program.

Guess who benefited? No surprise: it was the cronies running the system. In December 2020, *The Real Deal*, an L.A.-based real estate publication, broke the news that a hotel in Downtown L.A. was receiving Project Roomkey funding. The hotel's owner, Shenzhen New World Group, was implicated in an elaborate pay-to-play scandal involving former L.A. City Councilmember Jose Huizar. Shenzhen New World and its chairman, Wei Huang, were indicted on November 30 on racketeering charges.

Cronies are still benefitting. As recently as June 2023, cities are still using Project Roomkey funding to purchase motels at outrageous prices. The city of Chula Vista, near where I live, is doing that same thing as this is written. No funding for organizations that provide services, because they are mostly religion based, but plenty of money to buy motels at prices their owners love.

Here we see the same old story. Large government programs that sound good on paper offer little real-world viability. Our politicians prefer ideas generated within the swamp of Sacramento instead of forging practical solutions. I guarantee you that a team of builders, architects, and developers would be a thousand times more adept at solving these issues than lobbyists in their $5,000 suits.

There are examples for California to emulate. Florida has halved its total homeless population in the last decade. In just ten years, the number of homeless families decreased from 6,333 to 1,687. Florida posted the second-largest one-year homelessness decline in 2020: 3 percent. The Miami-Dade County metropolitan area now has a homeless population of less than one thousand. California reported the largest one-year gain of any state: 6.8 percent. Los Angeles County's homeless count stands at 63,706.

Florida has used a tough-love approach. Urban centers like Miami are clearing out homeless encampments. At the same time, they are partnering with various community organizations to house those living on the streets. Take a drive through the streets of Miami today and you will not see a single homeless person. It's a far cry from the multitude of tent cities we see daily in every California city. Governor Newsom should follow Florida's lead and fix our homeless problem.

We can end homelessness. With ample public and private resources at our disposal, our citizens should not have to worry about having roofs over their heads. We must make housing more affordable and provide the necessary healthcare to those in need. The key is affordable housing, which is the product of lower building costs. We need faster approvals, fewer mandates, less litigation, and lower impact fees. Homelessness has always been a tough challenge. But smart thinking and common sense, and a no-nonsense attitude such as the one Florida took in cracking down on homelessness, light the way forward.

CHAPTER 11

MAKING HOMEOWNERSHIP MORE THAN A MIRAGE

Californiaʼs sky-high cost of housing has made homeownership impossible for too many residents. Only 47 percent of Californians still believe in the part of the American Dream that says that by working hard, you can own your own home. This state of affairs should appall all of us.

The state needs over 1.4 million new housing units. The housing shortage and the increase in prices of available homes impact all aspects of daily life—from businesses to family budgets.

According to a September 2020 report in the *New York Times*, the median cost to buy a home in California has reached an astronomical $712,430. That's for the *average* home. Can the *average* Californian afford that? Will your children be able to? You'll have to save up for your whole life even to have a chance. A 2019 Home Affordability Report, put out by home equity co-investing pioneer Unison, found that the typical Los Angeles resident will spend *forty-three years* saving up to make a 20 percent down payment. Ironically, forty-three years is the amount of time the average LA worker will toil before retirement. If that math worries you, you're not alone.

The *Monterey Herald* interviewed Salinas realtor Chris Barrera about why middle- and low-income people are leaving California. Barrera reported that increasing numbers of his clients cite the cost of living as the main reason they are packing up and leaving. He estimates that one-fourth of his clients can no longer afford to live in California. "People are being priced out," he said. "I have a lot of clients who are selling, and they're just tired of California politics. Monterey County is one of the most expensive places to live in the U.S. When does this stop? When does this start evening out? All of us will be in that situation one day when we retire. To have to leave where our family is and where we are brought up, just because we can't afford it, is pretty sad."

He's right, and even Governor Newsom agrees. "Cost of living. It is *the* issue that defines more issues than any other issues in this state," Newsom noted.

I couldn't agree more. The problem starts in Sacramento. Unfortunately, the governor, the legislature, and the Sacramento political class ignore the importance of reducing excessive costs to build housing—impacting supply and affordability. But none of the political arguments matter more than the real issue: how to help all Californians afford a home—or even their monthly rent.

Unless we act soon, we will lose more of our residents and their needed talent. A recent survey by the global multidisciplinary research, analytics, and data consultancy Edelman Intelligence reported that 53 percent of Californians and 63 percent of millennials are considering fleeing to a lower-cost state. Yes, you read that right. Over half of the state is so fed up that they're considering pulling up stakes and heading for greener pastures.

The impossibility of buying or renting a home forces Californians to make painful choices. Older residents don't want to choose between spending their fixed income on rent or blood pressure medication. They don't want their adult children to move out of state because they can't afford to buy the house where they grew up. Young folks are choosing to leave after they graduate college because they cannot buy a home and put down roots in the Golden State.

How do we solve the problem of affordable housing? Step one is to repeal part of the legislation that has been an albatross around this state's neck: The California Environmental Quality Act (CEQA).

The Lord's Work

CEQA is a 1970s-era statute that allows virtually any interested party, under flimsy environmental pretexts, to file a lawsuit to stop a project. CEQA lawsuits can stop a project even after it has cleared a strenuous review and approval process. The heavy lift will be in reforming CEQA. Former governor Jerry Brown once called this "Doing the Lord's work."

Environmental lawyers, government agencies, lobbyists, and special-interest groups with a financial incentive use CEQA to delay housing projects an average of two-and-a-half years. As a builder, I can attest to how much those delays matter. The longer you carry a project, the higher the interest costs, real estate taxes, and other costs—costs then passed on to homeowners and renters.

I'm not alone in my indignation. In *The Sacramento Bee,* former governors George Deukmejian, Pete Wilson, and Gray Davis declared the need to reform CEQA's failing system. They wrote, "While CEQA's original intent must remain intact, now is the time to end reckless abuses of this important law—abuses that are threatening California's economic vitality, costing jobs, and wasting valuable taxpayer dollars. Today CEQA is too often abused by those seeking to gain a competitive edge, to leverage concessions from a project, or by neighbors who simply don't want any new growth in their community—no matter how worthy or environmentally beneficial a project may be."

A 2018 report by the Terner Center for Housing Innovation at UC Berkeley advises that factoring in added government fees and the enormous cost to defend CEQA-generated lawsuits tacks on $146,400 in added costs for a single-family residential unit. Development fees in

California are three times the national average. Green building standards in Los Angeles add 11 percent or more to the cost of building a home. Local land-use regulations drive up the cost of construction. All these fees are passed along to the consumer. If you've tried to buy or rent a home in California in the last ten years, I'm telling you something you already know.

In many other states, builders go before a single board for approval. Lawsuits and years-long delays are not *their* norms. In Indianapolis, for example, the approval process is typically six months. Building there, I'm still put through a rigorous review to make sure my project is environmentally sound and addresses traffic and every other impact. In the face of these obstacles, California builders are increasingly choosing to build housing in states with fewer regulations.

The knock-on consequences are far-reaching. The California Association of Realtors estimates that lost construction revenues cost California's economy $150 billion to $400 billion annually. Economists for the Southern California Association of Governments examined projects in their regional transportation plan and calculated the economic benefit of completing those projects just five years sooner. Cutting down on needless red tape and frivolous lawsuits would save taxpayers more than $1.25 billion on construction costs while creating an additional 102,000 construction jobs and more than 200,000 nonconstruction jobs each year. That would increase Southern California's GDP by about $31 billion annually. If policymakers reduce impact fees, minimize litigation, cut mandates, and streamline regulations, we can achieve this goal. Elected officials could remove these barriers. But that won't happen until they hear from constituents who stand up and speak out.

Even the Best of Us

The high cost of housing affects even the best of us. A January 2019 report by 10News, an ABC affiliate, documented the plight of San Diego's finest. They endure grueling daily commutes because they can't afford to live in the city they've pledged to protect.

Brian Avera is an SDPD sergeant forced to drive sixty miles to work each way from his home in Temecula, where homes are more affordable. "I usually get up at 4 a.m. and get on the road at 4:30 a.m.," he said. "The job by itself can be stressful, but adding a two-hour commute to the end of the day, and doing that a few days in a row, can get to wear on officers."

Detective Jack Schaeffer, president of the San Diego Police Officers Association, echoed his colleague. "There are more and more officers having to move farther and farther away from San Diego to be able to afford to have the quality of life that they want. Approximately 27% of our officers live in the city of San Diego. That's it."

For San Mateo Police Officer Jeff Brinton, the daily grind of an eighty-five-mile, two-and-one-half-hour commute was so demanding that he began sleeping in his van, parked in the police headquarters parking lot. Brinton said he's not the only member of the force who sleeps in a vehicle rather than drive home several hours after a twelve-hour workday. "A lot of (officers) are sleeping in their cars." That is inexcusable.

Here's a startling number: 68 percent of San Mateo's police officers live outside the county limits. The typical commute for officers living outside the county is fifty miles each way. The number-one reason: they can't afford to buy a home in the community they serve. The average midcareer peace officer in San Mateo makes about $101,000 a year; that's not nearly enough to buy the average $1.4 million Silicon Valley home.

Atherton is another affluent Bay Area city where not a single police officer can afford to live, given that the median-priced home approaches $7 million. Officers must endure commuting two hours or more from places like Gilroy and Tracy. In response, the city converted an eight-by-ten storage closet into a sleeping room where tired off-duty officers can sleep between their twelve-to-sixteen hour shifts. Treating police officers this way is shameful.

It's not just those who protect and serve us who have to make hard choices. Take the case of Chuck DeVore, a California State assemblymember from 2004 to 2010. When Representative DeVore was termed out in 2010, he had a decision to make. His wife's parents, both over eighty years old, had dementia. DeVore brought them into their family home in Irvine, but it was not large enough to accommodate everyone. Chuck found himself confronted with a decision he never expected to have to make: neglect his filial duty or flee the state he had represented and loved.

In the end, like so many other Californians, the DeVore family packed up and moved to Texas. The home DeVore purchased in Texas Hill Country, west of the capital, Austin, was 70 percent larger than the home he sold in California—and it cost $110,000 less.

According to NerdWallet, the median home price for three-bedroom two-bath homes in Orange County is $979,637. The same home in Austin costs $347,906. Overall, housing costs are 57 percent lower in Austin than in Orange County. Add to that transportation (28 percent lower) and food savings (20 percent lower), and you see why Texas is becoming an attractive alternative.

Austin used to be a sleepy college town that housed former president Lyndon Johnson's library. Times have changed. Today Austin is a mecca for high-tech start-ups and booming enterprises. It's not paradise. Austin now faces traffic congestion and other problems that fast growth entails. Still, the cost of housing in that lovely community is about a third of California's.

Back to DeVore. When asked about the difference between building things like critical infrastructure in Texas and California, he responded, "The bottom line is, in Texas, there's nothing like CEQA." He blames environmental lawyers and labor union bosses who conspire to "greenmail" projects with expensive and drawn-out litigation unless their demands are met—demands often unrelated to an environmental impact. This burdens developers, citizens, and the government. It increases the construction costs of everything from freeways to single-family residential homes while lining the pockets of special-interest groups. Who pays? No prize for guessing.

If a Shoe Drops

Approximately 45 percent of Californians rent their homes. Think it's any better for renters than buyers? Think again. An April 24, 2018, analysis by the nonprofit Economic Roundtable found that 600,000 Los Angeles County residents spend 90 percent or more of their income on housing. Daniel Flaming, president of the Economic Roundtable, sounded the alarm. "Virtually all of the liquid resources of the family are going to pay for rent," he said. "And if a shoe drops—if someone gets sick or someone loses a job, or if someone leaves the household that's contributing to paying rent—then that family can easily find itself on the street." NBC News reports severe housing shortages have caused rents to increase twice as fast as the national average. The monthly rent bill claims half of the household income for approximately 50 percent of those living in and around the state's major cities. The 1.3 million families earning less than $25,000 per year are walking a tightrope between being able to make their rent and living on the streets.

A California Housing Partnership Corporation study in 2015 reported that renters in Orange County need to earn $42.12 per hour to afford the median monthly rent of $2,190. Today, the average low-income resident spends 78 percent of their wages on rent. When we consider housing costs, Orange County's poverty rate rises from 11.9 percent to 21.3 percent. That's over double the national poverty rate.

In a January 2020 interview with the *Monterey Herald*, Randa Moore cited the cost of living as the number-one reason she left Santa Rosa for a three-bedroom house with a pool for $1,400 a month in Florida. In California, Moore says, "We were working ten to sixteen hours a day, seven days a week, every holiday, and were still struggling to buy groceries. We don't make California money anymore, but we have more money at the end of the month. The difference is in thousands of dollars and hours working. Do I miss my home state? I miss what it was before high costs destroyed the middle class. California has become a two-class system, the haves and the have-nots. The poor have no chance."

In my travels around the state, I talk to many people. One was Felipe Martinez, whom I met at the Sriracha Hot Sauce Factory in Irwindale. Felipe is renting a one-bedroom apartment for himself and his four children. He pays $1,500 a month. His four girls share the bedroom in the San Dimas apartment while Felipe sleeps on the living room floor each night. He doesn't want to move to Texas because he loves the Dodgers. But, like a lot of Californians, he's struggling.

We need to help Californians like the Martinez family. We *can* build housing that's a lot less expensive. I do it in Indiana, and Indiana is a great place to live. They're not environmentally backward there. They have high environmental standards. They have stringent building standards, but they do it in a way that allows residential construction to be cost-effective. Here in California, it's all about making builders jump through hoops—the kind of hoops that raise costs.

Gavin Newsom is part of that political class. He's done nothing to solve the problem, and you can bet he's not going to do anything. The correct action would step on the political toes of the special-interest groups who bankroll him as well as control the California legislature—a situation Hear the People would remedy. It bears repeating: California's high cost of residential home building stems from regulations: first and foremost CEQA, then litigation, mandates, wage rules, and impact fees. Municipal fees, permits, codes, and city requirements can tack an additional 6 to 18 percent on building costs. Various mandates and prevailing wage rules imposed by special-interest groups in Sacramento add up. The result is that rents are still sky high, and the cost of living in these housing units continues to consume a considerable share of a renter's total monthly income.

Any comprehensive solution to bring down the housing costs in California has to include reform of CEQA. The state needs to give local authorities incentives to approve new housing development and new commercial areas. We need innovative products.

Utilities, food, healthcare, clothing, and services of all sorts cost more because the high cost of living forces employers to pay more. Those higher salaries don't yield a better standard of living because they get eaten up by the rising costs of everything else. A vicious cycle.

If we had the kind of electoral system with small districts like Hear the People, politicians would be able to change CEQA to allow more building and bring down the costs of construction. Special interest groups and environmental lobbyists wouldn't be able to hold up corrective legislation. This is a major issue directly impacting the lives of many Californians and it won't change until we change the way we elect our leaders.

CHAPTER 12

SENSIBLE ENVIRONMENTAL POLICY

On a rainy afternoon in January 2021, I spoke to a Central Valley farmer named Joe Del Bosque over a Zoom call. Joe looked like he stepped off a Western movie set with his rugged features, Wrangler jeans, and red checked shirt. His hair was silver under an off-white cowboy hat. His hands were calloused from a life spent working the land. Joe told me his American story and how it bears upon California's current water restrictions that impact thousands of farmers like himself.

"I have to go back to my parents to start my story," Joe said to me in his easy, open manner. "They were migrant workers from Mexico back in the '30s and '40s. They settled in this area in the '50s when I was three or four years old. I grew up on a farm not very far from here. My father put me on a tractor when I was ten years old, and off I went. I worked on the farm every summer for seventy-five cents an hour and saved enough money to go to Fresno State."

"After college, I came back and worked on the farm as a manager for ten years. I learned a lot from my dad about growing melons," he continued. "In 1984, something got into me, and I struck out to start my farm. It wasn't easy because I had no money, but I was able to do it. I started with nothing, renting land. It went well because I worked hard. Today I farm two thousand acres, half of which I own. We grow organic melons, sweet corn, asparagus, and almonds and employ between two hundred fifty and three hundred people at harvest time."

Joe raised six daughters on the farm. Two still work for him. His wife manages the employees and is in the fields every day. "One of the huge challenges we've gone through started in 1990 when we first began getting water restrictions," he said. I could hear a much-needed rain coming down on his roof as we spoke. "They only gave us 25 percent of our supply. It was scary because we didn't know what we were gonna do. We could only plant 25 percent of our land: three-fourths of our land was fallowed [left unplanted]. Many of the people I had working for me had to be laid off and lost their jobs. We had water restrictions for a number of years in a row, and it was tough. I realized we can't farm like this. We cannot succeed by fallowing land and laying off people. We had to do something."

When I asked Joe how much water the state allocated to him last year, he told me: "In 2020, we received about 20 percent in the spring and a bit more in the summer when it was too late. We didn't make much money last year because of that. We're trying not to lay off more people because they're good people. We'll just bite the bullet and keep them on board. They have families. A lot of them have kids in college. They're poor, but they want to go to school and improve their lives." I asked what the outlook was for this year. "This year we were told to expect *no* water."

Where are you expected to farm with no water and infrequent rainfall? Only in California. Bosque's story points to a statewide problem. Nearly one million acres of California farmland lie fallow because the farmers don't have enough water. It's land that could be producing food and making us more prosperous. These are not large farms owned by corporations that can afford to take the financial hit. The average farm in California is *25 percent smaller* than the national average. These are farms that have been in the family for generations. Lost farmland means hundreds of millions of dollars of lost income for farmers, with tens of thousands of jobs lost. It is heartbreaking to drive through the Central Valley and see a desert where crops once grew. Our farmers deserve better.

We love our sunny weather in the Golden State, but it doesn't rain for long stretches of the year in the Central Valley and Southern California. Because of the arid climate, large swatches of the state often run out of water before the rains return. We need to store it during our short rainy season to make it through the dry months. Usually, that doesn't happen because no one is building new reservoirs. We built the last major reservoir in Southern California in 1999. In Central and Northern California, the last dam was completed during Ronald Reagan's administration. Since that time, our population has increased by over ten million people. The urgency speaks for itself.

Another farmer I spoke with asked what would happen if California had built no new roads over the last thirty years. We continue to upgrade and expand our highway system, so some of our roadways aren't as congested (although they're still plenty congested in many places despite the added lanes). Yet, we have failed to expand our water capacity even as our needs have multiplied. Farmers, businesses, and Californian citizens all need reliable and plentiful water sources. Our cities, towns, agriculture, and industry cannot thrive without it. Can you imagine if we had not improved our freeways since the Reagan years? That would be unconscionable—yet we have done exactly that in neglecting our water supply.

The massive winter rains and snowpack of 2022–23 serve to highlight the results of inaction and the malign influence of environmental lobbyists. This year, California experienced a once-in-a-generation confluence of storms that have filled reservoirs and created a snowpack of such epic proportions that the prime worry statewide is of flooding, not drought. Voters in California approved major bond issues to build reservoirs and improve the state's water distribution system. Was anything spent? Hardly. We are thus seeing the result of this inaction—a huge wasted opportunity as most of this year's huge rainfall will end up flowing to the Pacific, unavailable for people fish or agriculture. It may even result in huge flooding.

Special-interest funding begets bad policy, which begets human suffering—an old story in California.

This issue of water access is central to our future. California has a tremendous agricultural economy. It generated *$50 billion in sales* in 2019, or nearly double second-place Iowa's sales. Many people don't realize that we have more cattle than Texas and more dairy farms than Wisconsin and Vermont combined. We farm over four hundred different crops here. California grows more fruits, vegetables, and nuts than in the other forty-nine states combined. We grow 80 percent of the world's almonds in California. We are the top producer of sixty-six different food crops. We grow nearly all the oranges, dates, figs, raisins, prunes, walnuts, pistachios, almonds, olives, artichokes, kiwis, pomegranates, and sweet rice in the U.S. California sells more organic produce than the following top ten states combined. What would our supermarkets and tables look like if all that went away?

To gain insights into the economic impact of water rationing, I spoke with Mike Wade, the California Farm Water Coalition's executive director. "When water is reduced or eliminated, jobs go away, and we end up with poverty," he said. "We have a situation where local economies suffer. It's not just the workers who lose their jobs. Local businesses depend on those dollars to keep their grocery stores, gas stations, and barbershops operating. What happens after a long period of reduced water deliveries is that people move away. We end up with disadvantaged communities with unstable economies thanks to an unstable water supply."

While the recent past has created significant hardships, the situation was not always like this. In 1938, the Central Valley Project (CVP) began building dams, reservoirs, hydroelectric plants, and aqueducts. A series of twenty dams and reservoirs provided water to the Central Valley and controlled flooding. Once barren land turned green and productive. Our agriculture industry blossomed. The CVP has returned the $3 billion investment in our water supply over one hundred times.

In 1960, Pat Brown, Jerry's father, created the California Water Project (CWP). That program built a new series of dams and aqueducts, and the water flowed. However, in the 1980s, environmental groups began attacking the CWP and the CVP because they dammed rivers to create reservoirs. Environmental extremists want no rivers dammed, no matter the cost to farmers, our economy, or the general population.

Environmental group lawsuits led to the San Joaquin River Restoration Act of 2009. Salmon had been absent from that stretch of the river for over one hundred years. The goal of this act was to restore salmon to the upper reach of the San Joaquin River. Five hundred salmon returned, and the government deemed the initiative successful. The cost to taxpayers: $4 million per fish. The cost to farmers: sixty billion gallons of water lost each year. The cost to you and me: higher food prices. The logical rationale for this "Restoration Act" completely escapes me.

There is a widespread misconception about farmers wasting water. It's a myth. In California, the government rations water. Farmers do not waste water. Rationing forces them to find innovative ways to use water efficiently and responsibly. For decades California farmers have been growing more food with less water. Crop production has increased by 38 percent during the last forty years, while water usage has decreased by 14 percent.

Like any entrepreneur, farmers like Joe Del Bosque have had to be adaptable, and he tried. He transitioned to higher-value crops that used less water and were more profitable. As he explained, "Farmers in this area have had to adapt and become more efficient, become better farmers. A lot of us had to learn to grow new crops, something different, something better," he said. "We made a great effort to change our farms from what they were thirty years ago."

Joe told me that he began using drip irrigation in 1997 and that by 2010 the whole farm had evolved to drip irrigation. Central Valley farmers have spent $4 billion on modernizing their water irrigation systems in the last fifteen years, primarily drip, microsprinkler, and subsurface irrigation. But then came the drought of 2011–2019. Increased restrictions brought hard times, and things went from bad to worse for Joe and the other farmers. "In the years 2014, 2015, and 2016 we had zero water allocation,"

Joe said. Extensive idle land meant Joe and other farmers lost customers like Safeway, Whole Foods, and Trader Joe's. To keep in business and not lay off his workers, Joe had to buy water from other farmers. He then had to pay those farmers for their water *and* the lost revenue from crops they couldn't water themselves. "We basically went out and bought their crops so we could take their water. It was very, very expensive, but it was the only way to try to keep going," he said. "We had some really tough times. There were years I spent over a million and a half dollars on water. It was horrendous, but we did what we could."

On Valentine's Day 2014, President Barack Obama visited Joe on his farm to discuss the California farmer's plight. They walked through 125 acres of dry, empty fields that should have been capable of producing a million melons. That visit raised awareness but brought no relief. Bureaucracy in Sacramento is still leaving the working farmer out to dry.

Water Wars

Farmers are an important constituency, but their numbers are dwindling, and water restrictions persist. Their funding is usually far exceeded by outlays for radical environmental groups who push their dogmatic views on the rest of us. Central Valley farmers are powerless to stop the regulations that choke off their water supply and turn farms into government-created dust bowls.

Finally, the federal government decided to take action, most notably with *Modernizing America's Water Resource Management and Water Infrastructure Jan. 2021*, a national plan to increase California and the West's water capacity. This initiative aims to modernize delivery systems, increase water storage, streamline bureaucracy, and improve drought resilience and water reliability. Predictably, environmentalists lined up against the plan. Governor Newsom piled on board with the radicals and filed suit.

Now that you know more about California's water problems, would the idea of raising an existing six-hundred-foot dam by eighteen and a half feet to supply water to an additional six million Californians seem like a good idea? That was the plan for expanding Shasta Dam in 2019. It seemed like a great idea to me—and almost everyone on the state and federal levels thought so. Once again, politics beat out sound management. Left-wing California Attorney General Xavier Becerra and an army of environmentalists quashed the project.

Becerra filed over 110 lawsuits against the federal government from 2017 to 2021 *at* the cost of $41 million to taxpayers. Becerra wasted $41 million of our tax money to prevent Californians from getting more water. The Center for Biological Diversity has filed over five hundred lawsuits, all in California. Earthjustice, a San Francisco-based environmental group, had 375 active cases pending in 2014 and collected over *$18 million in attorney fees* in five years. You, the taxpayer, footed the bill for every dollar the environmental radicals wasted. Only in California.

Only in California, indeed. That is a phrase you hear a lot in other states. Why? Because California is the only place where a handful of environmental extremists can routinely hold the population ransom on any project they don't like. Their plan is simple: get one judge to overturn the will of forty million citizens. And guess what—their scheming has worked. These special-interest lawsuits undermine democracy. They represent tyranny by the few. We cannot allow a handful of environmental zealots to hold hostage our water, our citizens, and our future.

There is a way forward. Mike Wade of the California Farm Water Coalition sees encouraging signs that we may be moving forward positively. As he relates, "We're starting to see more cooperation between some conservation organizations, farmers, and public agencies in implementing joint projects that help improve habitat, reduce the impacts on fish and allow more water to flow to farms. There have been projects completed for decades that were cooperative between conservation groups and farms which provided many benefits for both sides."

Wade cited the collaborative effort called the Voluntary Agreements, formed by over 180 stakeholders (NGOs, government agencies, and water agencies representing farmers) to find long-lasting solutions based on modern science. The idea is to substitute cooperation and collaboration for the endless cycle of litigation. These Voluntary Agreements, Wade explained, are a break from outdated science and impasses of the past and set California on the path toward responsible environmental and water management. They are supported not only by farmers but by 62 percent of Californians.

Joe Del Bosque echoes his fellow farmers when he says, "Let's work together and structure this, so we meet everybody's needs as best we can. Many farmers want to bring everybody to the table to agree on something rather than imposing restrictions and bringing lawsuits. It's hurting the economies of our agricultural communities. It's hurting the people who work in these communities. We just have to find a better way."

Summing up the Voluntary Agreements, Mike Wade explained his enthusiasm. "We are a strong supporter, given that this plan lays out a framework for smart projects that provide environmental protection, improve habitats, improve in-stream flows, and make conditions better for fish." Wade wrote in his February 2020 op-ed for the nonprofit news organization Cal Matters, "More top-down regulation will only continue to breed endless lawsuits. In contrast, the Voluntary Agreements offer a positive path forward in which all water users have a voice. And once completed, these Agreements will begin making things better immediately. They will provide more water stability to agriculture in the San Joaquin Valley while still providing meaningful, real protections for fish while maintaining all of the protections under the Endangered Species Act. There is only one choice if you care about the future of California, and that's the completion of the Voluntary Agreements."

Predictably, six environmental groups filed suit. There was a conflict between the federal government and state agencies. As a result, the Voluntary Agreements have stalled. I believe that no lawsuit, no special-interest group, and no disagreement between governmental agencies should ever be able to sabotage the common good. Water is a fundamental right. No one should have the power to withhold water from our farms and our citizens.

We must champion pragmatic solutions to complex problems by providing leadership that equally values all Californians' voices. We should increase water storage capacity by building new dams and expanding the capacity of existing reservoirs. We must use technology and innovative ideas to improve efficiency and reduce waste. One solution I believe is workable to help ease California's water shortage comes from Israel. Israel is 60 percent desert, and rain falls only in the winter and only in the northern part of the country. In 2007, the nation risked running dry. Water shortages posed an existential threat to the nation's survival. Energetic and talented, they refused to allow a big problem to hold them back. They innovated and built large desalination plants to process saltwater from the Mediterranean Sea. Removing sea salt and other impure minerals makes it drinkable and suitable for other uses.

Israel's plants now provide more than six hundred billion gallons of drinkable seawater a year. It exports water to the Middle East region. Fully 80 percent of the small country's water comes from desalination. While we have three hundred desalination plants in the United States, they are used almost exclusively for industrial purposes. Just 13 percent of our drinking water and water for cooking and bathing comes from desalination.

In May 2014, Bloomberg Television interviewed the Israeli prime minister. In that interview, he said: "California, I hear, has a big water problem. How come we don't have a water problem? Because we use technology to solve it." Why don't we have more such plants in California? One built in 2016 in Carlsbad, California, was triple the projected cost (and almost five times what Israeli facilities cost) due to litigation. Still, it brought fifty million gallons of fresh water a day from the sea to serve the needs of about three million people. But the follow-through hasn't been there, and we haven't continued down this road.

In addition to desalination, Israel reuses treated sewage water for agriculture, runs a public education campaign to conserve water, monitors leaks in its infrastructure using advanced software, and runs computerized deep drip irrigation systems. According to Heather Cooley, water program director for the nonprofit Pacific Institute, those areas are ones on which California and the U.S. need to work. As she told the online magazine *Governing*, "Water conservation and efficiency is typically the cheapest, fastest way to reduce demand and essentially develop a new supply. We've made significant improvements in California, but we still have a long way to go."

We do indeed. But with forward-thinking ideas, we will get there while remaining good stewards of the environment by supporting healthy and diverse ecosystems. We must move forward with pragmatic solutions like the Voluntary Agreements. We will solve California's water issues and strengthen our commitment to those that grow the food we put on our tables each day.

Paradise Is Burning

Tomoyo and Shigeo Kojima arrived in California with one suitcase between them. Working twelve-hour days, they opened a Japanese restaurant to share their culture and, with its success, bought two homes in the Sierra foothills in a town called Paradise.

On the morning of November 8, 2018, Tomoyo looked out her window and saw a wildfire approaching. In an interview with the *Los Angeles Japanese Daily News* in December 2018, she recounted what happened next. Within minutes, her backyard was burning. She ran to put it out with a garden hose, then called her husband at the restaurant and told him to "come back home immediately." Thirty minutes later, they began evacuating, joining the line of traffic as people fled the blaze engulfing the town. Rising ash made the sky as dark as night. The fire raged on both sides of the road around them. Propane tanks exploded in the chaos. Traffic crawled at a snail's pace. Some residents abandoned their cars and fled on foot. "I might die here," Tomoyo thought.

The Kojimas escaped from the fire with their lives, but their homes and their restaurant burned to the ground. "We never imagined our houses would burn. Those were our dream houses," they remembered. "We had hoped at least one of our houses or the restaurant might be able to survive. However, everything was burned down. We never thought we would be homeless."

The couple relocated to a Red Bluff RV park to start their life anew. "Precious memories and two suitcases—this is our new start," they told themselves. Their employees had scattered to places like Nevada and Georgia. A month after that fire, the couple began to sell takeout from a food truck, but they have bigger plans for the future. "One day, we want to reopen the restaurant together," they told the newspaper. "We want to go back to our happy days. We don't want it to end like this."

The fire that destroyed everything the Kojima had built, the Camp Fire of 2018, was the deadliest blaze in California's history. It killed eighty-six people, destroyed 18,808 buildings, and decimated the town of Paradise. California averages over six thousand wildfires each year, burning more than one-quarter of a million acres annually. That is one part of the cost of wildfires that burn out of control. Disasters like these tear communities apart and turn dreams into smoke.

The tragedy that befell the Kojimas was possibly preventable, but it will continue to happen. Thousands of homes burn to the ground each year in California. Sacramento's response is to pass the buck by blaming "climate change." Instead of proposing actionable solutions, career politicians and the environmental lobby that helps elect them will use wildfires to further a radical agenda that imposes severe costs on Californians while returning limited, often questionable benefits.

What was Governor Newsom's response? He hired a New York law firm to draft new legislation, AB 1054, to *protect* Pacific Gas and Electric at a cost of $3.7 million to California taxpayers. PG&E was responsible for the deaths of eighty-four people and our governor chose to protect the criminals who contributed $208,400 to his 2018 campaign instead of protecting the people he is elected to represent.

Ethel Colleen Riggs was one of those people. She was burned to ashes in her laundry room in Paradise during the Camp Fire blaze. Mrs. Riggs's grandson, Steve Bradley, a former volunteer firefighter in Paradise, drove from Sacramento to Paradise hoping to save his ninety-six-year-old grandmother. He was too late. Steve told ABC News10, "I don't talk about it enough, but that really keeps me up at night. You know, was she expecting me? Was she expecting me to be able to get there at the last second?"

Steve Bradley and other fire victims were outraged that Governor Newsom protected PG&E, but left Bradley's grandmother to perish in the flames caused by the utility company's negligence. Gavin Newsom went even further to protect his benefactors at PG&E. He had the audacity to award a state certificate of safety to the corporation convicted of felony manslaughter in the killing eighty-four Californians.

What safety procedures did PG&E put in place to qualify for the safety certificate? None. Former Volunteer Firefighter Steve Bradley echoed the opinion of many in California when he stated, "If it were me, I would have been in jail a long, long, long time ago. But PG&E gets a pass because they're a corporation." In fact PG&E got something even better than a pass. The safety certificate gave the company access to a $21 billion state insurance fund to cover costs due to the fires it causes. It's good to be friends with the governor.

The catalyst for the continuing increase in deadly wildfires is that environmental laws enacted over the last twenty or thirty years forbid any disturbance of the forests. Federal and state laws prevent people from taking dead trees out of the woods. We have one hundred and twenty million dead trees on the floors of our forests. Wildfires are not growing in severity because of healthy trees: dead trees and tinder are going up in flames.

A proven solution exists. Yet the environmental extremists and influence peddlers in Sacramento refuse to use it. California had logging companies go into forests and take out the dead trees in the past. They would get to keep the wood. Arizona does this extensively. People think Arizona is all desert, but it's not. There are a lot of forests in the northern part of the state. Arizona has had tremendous fire risk over the years but has dealt with it by contracting with logging companies to go in and take dead trees and tinder out of the forests.

These companies get to keep the wood. So, mitigating the fire risk is a win-win for the state and the logging industry. California has forbidden that. If we allow logging companies to cull and clean the forest responsibly, we can reduce wildfire severity. California used to have almost a hundred forestry concerns and sawmills. They did a pretty good job taking care of the forests; they had to because it was their livelihood. We're down to a handful now. That's one of the big problems. Most of the lumber industry has moved north to Canada. One knock-on consequence is that consumers pay higher and higher prices for lumber. That's avoidable.

A second solution has been around for hundreds of years: firebreaks. Historically, Native Americans used firebreaks. A firebreak is clearing a lane in a forest at various intervals. You build these firebreaks and cut a road in the woods to suppress a blaze about to burn out of control. Firefighters use fire roads to get their equipment into otherwise inaccessible areas. We don't allow cutting firebreaks or fire roads anymore because environmental purists won't allow any trees to be touched or any wildlife disturbed.

Environmentalists use their fundraising to influence politicians. Politicians don't want to vote against these environmental bills because they will get an opponent funded by these environmentalists. That is a crucial problem. But it's worse than that. The radical environmentalists want us to believe they are nature's guardians, just interested in doing the right thing. Jerry Brown once pointed out astutely that in politics, follow the money. He's right. Much of the propaganda and disruption that these radical groups perpetrate is about raising money. This money pays them fees, media commissions, commissions on coalition building, and retainers. Once you grasp that, the picture grows clearer. The radical groups are not engaged in honest debate. It's a rigged game and trust me, and big bucks are at stake.

The sad thing is that the radicals are misleading you on the merits. A September 2017 Public Policy Institute of California report, financed in part by the Environmental Protection Agency, argued for forest thinning. The report stated, "The strategic removal of high-density smaller trees and fuels is essential to increasing long-term resilience of headwater forests" and that culling flammable biomass "reduces the risk of high severity fires while promoting low-and moderate-severity fires that increase habitat heterogeneity and do not kill many large trees. Lower biomass also reduces the overall water demands of forests. In drier areas, less competition for water will lead to greater tree growth, healthier trees, and eventually more large trees."

The report stressed that forest thinning "mimics some of the effects of fire and provides wood products for commercial uses. Commercial uses of wood products include constructing housing in urban and suburban areas—which has the added benefit of sequestering carbon. Reducing the density of forests using a mix of fire and mechanical thinning can make them less vulnerable to current and future stressors, particularly those associated with climate warming and increasing variability of precipitation."

Another uncomfortable fact that radical environmentalists conceal is that wildfires emit vast amounts of greenhouse gasses. Greenhouse gasses from wildfires have increased each year since 2011 when the Democrats took control of Sacramento. Since then, CO2 emissions from wildfires have risen from five million metric tons in 2011 to a projected 111.7 millionmetric tons in 2020, as reported in December 2020 by the California Air Resources Board. That's more carbon dioxide than every single power plant in the state produces.

The Sacramento solution is to mandate more green energy. You and I pay that cost. Those 111.7 million metric tons of CO2 spewed into the atmosphere due to forest fires is only slightly less than every California car produces in one year. Gavin Newsom and the radical Left's solution? Mandate that all new vehicles sold in California by 2035 be electric. That cost passes on to working-class Californians, the same people who can't afford to buy a home or pay rent in large cities, let alone drive a new $80,000 Tesla.

Reducing carbon emissions and mitigating some of the effects of climate change and drought while saving people's lives and property sounds like a no-brainer. The Public Policy Institute of California report has blasted the political paralysis in Sacramento, stating: "Yet these tools remain underutilized due to many political, social, historical, and budgetary reasons."

Gavin Newsom could do something about this tomorrow. Yet he refuses to champion practical forestry policy. Some people attribute that to pressure from environmental groups. Let's be clear: this issue is not conservative versus liberal. The harsh reality is that Newsom has left us behind on this issue because he doesn't know what he's doing. Let's face it: it's easier to hold a press conference than roll up your sleeves and solve a complicated problem.

To fight wildfires, we need a common-sense, science-based approach. We *can* be responsible stewards of our forests. Thinning dead trees and underbrush, cutting firebreaks, and clearing firefighting equipment paths are all solutions that fire crews have used effectively and responsibly before. We need to start thinking outside the box about solutions.

Think of the billions in added taxes and fees Californians pay every year to supposedly mitigate CO2 emissions. Wouldn't it make more sense to spend money on sensors in the forests along with cameras that would allow authorities to pinpoint fires the moment they occur? We could then make an appropriate response and limit the damage and pollution from these fires.That would do a lot for the environment.

In 2020 as the pandemic shuttered the airline industry, I proposed an idea called the Air Armada, a fleet—as many as one hundred large airplanes (737s and 747s) equipped with tanks and ready at a moment's notice to fly over fires and apply an overwhelming force of water or retardant. Each plane can carry 24,000 pounds of water or retardant that we can deploy. The four DC10 jets California now uses have only half that capacity. If you concentrated the capabilities at critical points and allowed planes to take off at dawn when winds are less and fires are not as hot, we could retard the progress of fires and save lives and property. Common sense tells us to put overwhelming force on a fire. Douse it before it becomes an inferno that is incredibly difficult to put out.

Since I'm budget-minded, I know how we'll pay for the Air Armada. We can funnel funding from an $80 billion high-speed rail train that *might* someday connect San Francisco and Los Angeles. We can take some of that money spent on that train, which is way behind schedule and will be obsolete before completion, and use that money to buy or lease those airplanes.

Our current leadership doesn't think innovative solutions like the Air Armada are worth pursuing. The California way has always been about thinking big. Let's start thinking that way again.

We know why our leadership doesn't do this—they are too easily manipulated by funding interests that favor higher taxes on gasoline and elimination of fossil fuels as their way to fight pollution. Those funding interests don't want the forests managed or firefighting response done with aircraft. They use their money and their political muscle with the media to move our leadership in the direction they want; not the best way for the rest of us. That's why we need an election system that focuses on good policy not money and media.

CHAPTER 13

WHY POLITICIANS AND REGULATORS MAKE CRIMINALS LOOK LIKE AMATEURS

California was once a bastion of entrepreneurial spirit. In the California Gold Rush of 1849, tens of thousands of courageous men and women braved the arduous cross-continental journey by wagon train, eager to seek their fortunes. Those that didn't find gold nonetheless stayed and farmed or opened businesses. They reinvented themselves. This culture of risk-taking fueled innovation. California's economy boomed, and more people came over the ensuing years and decades. They created new businesses and got good jobs, whether in oil, aviation, entertainment, aerospace, or technology. The middle class grew. People were prosperous and happy.

Then came the regulators—transforming California into the antibusiness state we have now become. California is the most regulated state in the nation. We have 395,608 regulations, one hundred thousand more than runner-up New York, according to a 2020 report by George Washington University—and with no end in sight. Our labor markets alone are among the most heavily regulated in the country.

Annual surveys of top executives paint California as one of the most toxic places to do business. The 2021 State Business Tax Climate Index placed California second to last in business friendliness among the fifty states. The Hoover Institution of Stanford published a study stating: "California is too expensive, and its taxes and regulations are too high." We outpace the number of lost manufacturing jobs nationally. Many companies have abandoned expansion plans or moved out. I listed these before, but it bears repeating: Toyota. Hewlett Packard. Charles Schwab. Tesla. Oracle. The list goes on.

State regulatory agencies don't only hurt business—they hurt *people*. The rampant cronyism, nepotism, ineptitude, and staggering fraud plaguing our regulatory agencies are crippling our economy *and* placing our citizens in harm's way. Bribery, campaign contributions, and funneling money through nonprofit shell organizations are all too common. The massive avalanche of regulation comes from an entrenched bureaucracy of public employee unions, lobbyists, and politicians, all of whom want to maintain the status quo.

Nothing illustrates the criminality of regulators better than the story told by Alice Stebbins, the former executive director of the California Public Utilities Commission (CPUC). The Commission regulates electric, natural gas, telecommunications, water, railroads, and passenger transportation companies like Uber and Lyft. According to Stebbins and most people you talk to, the CPUC is "truly the most powerful state agency."

I spoke with Stebbins from her home near Sacramento. In 2018, the commission hired her "to bring fiscal integrity to the CPUC." When she took the job, her boss warned her: "You're going to get invited to luncheons with the utilities. Do what I do: bring a sack lunch." Stebbins audited the agency's books as part of her duties as executive director. What she found was shocking.

Stebbins dug into the CPUC's finances and discovered that a staggering $200 million was missing from accounts that fund services for the blind, deaf, and poor. One of the programs in question was Lifeline. Lifeline is a program that gives free cell phones out to disadvantaged Californians. For example, the program handed out phones to at-risk youth in the state foster-adoption system. The kids could use the phone to call someone if they were in a home that wasn't safe. The funding comes from a monthly fee on your phone bill. There were no checks and balances on vendors who supplied the phones. The phone providers simply submitted a statement to the CPUC and were paid, no questions asked. Many of the phones simply didn't exist. Stebbins saw that it was fraud. "As I started digging, there were some companies—and boy did they not like me. I mean, they *hated* me because they saw what I was doing," she told me.

"The problem was the programs were controlling the money, and the commissioners had access," she continued. "You're looking at a system that is just terrible, with no controls in place whatsoever. They wanted me to go away." Bernard Azevedo, an auditor Stebbins brought on board, found $6.3 million missing from the Deaf and Disabled Telecommunications Program. In an interview with ProPublica, he said, "I have real concerns. That's a lot of money." Stebbins added, "I think there are millions of dollars out there that haven't been reported." Stebbins and her staff were alarmed that such programs, designed to help the neediest Californians, were rife with fraud. When Stebbins went to the commissioners with her concerns, she was told: "Just make things work out and don't make waves."

Stebbins accused the new commission president Marybel Batjer of obstructing her investigation into the missing funds and stymying her reform efforts. "Governor Newsom put in Marybel Batjer. Batjer had no experience in energy. She supposedly revamped the DMV," Stebbins said with a touch of sarcasm in her voice.

When Batjer took the reins of the agency, Stebbins said she "felt her support start to fade." Batjer illegally emailed other commissioners about Stebbins, writing: "I fear she is working up to a scorched earth approach," and "I can't imagine her staying." The other commissioners lined up behind Batjer. Her bosses told her: "You really need to toe the line. Maybe you should back off on some of these issues." Stebbins was floored, but she didn't stop.

Deserted By the Higher-Ups

In April 2020, an investigator from the state personnel board called Stebbins and told her she was under investigation for ethics violations for selecting six of the auditors she hired. "In June, I got a special report that blasted me for my hiring." Stebbins maintains that all the auditors were qualified, and she followed the agency's hiring process. When Stebbins looked for support from her superiors, "there was a wall that went up."

Stebbins is confident that the governor's office brought in Batjer to take her down. "That was a tough pill for me to swallow. It was terrible. They destroyed my career. I was terminated at a hearing on August 31 where I was chastised by the president [Batjer] who said that there was nothing to any of my findings." Stebbins put on a brave face but shared with me, "Behind the scenes, I was crushed. I was hurt. And I was disgusted because I knew they wanted me to stop fixing all the broken parts of the [C]PUC. More importantly, they wanted to continue with their corruption. Who knows what money was exchanging hands?"

Stebbins believes the ethics violations were trumped-up charges. "That was the cover they used to fire me." She claims it was the missing $200 million that got her fired. As Stebbins told the *San Francisco Chronicle*, "I get the feeling that maybe I'm on the path to uncovering more. I know I am...and I think I've made people nervous." In an interview with ABC10 Sacramento, she said, "We are a watchdog, and my teeth were being removed."

There's more. The California Public Utilities Commission oversees privately owned electric and natural gas utilities, none more potent than Pacific Gas and Electric (PG&E). The largest private utility in the nation, the company services 5.45 million customers. PG&E has a monopoly on power in California. It reported revenues of $17.12 billion in 2019. Its money and power to influence regulators knew no bounds.

Stebbins believes Pacific Gas and Electric lobbied to have her terminated because she posed a risk to their inappropriate and illegal relationship with the regulators at the CPUC. PG&E routinely puts profits over safety, and nobody minded the store to stop them—until Alice Stebbins began asking questions.

Stebbins said, "They [PG&E] are a massive, powerful business in California. And they seem to be able to get away with a lot."

On September 9, 2010, a PG&E natural gas pipeline exploded in San Bruno, California. The blast killed eight people and injured sixty others. A jury convicted PG&E on six felony counts. A November 2015 motion by the cities of San Bruno and San Carlos alleged, "PG&E's employees and agents engaged in communications with decision-makers at the Commission [CPUC], as well as related conduct that was harmful to the regulatory process." In January 2017, the judge ordered PG&E to pay a $3 million fine for its role in the disaster. The judge placed PG&E on probation for five years, the maximum penalty allowed by law.

How did the CPUC respond? Former CPUC president Michael Peevey was in charge of protecting consumers and regulating PG&E. Instead, Peevey used his position to protect the utility giant. The State Attorney General's Office opened an investigation—since stalled under Attorney General Xavier Becerra—into the allegation that Peevey helped PG&E find a judge who would be sympathetic to the $1.3 billion rate-increase case. PG&E needed the $1.3 billion to offset costs related to the San Bruno explosion. In January 2015, a search warrant authorized state investigators to raid the house of Michael Peevey and his wife, Carol Liu, a California state senator, and the Orinda home of former PG&E executive Brian Cherry. The search and seizure targets were "Ex parte communication, judge-shopping, bribery, obstruction of justice, or due administration of laws, favors or preferential treatment." The powers that be forced Peevey to resign as the agency head.

On March 28, 2017, PG&E agreed to pay an $86.5 million settlement for illegal email communications with the CPUC relating to the San Bruno investigation.

Explosions weren't the only disasters caused by PG&E. From 2013 to 2019, failure to maintain their power lines and towers caused fifteen hundred wildfires in California. On April 29, 2020, U.S. District Court

Judge William Alsup found PG&E "cannot safely deliver power to California." Judge Alsup wrote, "PG&E wildfires killed at least 108 and burned 22,049 structures." The judge blamed PG&E for the Camp Fire that destroyed the town of Paradise and killed eighty-five people. Judge Alsup laid the blame squarely at the feet of PG&E. "This failure is upon us because for years, to enlarge dividends, bonuses, and political contributions, PG&E cheated on the maintenance of its grid—to the point that the grid became unsafe to operate during our annual high winds, so unsafe that the grid itself failed and ignited many catastrophic wildfires."

On June 16, 2020, PG&E pled guilty to eighty-four counts of involuntary manslaughter for causing the Camp Fire. The California Public Utilities Commission failed in its primary responsibility of regulating PG&E and protecting the public. The CPUC was responsible for enforcing power line and tower safety regulations. They did not, and eighty-four Californians died. At the court hearing, Bill Johnson, PG&E's CEO, admitted, "Our equipment started that fire." He stood in the courtroom and repeated, "Guilty, your honor," eighty-four times as the judge read out each victim's name.

The California Public Utilities Commission quickly came to the defense of the utility it was supposed to regulate. The CPUC threw its support behind AB 1054. The 2019 bill amounted to a $13.5 billion bailout of PG&E. It established the Wildfire Relief Fund, paid for by public bonds and rate hikes, to satisfy claims from victims of the fires. PG&E's lobbying efforts intensified to pass AB 1054. Sacramento ABC10 reported PG&E made campaign contributions to ninety-three California legislature members totaling over half a million dollars. PG&E gave Gavin Newsom $208,400 in campaign contributions. In addition, PG&E gave donations to the charitable foundation formed by Newsom's wife. PG&E spent $844,000 more lobbying the California Public Utilities Commission in the two years following the Camp Fire.

Stebbins says PG&E's lobbying efforts allowed the corruption to continue. "I mean, PG&E, how many passes can we give them?" she asked. "San Bruno. Paradise. It's not OK."

Back to Marybel Batjer. She was one of the chief architects of the AB 1054 corporate bailout. Gavin Newsom signed AB 1054 into law on July 12, 2019—the same day he appointed Batjer as the new president of the CPUC. Less than two months after her appointment, the CPUC approved billing customers for most of the losses incurred by PG&E due to fire victim settlements. The CPUC failed to hold a public hearing, as required by law. It was yet another backroom deal between the regulators and the industry. Under the agreement, every PG&E customer would have about $2.50 a month added to their electricity bill for fifteen years.

Profits over People

Alice Stebbins commented, "PG&E was caught in a whirlwind of fires, and they knew the liability they were going to incur was going to be large. Let's face it—PG&E is a publicly-traded company, and their number one priority is making money. That's what they do. It was always a profitable, money-making company. That's what their job is. Yes, they provide electricity and gas, but that was just the mechanism to make money. Taking care of the ratepayers was secondary to making money." When asked by ABC10 Sacramento reporter Brandon Rittiman what she would say to the people of Paradise, Stebbins replied, "I'm sorry, and I'm sad. I don't think we held PG&E accountable."

The California Public Utilities Commission failed to regulate PG&E due to lax oversight and outright collusion. It chose to serve its interests and those of the utilities it oversees. Regulatory agencies like the CPUC harm Californians because they place big-money donors before the constituents they serve. Special-interest groups continue to use their money and political support to bend the government to their wishes. The results are plain—a dysfunctional state that's going up in flames before our very eyes.

Alice Stebbins echoed my views when she asserted, "We are accountable to the taxpayers and ratepayers of California." She and I believe the number-one priority for reforming the broken regulatory system is eliminating waste and corruption. "That's what I wish the state of California would do," Stebbins summed up. "We have to be transparent. We have to tell the public what's going on and what we're doing. But it's always this big secret."

California's regulatory agencies don't want transparency, nor do its politicians. Waste is their bread and butter, and creating excessive regulations is how they justify their existence. Corruption and cronyism are commonplace. Nepotism is the norm. The corrupt regulatory system is choking the life out of our economy. Examples abound. Again, the election system perpetuates this misery—more regulations and regulatory actions mean we need more regulators who pay dues to public sector unions that allow those unions to fund the big campaign spending needed by the politicians. If we had Hear the People, we would be electing leaders who didn't have to fear public sector unions and could act for the benefit of all Californians, not just unions and their bosses.

Talk About Cronyism!

The Board of Equalization (BOE), the state agency that regulates and collects taxes, was so rife with nepotism and fraud that it was dismantled. A state audit found that one in five employees had a relative who worked at the BOE. One employee characterized the agency as "pretty much a family affair." The BOE was accused of misappropriating nearly $50 million. Highly paid employees performed parking lot duties at unsanctioned events. A commissioner spent over $130,000 on office furniture. Those are your tax dollars hard at work. The whistleblower that uncovered and reported the fraud was—you guessed it—fired.

Things were no better at the Department of Industrial Relations. The corruption went all the way to the top. The director, Christine Baker, hired her daughter, even though she did not have the requisite qualifications for the job. The daughter was a virtual no-show, some weeks only writing one work email and completing zero projects. When her manager attempted to discipline her, he was asked by his supervisor, "Are you trying to lose your job?" When the daughter complained about another manager, he was reprimanded and reassigned. The director promoted her daughter.

A state audit exposed gross misconduct and fraudulent nepotism at the Department of Industrial Relations. When questioned by auditors, a government employee and fraud investigator named Socorro Tongco told the truth and was—well, you know by now how this ends. Anyone who dares to do their job and expose corruption faces retaliation and is forced out, often on trumped-up charges. Tongco was awarded a $250,000 settlement for wrongful termination. Christine Baker was forced to resign amid a public outcry. But, like so many in our government, she failed *upward*. Within months, former governor Jerry Brown appointed Baker to the California Fraud Assessment Commission.

When asked how she would fix the regulatory mess in California, Alice Stebbins was clear as day. "I can tell you how many agencies don't need to exist in California," she said. "I can tell you how many programs need merging. I wish somebody would have, excuse the expression, the *balls* to do it. We all know where the waste is. We all know the departments that don't need to exist. One of those agencies is being led by one of the governor's old drinking buddies."

The regulatory climate in California hurts everyone in California. As the cost of compliance with regulations increases, businesses become less competitive. Regulation drains productivity. Productivity decreases as time and money evaporate to comply with the mountains of red tape and endless paperwork. When you fill out a form for a government agency or fight a battle with the government, you waste valuable time shuffling paperwork back and forth and having hearings and arguments with government bureaucrats. It reduces the time you spend on innovating and producing your products.

We all feel the impact of regulations. The state tax base erodes when corporations and small businesses leave to set up shop in business-friendly states such as Texas and Nevada. That means higher taxes for the rest of us. The good part of the regulation is when it rewards people who do things the right way. That is what we want to have here. We want full transparency. That is where a free press and complete disclosure of information comes in. A lot of regulation gives bureaucrats the power to review products and other services to "make sure" that the customer is treated right. I would trust the free market to do that better. I want competitors out there to have the freedom to point out where their product is better because it does a better job. If a free market allows that information to be transmitted, people can choose among different products and services, with a much better result.

Governments grow regulations because bureaucracies favor things that allow them to grow. As head of a bureaucracy, you want an enormous budget and the most people under you. In 2019, California had 543,000 full-time government employees. In 2017 alone, the state payroll increased by $1 billion, and it keeps on growing. When your sphere of influence grows, so does your importance and power. When does it stop? Where will we end up if these trends continue? History abounds with examples, none of them good.

Unfortunately, regulators do things that benefit themselves instead of the marketplace. We need to make sure the playing field is level for all players. A vibrant, competitive marketplace, not one steeped in self-serving and obstructionist regulations, is the best way to ensure people do the right thing.

Is the situation hopeless? Not if we elect leaders who will do everything in their power to create a better balance between regulation and productivity. Elected leaders need to stand for regulations that keep the scales balanced for everyone. Politicians herald regulations as the best way to make sure we have affordable and safe products and services that will ensure a safe and prosperous California for all. Doing the job better requires a genuinely competitive and transparent free market where market actors are encouraged to do their best to compete and do the right thing for the greater good. Enacting real changes to our election system, such as Hear the People, would go a long way towards providing the impetus for a return to a genuine free market.

CHAPTER 14

STATESMEN DON'T MAKE MILLIONS PEDDLING INFLUENCE

"I am a special agent with the Federal Bureau of Investigation...I am currently assigned to the Public Corruption Squad in the Los Angeles Division, where I specialize in the investigation of corrupt government officials." So begins a sealed affidavit filed on May 2, 2013, in the U.S. District Court in Sacramento. The once-classified document, now a matter of public record, spelled out the case against former California state senator Ron Calderon. You might remember Senator Calderon. A federal court convicted him in October 2016 of accepting over $150,000 in bribes and sentenced him to three and a half years in prison.

Calderon served as a state senator from 2006 to 2014. He represented the thirtieth district, home to the scandal-tainted cities of Bell and Cudahy. His two brothers served in the California legislature. He used his elected position to enrich himself and his family. His is the story of a corrupt politician and his downfall. Stop me if you've heard this one before, California.

Ron Calderon's tale of bribery and influence peddling began in 2012. Working on a tip from the Fair Political Practices Commission that Calderon was engaged in shady dealings, an undercover FBI agent constructed an elaborate ruse. He posed as the owner of a film studio that provided funding for independent films and commercials under the phony name Rocky Patel. (Don't you love it when law enforcement has a sense of humor?) The FBI agent sat at a table in a downtown Los Angeles restaurant and waited. He was wearing a wire. His lunch guest was state senator Ronald Calderon.

Over lunch, the FBI agent and Senator Calderon talked about movie production tax credits. Calderon told the movie producer that his daughter was involved in a movie called *American Gigolo 2*. She was looking for someone to produce the picture. Calderon asked the FBI agent if his studio "might be interested in getting behind the movie." The next time they met, the counterfeit producer told Calderon his studio might invest in the film if Calderon could use his influence in Sacramento to lower the threshold for movie production tax credits from

$1 million to $500,000. This reduction in this threshold would benefit independent movie producers and might help *American Gigolo 2* get made. Calderon responded, "There might be a play, you know, to lower, to lower the tax credit" for independent movies.

"That's Diamonds for Me"

Senator Calderon proposed a plan that "helps us both." He would hire the movie producer's girlfriend to work as a staffer in his Senate office. The undercover agent would hire Calderon's daughter to work at his movie studio. This maneuver is an illegal tit for tat or quid pro quo in California. The FBI agent offered to put Calderon's daughter on his payroll—later negotiated at $3,000 per month—for consulting. She never worked a day. Calderon expressed his gratitude, "Any help you could do for my kids is…that's diamonds for me. That's diamonds."

The list of offenses committed by Calderon would make Huey Long blush. In addition to $27,000 paid out to Calderon's daughter, Calderon elicited $30,000 in bribes to employ the fake movie producer's girlfriend as a legislative staffer. California taxpayers paid her salary. On the way to the Miami airport, the undercover FBI agent slipped Calderon an envelope stuffed with $3,000 in cash. The phony movie producer also paid $4,000 for a VIP table in a Las Vegas nightclub where Ron Calderon got his picture taken with the rapper Nelly.

Senator Calderon funneled a $25,000 bribe from the FBI agent through a nonprofit controlled by his brother Thomas. Ron Calderon told the FBI agent, "We have this non-profit. It is called Californians for Diversity...We can put money into that...Then Tom and I, down the road, we build it up, we can pay ourselves." Thomas Calderon later pled guilty to money laundering and concealing bribes, according to the U.S. District Attorney's Office. Ronald Calderon served two years of his sentence, and they set him free in 2019.

I can't say it often enough: Sacramento is a den of thieves. Politicians sell their votes and their integrity for a few pieces of silver. Indeed, one of the amazing things about corrupt politicians is how little money it takes to hook one. In the movies, they want millions. They often want just a few hundred or a few thousand in real life. Ron Calderon and his brother were emblems of everything wrong in Sacramento. They lined their pockets instead of helping the people. They were not the only ones—take the case of Senator Leland Yee. Yee was the antigun activist who brokered an illegal arms deal with an undercover FBI agent. He pled guilty to felony racketeering, public corruption, money laundering, bribery, and gun trafficking in 2015. What happened to the ideals on which we founded this country?

The Calderon brothers were the poster boys of the elite ruling class running Sacramento. They used their position and power to enrich themselves at the expense of their constituencies. Government corruption erodes public trust in our institutions. According to a 2018 survey conducted by the Public Policy Institute of California, 61 percent of Californians distrust their state government.

That is unacceptable.

California needs statesmen, not politicians. Too many hacks like Ronald Calderon and Leland Yee enter politics for the wrong reasons. Many politicians view their office as a way to get their hands on the levers of power. Public servants believe in serving. Too many politicians are after a bigger slice of the pie for themselves, their families, friends, lobbyists, and campaign donors. Public servants seek to make the pie larger for everyone.

George Washington, Dwight Eisenhower, and Ronald Reagan were public servants and statesmen. They led by example. They worked for the common, and citizens revered them. They made you feel like you lived in the greatest nation on earth. We need governors who measure up to their high standard.

An Incorruptible Beginning

George Washington set the bar. In the first State of the Union address, President Washington declared, "The welfare of our country is the great object." Washington was a shining example of selfless service to his fellow man. In a letter he wrote to James Madison, he expressed the hope that the precedents he set "may be fixed on true principles." His legacy of integrity provided a roadmap. "I hope I shall possess firmness and virtue enough to maintain what I consider the most enviable of all titles, the character of an honest man." Thomas Jefferson noted that Washington's "integrity was most pure" and his character was incorruptible.

General Washington was the commander-in-chief of the Continental Army before he was president. He inspired loyalty. His moral fiber inspired awe and respect. Washington did not campaign for the appointment. He refused to accept a salary. He saw his duty as a moral obligation to his country.

General Washington and the Continental Army defeated General Cornwallis and the British at Yorktown. A conquering hero, the country lay at his feet, but Washington refused to pick up the crown. Instead, he resigned his commission from the Continental Army and returned to his farm. When King George heard the news, he remarked, "If he does that, he will be the greatest man in the world."

Washington returned to public life only when he could no longer deny the clamor for his return. As president, Washington held the reins of power loosely. He sought common ground between the rival factions of Alexander Hamilton and Thomas Jefferson. Washington balanced the competing interests of states' rights and federal control through compromise and cooperation.

Washington enshrined the ideas of the new republic into our institutions. On September 18, 1793, the second-term president laid the cornerstone of the United States Capitol building, literally laying the foundation for our representative government. The inscription on the metal plate affixed to the cornerstone praised the two-term president, "whose virtues in the civil administration of his country have been as conspicuous and beneficial as his military valor and prudence have been useful in establishing their liberties."

People trusted Washington because he was noble and incorruptible. His vision, goals, and methods stayed true to his values and those of the nation. He exhibited moral coherence between his vision for the future and his daily actions. Americans revere him today for these same qualities. I'll wager you cannot remember a single policy initiative or presidential edict from his eight years as president—but everyone knows the story of the cherry tree. Americans value honesty. No wonder he became "the father of our country."

Washington could have ruled indefinitely but chose to retire to Mount Vernon. This act established the precedent of a peaceful transition of presidential power after two terms. Many of these precedents stand today. His legacy endures because he was a man of conviction. After Washington's passing, his brother in arms, Light-Horse Harry Lee, eulogized him as "first in war, first in peace, and first in the hearts of his countrymen."

We must get away from the idea that politics is a profession or a business. It's not: it is a calling. Statesmen enter public service to give back for all the benefits bestowed upon them by our great nation. President Washington understood, above all, that freedom is a debt one must repay. Washington's motto was "deeds not words."

I aspire to that ideal. Let me give you two examples. In 1992, I started a Chicago affiliate of a community program now called Rebuilding

Together. We began with one home repair in 1992 and now repair fifty houses a year with about one thousand volunteers. In twenty-nine years, we have repaired almost fifteen hundred homes of low-income elderly and disabled persons in the city. I served on the USO board of directors for ten years in Chicago and ten years in San Diego. The USO supports America's troops and their families. Public service—two words that mean something to me. The rewards are not financial but are something far more significant.

A Fighter's Grit

Dwight David Eisenhower was a leader who believed in public service. Eisenhower led our troops to victory in World War II against the Nazis as Washington had fought against tyranny during the Revolutionary War. Both men exhibited steely-eyed determination under fire. These leaders embodied our fighting American spirit. They stood tall when it mattered most.

Eisenhower was not born into privilege. "I belong to a family of boys who were raised in meager circumstances in central Kansas, and every one of us earned our way as we went along, and it never occurred to us that we were poor, but we were," he said of his childhood. Nobody handed Eisenhower anything for free. After graduating high school, he worked at the creamery where his father was a mechanic. There he earned enough money to send his younger brother to college. Eisenhower embraced responsibility. He placed his brother's welfare above his own. He would soon do the same for his country.

A man who has earned everything he has, including his self-respect and the respect of others, understands the value of individual initiative and hard work. Eisenhower knew that people and not governments generate wealth and create jobs. Eisenhower encouraged private free-market solutions to public problems. His vision, which he called modern Republicanism, was hewn from common-sense Midwestern values. He knew the farmer in his field was the expert, not some bureaucrat sitting behind a desk. In his homespun wisdom, he said, "Farming looks mighty easy when your plow is a pencil, and you're a thousand miles from the cornfield."

In his first inaugural address, Eisenhower declared, "A people that values its privileges above its principles soon loses both." He understood that moral authority is the source of a statesman's power. "The supreme quality for leadership is unquestionably integrity. Without it, no real success is possible." He was instrumental in adding "under God" to the Pledge of Allegiance. He was courageous in his commitment to the principles of our nation, even when politically unpopular. He sent National Guard troops into Little Rock, Arkansas, in 1957 to enforce the court-ordered desegregation of Little Rock High School. He ordered the U.S. armed forces to desegregate, asserting, "There must be no second-class citizens in this country."

Eisenhower gave voice to the responsibility all statesmen embraced when he said, "I have one yardstick by which I test every major problem—and that yardstick is: Is it good for America?" Eisenhower established the interstate highway system in 1956. Its 41,000 miles of roadway poured enough concrete, Ike reported, to build "six sidewalks to the moon." This infrastructure project spurred economic growth by making interstate commerce and travel more efficient.

Federal spending relative to GDP declined during the Eisenhower administration. He loosened the government's grip on the economy, facilitating rather than restricting free enterprise. Personal income increased dramatically, and America enjoyed eight years of prosperity. A burgeoning middle class used its newfound purchasing power to acquire the new technology of the day, including television sets. Its members bought homes in the suburbs and commuted to work on new ribbons of concrete highway.

But with increased prosperity came increased pressure to enlarge entitlement programs. Yes, our government must provide a safety net for our most vulnerable, but Eisenhower understood its limitations. After leaving office, he lamented that the incoming administration had turned the government "into a giant federal Santa Claus."

1950s America was an idealistic time. A stable middle class was driving our economy. Our place on the world stage was secure. But good times never last forever. The upheaval of the 1960s and the economic malaise of the 1970s would soon test America's mettle.

From the Heart of a Nation

In 1980, that all changed when Ronald Reagan was elected the fortieth president of the United States. While not perfect, Reagan was a statesman who towered above the political landscape and became a symbol for the rebirth of American ideals and power. Reagan saw a nation that had strayed from its traditional Judeo-Christian values. He worked to correct the course and steer us in the right direction, and he galvanized a nation. I'm proud to call myself a Reagan Republican.

Reagan said: "Government's first duty is to protect the people, not run their lives." He drew a distinction between the Soviet Union and the United States. The choice was clear: total government control of every facet of life or the freedom to choose one's destiny. Reagan embodied the American spirit of self-reliance and rugged individualism we hold so dear.

Ronald Reagan did not become governor of California or the United States president to enrich himself or his friends. When he saw problems, he looked to the free market for answers. President Reagan spoke out against the big government. He declared, "Liberals called on government to play an ever-increasing role in the lives of our people. They relied on central planning, regulations, and bureaucracy. Is there any doubt about why our country in the late 1970s seemed to be humming along with all the efficiency of a Bulgarian shoe factory? If central planning were the way to a better world, we'd be importing our grain from the Soviet Union and not the other way around..." The fall of the Soviet Union and the Berlin Wall are potent reminders that Reagan was right.

Reagan put his faith in the American entrepreneurial spirit. He understood that an individual in the private sector, motivated by self-interest, will be more innovative and productive than a public-sector employee inspired by self-preservation. Steve Jobs sold his Volkswagen bus to get the money to found Apple in his garage. He was unflinching in his dedication to perfection. He insisted that the Mac personal computer be not merely great but "insanely great." The public sector cannot replicate that commitment to excellence. There simply isn't the incentive. Why be extraordinary when mediocrity pays the same? Name one thing the government has created that has improved your life as much as the personal computer or the iPhone.

The Great Communicator said it best when he quipped, "The most terrifying words in the English language are: "I'm from the government, and I'm here to help." Reagan understood the government isn't the solution to our problems: it *is* the problem. And the government never gets any smaller. Sacramento keeps adding more governmental agencies and more regulations, creating a sea of red tape. Have you noticed how state agencies never complete their objectives and disappear? Reagan called them "the nearest thing to eternal life we'll ever see on this earth." Every business owner must be efficient to stay solvent. That rarely happens in government. There is almost no accountability. Governments never go out of business—they just raise your taxes.

Our election system continues to foster this misery—the bigger government grows, the more powerful lobbying becomes. Lobbyists then cement that power by handing out big campaign contributions to politicians who need that money to buy media in large electoral districts. The media has a liberal bent and exercises a lot of power over election results in the way they report the news and provide news-making opportunities to candidates. Shrink election districts down to a level where door-to-door campaigning is required and we will eliminate this corrupt game.

President Reagan gave voice to the ideals of a nation. His ethos sprang from the American dinner table, not the halls of government. He explained the appeal of his message when he said, "I wasn't a great communicator, but I communicated great things, and they didn't spring full bloom from my brow; they came from the heart of a great nation—from our experience, our wisdom, and our belief in the principles that have guided us for two centuries."

Reagan regarded democracy as a system meant to limit the power of government over people's lives. The government's function was to uphold the rule of law, protect its citizens, provide infrastructure, and foster the private economy. In 1984 he said, "The difference between the path toward greater freedom or bigger government is the difference between success and failure; between opportunity and coercion; between faith in a glorious future and fear of mediocrity and despair; between respecting people as adults, each with a spark of greatness, and treating them as helpless children to be forever dependent; between a drab, materialistic world where Big Brother rules by promises to special-interest groups, and a world of adventure where everyday people set their sights on impossible dreams…"

I set my store in a society "where everyday people set their sights on impossible dreams." Californians can achieve great things if the government gets out of our way. The individual entrepreneur and the small business owner know more about their businesses than some paper pusher in Sacramento who never ran so much as a lemonade stand. It's time to give the power back to the people of California. It's their ideas, their hard work, and their expertise that will drive our state forward. We must invest more capital in the people and businesses who add value to our economy and spend less on the bureaucracy constraining business and draining our productivity.

Corrupt politicians, bureaucrats, special-interest lobbyists, and public employee unions have a vested interest in a larger, more intrusive government. It is the source of their power. They seek to preserve the status quo. Reagan called the status quo "Latin for the mess we're in." No wonder so many Californians don't believe their vote matters. They read the headlines and watch the news: corruption, influence peddling, bribery, and fat-cat lobbyists. Voters become apathetic because their voices go unheard. They feel disenfranchised. They despair over choosing the lesser of two evils. They stop voting or never vote at all. Voter apathy allows the media, party bosses and vocal, well-financed special-interest groups to exert undue influence on our democratic process.

President Reagan commented on this sad state of affairs. "It has been said that politics is the second oldest profession. I have learned that it bears a striking resemblance to the first." Like Ronald Reagan, I am not a politician. I am a husband, a father, a volunteer, and a businessman. Like Dwight David Eisenhower, nobody ever handed me a dime. I paved my way through initiative and dedication to the principles ingrained in me from an early age. I have earned the respect of my clients and investors, and we have all reaped the rewards. I don't need a public office to make money. I make my money the old-fashioned way—I earn it. Influence peddling and corruption are anathemas to me, as they were to Washington, Eisenhower, and Reagan. You cannot sell a statesman's integrity to the highest bidder.

We need leaders who feel a deep sense of moral obligation to our founding fathers, state, and country. We need statesmen with a vision that includes all Californians, not just the political elites and their well-to-do friends. Californians should elect leaders who pledge that they will never benefit personally from holding office. Who will make that pledge? Will the next generation of leaders serve the interests of the citizens of California, not their own?

As I detail in the chapter on Hear the People, we need to reform our electoral system to make it possible for statesmen to win office and change the tenor or our leadership. We need a reform which encourages statesmen to enter the arena in the first place. This won't happen on its own. We need a change in the system—a revolutionary change—to enable it.

CHAPTER 15

CALIFORNIA'S BUSINESS LITIGATION NIGHTMARE

Rick Roussin hit rock bottom in September of 1985. After growing up in a home dominated by alcoholism and violence, drugs and alcohol took over *his* life for many years. When one party night turned violent after a dispute over a keg of beer, Roussin was stabbed in the stomach, lacerating his liver and diaphragm. Doctors rushed him into emergency surgery, and he barely dodged the long beep of the flat-line. Nearly bleeding out from a stab wound was a watershed moment for Roussin. He has been sober since the moment he woke up from anesthesia in the recovery room.

Motivated to turn his life around, Roussin did what many Californians dream of doing: he started his own business. Roussin wasted no time; the same year he got sober, he founded Coast to Coast Computer Products. He started by making cold calls from the living room of the house he rented, and within a few months, he hired his first employee, a fellow addict in his twelve-step program.

As his business grew, he continued to hire people who "needed a second or third chance, because that was me," Rick told Tom Manzo, director of the California Business and Industrial Alliance, in a YouTube interview in February of 2021.

Today, about one-fourth of his employees and seven of his top ten salespeople are recovering alcoholics. Collectively there are over 450 years of sobriety at the company. Roussin encourages these employees to better themselves and maintain their sobriety. At Coast to Coast, convicted felons can get a steady job and a support system in an understanding environment, a rare oasis of security in their lives after prison. Today, Coast to Coast employs 230 people and sells about $60 million of ink and toner per year.

In four years, one of Roussin's employees went from being homeless to a homeowner. Rick is the kind of businessman California is lucky to have. He believes in his people, and they believe in his vision. They become dedicated, loyal employees. When his people grow, the business grows with them. "I truly care about my employees," Roussin said. "I know I am where I am because of them. I'm proud to be an entrepreneur that created a lot of jobs and changed lives."

Then Coast to Coast was hit with a Private Attorneys General Act (PAGA) suit. PAGA was enacted in California in 2004 to enforce the state's complex labor laws. In his final days in office, Governor Gray Davis (later recalled) gave PAGA to trial attorneys as a parting gift.

The idea behind PAGA was to shift the cost of enforcing labor regulations from the state to the private sector at the height of a state budget crunch. The law stipulates that the state receives 75 percent of any PAGA settlement award without lifting a finger. The plaintiff and their attorney split the remaining 25 percent.

PAGA is commonly known as the "sue your boss law." It is a form of legal confiscation, and it can happen to any of you who run a small business. Any private citizen can sue their employer for labor code violations on behalf of themselves *and* every other aggrieved employee who works for the same company by filing a class-action suit. Most states recognized that class-action lawsuits have gotten out of hand and cause more harm than benefit. They took action to restrict class-action suits.

No gift is too small or large for the trial lawyers in California. PAGA lets anywhere from two to two thousand coworkers file suit, ostensibly on their behalf, without their informed consent. Did you ever receive a random check, usually some pittance like $2.89, in the mail as your share of a class action suit? If so, thank PAGA. Even though the U.S. Supreme Court recently put some limits on PAGA's reach, the state legislature is now readying changes that would amend the law to make that decision nonconsequential.

Roussin has some choice words for PAGA. None of them are "thank you." "It started with one individual who got upset over being demoted," Rick said. The employee found a labor attorney who attempted to recruit other Coast to Coast workers to sue their boss. Not a single employee agreed. "Bent on revenge—although the problem lay in the employee's own failure—he looked for another avenue," Roussin continued. The attorney filed a hybrid PAGA lawsuit, and, Roussin reports. "They came after us with guns blazing."

Hybrid PAGA/class action suits allow employees and labor attorneys to enjoy the lower bar and more significant advantages than accorded pure PAGA lawsuits. Trial lawyers like class-action suits because they can reap greater financial rewards. In California, the charges levied against businesses are often ludicrous minutia.

"We were doing some horrible things," he said. "Here's one example. The paycheck stub had a typo. That cost about a million bucks right there." The payroll company that Roussin hired made a mistake on the address of his company on the pay stub. Roussin understood he had made a mistake, but it was a fixable clerical error that hurt no one. "The punishment has to fit the crime," he said. "Your payroll company, a third-party company, making a mistake on your address does not justify a million-dollar fine."

In total, Roussin paid $4 million to settle the case against him. Roussin lost more than money. The lawsuit changed the culture at Coast to Coast. Worker morale plummeted. Speaking about his workers after PAGA, Rick said, "They were less happy with the changes that were necessary to comply with all the rules of the *California Employment Handbook*." The flexibility the workers once enjoyed was gone, replaced by rigidly timed shifts and regimented lunch breaks. Dads used to change their hours to watch their sons' baseball games or attend their daughters' recitals at school—but no longer. California straightjackets Rick and his employees into schedules that don't allow the freedom his workers desire.

"It didn't benefit employees, as it claims it does. The state didn't get any money, the employees didn't get any PAGA money," Roussin said of PAGA. "The lawyers got a big, fat cut of the class action. We paid millions of dollars. We borrowed the money to keep the company alive and to pay those fees. A good portion of that went to the lawyers that filed the lawsuits. California is a beautiful state. I love this country. But this has to change. This has to be reformed."

Roussin is spot-on when he claims the attorneys are the real winners with PAGA. In his case, the state of California received just $20,000. In most PAGA suits, lawyers take home the lion's share of the settlement. In a recent high-profile $7.8 million settlement with Uber in 2018, attorneys walked away with $2.3 million. Each driver in the class action received an average of $1.08. "When you put the power into the hands of lawyers who are working on commission—and the higher they can get the number, the more they line their pockets—you create a devastating situation. You incentivize private citizens to do public work," Roussin observed.

Before PAGA, the state used noncommissioned state employees to enforce labor laws. The budget crisis forced the state to seek cheaper alternatives. "But because they were short-handed, they decided to deputize all of these—I've gotta be nice here—all of these lawyers to do the job for the state, but they don't give two craps about the state," Roussin explained.

In all of their infinite wisdom, the Legislature created the Private Attorneys General Act to deputize every citizen and shady lawyer in California as an attorney general with the power to represent the state of California legally. These "attorneys general" bring litigation for an entire class of workers—lawsuits that can force a company to its knees. Initially devised to protect workers from unfair labor practices—primarily wage theft—trial lawyers and disgruntled employees have inverted the law's intent to target employers unfairly. Any current or former employee can sue their employer for any number of labor code violations. Worse, the law inverts the usual civil suit rule that requires plaintiffs to bear the burden of proof by a preponderance of the evidence. Under PAGA, the burden of proof falls upon the employer to prove the claims false. That can be an expensive process that drains a company.

The settlements awarded to plaintiffs bear no relationship to the magnitude of harm inflicted by the code violation. PAGA's fine structure multiplies the number of pay periods during which the violation occurred by the number of affected employees. For example, a company that inadvertently forgets to put their address or the correct address on pay stubs has committed a code violation. The company is penalized one hundred dollars per week for each employee. If you employ fifty people and made this mistake for one year, you would be liable for over $250,000 in penalties. Two years of honest mistakes? That is going to cost you half a million dollars. Yet, no one was hurt by the simple clerical error at Coast to Coast. The penalty does not fit the infraction.

PAGA attorneys are driving the increase in litigation. They take a 30 to 40 percent cut of the total settlement. There is a burgeoning PAGA industry in California. Type in "fired" or "lost my job" on Facebook, and PAGA attorneys will contact you, promising colossal cash awards. Some especially greasy PAGA attorneys even hold barbecues at local parks with jumpers for the kids as a marketing tool. Entire companies specialize in finding PAGA clients for labor lawyers. One labor attorney in Southern California who has filed 696 PAGA claims has a "MR PAGA" vanity plate on his Rolls Royce. Is that our new idea of fair play?

Business owners are too frightened to speak out. They worry that PAGA attorneys, the state, or organized labor will target them if they stand and fight. Business owners estimate they pay about 30 percent of the plaintiff's damages to defend the lawsuit. For a $250,000 case, the price tag to the business owner would be $75,000—if they *win*. The price tag, if they *lose*, would be $325,000. Insurance does not cover PAGA claims. The company must pay the entirety of the claim out of pocket. Most companies choose to settle out of court, regardless of their innocence. It saves time and money and exposes them to less risk. If they can pay a $50,000 ransom to eliminate a $325,000 risk, they'll often choose the lesser of two evils.

The labor code violations are often minor or technical but cost companies millions. If a bathroom temperature dips below sixty-eight degrees, you are out of compliance. *Yes*, you read that correctly. It sounds preposterous to you and me, but for Big Lots it was an unfortunate reality when its employees filed a bathroom temperature lawsuit. Big Lots had to prove it maintained its restrooms at the correct temperature.

Starbucks recently settled a PAGA lawsuit because workers were required to turn on the alarm and lock the door after they clocked out. The employees averaged forty seconds of unpaid time for this labor code violation. The amount owed for the forty seconds of "unpaid work" came out to about twenty-one dollars for the year. The penalty assessed was $67,500 per employee.

My stepfather always told me to show up for work ten minutes early every day. In California, he would be subject to a PAGA suit. I cannot begin to calculate the number of hours my mother worked "off the books" as a public school teacher. I succeeded in life by working harder than my competition. Why are we penalizing people for showing the initiative to get ahead? I fear we are raising a new generation of workers who view locking the door after a shift as an "unfair labor practice." That kind of thinking is hostile to everything that has made this country great.

Passanisi's Deli

Santa Fe Importers is a seventy-four-year-old business started by Vincent Passanisi in 1947. In his twenties, the Sicilian immigrant moved to America and settled in California, where the weather reminded him of his beloved Sicily. At 1401 Santa Fe Avenue, he opened an ethnic delicatessen and market catering to Italian, Polish, and other recent immigrants near the port in Long Beach. For decades, the business thrived, allowing

Passanisi to build a meat-manufacturing plant making sausage, pepperoni, and meatballs in the building next door. In 2003, Vincent's grandson, also named Vincent, opened a second location in Seal Beach. Sante Fe Importers now employs between sixty-five and seventy people.

Santa Fe Importers is a California success story. Entrepreneurs like Vincent Passanisi and his grandson provide jobs, generate wealth, and supply their communities with the products they need. Businesses pay taxes. Their employees pay taxes. This provides revenue for the public benefits we all share. PAGA puts all of that at risk.

Vincent Passanisi sat down with me over Zoom on a cold March morning in 2021. His PAGA nightmare began in 2017. He let a janitor go when he had to downsize. Unknowingly, his troubles started with that disgruntled janitor. "I got this notice. I didn't know what it was, so I gave it to my attorney. My attorney was horrified and said, 'This is really bad news,'" Passanisi told me, clenching his hands.

"Our employees come in at 5:30 or 6:00 in the morning and wanted to take their lunch at noon because that was lunchtime for them," he continued. "This meant their lunches would fall outside of the regulated time period for lunch breaks." The workers asked Passanisi if they could combine their two ten-minute paid breaks into one longer twenty-minute break in the morning and take a later lunch. Even though the employees signed waivers stating they wanted their lunch at noon, Sante Fe Importers was out of compliance according to labor regulations.

Passanisi's mistake was trying to be a nice boss. "We were giving them the flexibility to determine when they wanted to take their lunch. I didn't realize you couldn't do that," Passanisi said. "We were giving the employees the freedom to do what they wanted to do, and that's what got us into trouble. Since PAGA, we've had to buckle down, so employees now take their lunches at 10:30 in the morning, which they don't care for at all."

"Our lawsuit was for two million dollars, and that's when we thought, 'We're going to go out of business. We're not going to be able to make it,'" Passanisi told me. He knew if they lost the lawsuit, they would be forced to go out of business after three-quarters of a century. He set up a meeting with a bankruptcy attorney and decided to go into mediation.

"The problem with these penalties is they keep adding up. Every time our employees took a late lunch, it created a penalty. If we didn't pay a wage penalty for them taking the late lunch, that's a second penalty. So now we've got two penalties. Because of those two penalties, your time records are considered inaccurate. Therefore, they say you're falsifying your records. That's the third penalty. One person with three penalties on one day, multiplied by all your employees, multiplied by each day, is how these things balloon out of control. That's the barrel they have you over when they get you into mediation," he said.

Passanisi was able to settle for $300,000. His lawyer fees were another $250,000. The 180 employees in the class action each received between tens and hundreds of dollars. The plaintiff got $10,000. The state of California received $10,000. The plaintiff's lawyers took home $100,000.

"We really had to struggle for a few years after that. I raised prices, and I had to let some employees go because I had to write a check for $300,000," Passanisi said. He estimates complying with every state regulation, and the cost of the PAGA suit adds between 30 percent and 40 percent to the price of everything he sells. "The whole thing ended up costing us about a half a million dollars. This year we're finally coming out of the hole, but it really took us quite a few years to come out of it," Passanisi told me. Seventy-four years of a family business nearly destroyed—all because of a disgruntled janitor and a law called PAGA.

When I asked Vincent if he saw a way forward, he pointed to his company's productive relationship with the Food and Drug Administration inspector at his sausage and meatball plant. "If there's a violation, it's usually because a mistake has been made; there is never a willful intent. We're doing the right thing because we don't want to hurt our customers. I see the inspectors as another watchful eye, another helping hand. Sometimes they see things that we don't see. When something happens, we institute corrective action, and we fix it. We are constantly trying to get better," Passanisi said.

"There needs to be a greater respect for the relationship between the employee and employer," Passanisi continued. "So often, in the media and in people's minds, the employers are these big businesses that just want to take advantage of the employees. I could not do what I've done without my employees. They are so valuable. Employees are not an expense; they are an asset to the company. Without them, we have nothing. I want to do the right thing by my employees. We want our employees to be happy. We want to pay them a fair wage and give them the benefits they want. But the state is creating more and more restrictions and denying workers the freedom to have the things that they want."

Small businesses cannot easily absorb the exorbitant legal fees required to defend lawsuits. The average cost to defend a frivolous lawsuit is nearly $200,000. The estimated cost to defend lawsuits is typically 30 percent of the total damages sought. To protect themselves from the added cost of doing business in sue-happy California, many small businesses relocate to states with more business-friendly environments.

Tom Manzo is the founder of the California Business & Industrial Alliance, which advocates for PAGA repeal and reform. He interviews people on his YouTube channel, which is how I learned about the plight of Rick Roussin's business that I discussed earlier. Tom told me, "I talk to entrepreneurs every day. They tell me, 'I want to move out of California. I'm not expanding in California. I'm selling and getting out.' I was just talking with a child psychiatrist who has her own business. She helps children who want to commit suicide, and she is embroiled in a PAGA lawsuit. She became so frustrated she decided to sell the business. Emotionally, she can't take this. She and her husband have decided to retire early."

Manzo thinks PAGA is stifling the creative business minds that used to flock to California. "If Steve Jobs tried starting Apple in today's business climate, he would never have been able to," he said. "Those guys worked long hours. I'm sure they skipped lunches. They are destroying the entrepreneurial spirit, the greatest trait the United States has. Anybody can create something from nothing. That's the American Dream—and they're ruining it."

Companies whose employees work independently are among the biggest targets for PAGA litigation. For instance, janitorial service companies that employ people to clean homes and offices rely on their employees to take their meal breaks independently. The company trains its employees to follow company rules but is not physically there to ensure compliance. Their janitorial staff is scattered over large areas and are not under direct supervision. This lack of strict oversight makes these companies a prime target for unhappy employees and unscrupulous attorneys.

Disgruntled employees use PAGA to settle personal grudges against their bosses. A worker with an ax to grind can walk out the door, see an attorney, and wage a scorched-earth campaign against their former employer.

Even if companies try to comply, it can be impossible. I asked Tom Manzo about compliance with labor regulations. "You are always going to get something wrong," he warned. "I don't care what anybody says. You are always going to get something wrong." He held up the 2018 *California Labor Law Digest*. The most recent edition contains over 1,110 pages with nine thousand regulations employers must follow. "What the state is asking business owners to do is an impossible task."

The current litigation climate in California is one reason businesses are fleeing the state in record numbers. The litigation nightmare is a drag on our economy. Every dollar that goes to defending lawsuits is a dollar taken away from research and development, stifling innovation. That makes California products more expensive and less competitive in the global marketplace.

Cutting the Cord on CEQA

PAGA isn't the only nightmare law on California's books. In the 1960s, the environmental movement successfully passed the California Environmental Quality Act (CEQA). I mentioned this troublesome piece of litigation in the chapter on affordable housing, but it warrants a more profound look because of its disastrous impact on the state's building costs.

CEQA purports to protect the sea and air, which are noble goals. The trouble is that its provisions have been extended to housing and are used to hold up the construction of sorely needed homes. It takes years of litigation and board approval processes to get anything built in California. This log jam drives up the costs, resulting in expensive housing.

Businesses incur high litigation costs to get anything built in California. Increased costs to construct housing and commercial developments means salaries in California have to be higher to pay the higher cost of living. If you hire a blue-collar worker, a nurse, or a secretary, you have to pay that person a lot more in California because they have a higher housing payment. Those higher salaries translate into higher costs for healthcare, clothing, food, anything you buy. The high cost of living is hurting families across California. Our most vulnerable citizens feel the most significant impact. When we factor the cost of living into the poverty equation, our high cost of living is one of the main reasons California has the highest poverty rate in the nation.

Sometimes a CEQA lawsuit is brought by a builder's competition, and the goal is to keep competing developers out of the marketplace, not to save the environment. This practice is particularly harmful to smaller businesses that lack the time or money to fight expensive litigation.

Labor unions gain leverage by threatening environmental lawsuits against builders. A developer will receive a call from a union representative who offers a union labor agreement for the construction project. If the developer refuses to employ union labor, the union informs the builder of the "environmental concerns" it has with the project. This thinly veiled threat is known as "greenmailing." It is an illegitimate use of CEQA but is still done on a constant level. The unions, masquerading as innocuous-sounding neighborhood grassroots groups, exploit CEQA provisions to hold projects hostage until the beleaguered developer decides to meet the union's demands.

The scope of CEQA has grown over the years to include more environmental impact studies. CEQA now requires projects to be vetted over greenhouse gas emissions and Native American artifacts. To understand the complexity and breadth of CEQA regulations and the potential for litigation abuse, let's examine the Newport Crossings mixed-use project in Newport Beach.

Newport Crossings is a proposed residential, commercial, and retail project. It would create a 350-unit apartment complex. The developers designated seventy-eight of the apartments for low-income residents. The state requires developers to hire an archeologist to identify possible Indian artifacts or dinosaur fossils. The Environmental Impact Report for the project was 493 pages long. That is longer than *Moby Dick*.

On the last day allowed under CEQA, the Southwest Regional Council of Carpenters (SWRCC), a union representing over 55,000 carpenters, filed an opposition to the project, claiming the city's environmental impact study was inadequate. When the city planning commission approved the project, the SWRCC appealed. The appeal threatened the project with weeks or months of costly delays.

Erik Weigand, the vice chair of the Newport Beach Planning Commission, told *Reason Magazine* in August 2019, "They are just trying to force the developer to get their guys the work. Basically, you have these carpenters trying to shake down the process." Hiring union workers can increase project costs by about 20 percent, making many projects financially unfeasible. Once the developers hired union workers for the project, the SWRCC dropped the appeal against Newport Crossings.

Radical environmental groups routinely abuse CEQA. These groups often serve themselves—paying salaries, overhead, fees, and commissions. It's all done in the name of protecting the environment. It's a sham. They stuff their coffers with donations and litigation award fees while their directors pay themselves handsomely.

In 2019, the Center for Biological Diversity filed, on average, one lawsuit in California every two and a half weeks. These suits netted $750,000 for the organization in legal settlements. In 2013 the board of directors approved a $1.79 million payout to the directors and a handful of long-term employees. In 2017 the total annual compensation for their four directors was nearly $950,000. The director, Kieran Suckling (a former protester for the radical environmental group Earth First!), paid himself $295,823. The group's payroll, benefits, and taxes totaled over $16 million in 2019. These are not your altruistic tree-hugging environmentalists. They are well-oiled money-making machines who use people's concern for the environment to enrich themselves and further their agendas.

Why should we put up with these fraudsters?

Waking Up from the Nightmare

Fear of litigation is turning the California Dream into a nightmare. We need common-sense regulations that protect workers' *and* employers' rights, protect the environment in substantive ways, *and* allow construction of badly needed housing.

We must repeal PAGA. Labor violations and protection of workers are under the Division of Labor Standards Enforcement (DLSE). The DLSE has a wage-claim adjudication process. The parties informally conference to resolve the matter. If that fails, the DLSE sets an administrative hearing for a final decision. We need to take labor claims out of greedy attorneys' hands and restore common sense and fair play into labor dispute claims and settlements. In the meantime, things are about to go from bad to worse.

Assemblywoman Lorena Gonzalez (now Lorena Gonzalez Fletcher after she married another politician, Nathan Fletcher—she is now head of the strongest and richest labor union in the state, a position infinitely more powerful than an assemblywoman) introduced a bill that criminalizes PAGA "wage theft" of over $950 for all employees in aggregate, not for a single employee. Under her proposed law, an owner of a company can be charged with grand theft. Grand theft is either a misdemeanor or a felony. Misdemeanors are punishable by up to one year in county jail. Felony grand theft can bring jail times of up to three years in the state penitentiary. Employers could spend three years behind bars for failing to provide ten-minute lunch breaks. No wonder businesses are fleeing the state. When Elon Musk decided to pack up and move to Texas—Tesla is now officially a Texas company—after he grew frustrated with California's oppressive regulations, Congressman Gonzalez snarkily summed the Democrats' dismissive view of business owners when she tweeted: "Fuck Elon Musk." Very classy. That's what kind of leader we get with the current election system.

If PAGA cannot be repealed, then we need substantive reform. Employers should have a reasonable amount of time to fix code violations before penalties kick in, called "right to cure." Some labor statutes have right to cure provisions, but they are too narrowly defined and cumbersome. We need to expand right to cure broadly. A clear line of communication and protocols to solve problems is essential in any business. Right to cure establishes a clear and common-sense pathway to solutions that treat employees fairly *and* allows employers to remediate issues without the fear of punitive lawsuits.

PAGA suits are de facto class action suits, but they are not subject to the exact requirements as class actions. PAGA cases should have to adhere to the same standards as class action suits. Employees need to have the ability to opt out of PAGA litigation, as they do with class-action suits. Employees often do not know or are outright opposed to litigation against their employer. Nonetheless, they are lumped in with the claimant. In most PAGA claims, the plaintiff has not suffered any harm. We can settle small wage disputes without liability to the employee.

We must amend PAGA to allow only claims where the plaintiff can show they suffered significant damage from a labor code violation. It is common sense to cap PAGA penalties and awards based on the severity of the damage caused. The Labor & Workforce Development Agency in California should investigate and substantiate PAGA claims before any party brings litigation against an employer.

"Loser pays" is a way to decrease the large number of frivolous lawsuits in California brought about by PAGA and CEQA. The concept is based on the British model and is widely used outside the U.S. In loser pays, the loser of the lawsuit is required to pay the winning side's attorney fees. Loser pays has been instituted in Alaska, Texas, Oregon, and

Oklahoma for a broad spectrum of civil cases but applies to only a handful of civil cases in California.

According to a survey of 452 small business owners, 88 percent support adopting a loser-pays system. Loser pays discourages people from bringing or even threatening baseless lawsuits. Often businesses will settle almost any case because it costs more to defend the suit than to settle out of court. Lawyers know this and take a shotgun approach: shoot at everything and hope you hit something. Loser pays addresses this problem.

There is empirical evidence that implementing a loser-pays system significantly reduces speculative lawsuits and limits the leverage plaintiffs with weak or fraudulent cases enjoy by threatening their bosses with expensive litigation. Furthermore, it deters the filing of unnecessary motions and discoveries meant to delay the legal process or allow lawyers to pad bills.

Loser pays paves the way to redress the wrongs perpetrated against business owners who get dragged into court on baseless claims. Someone falsely accused of an offense should not bear the financial obligation to defend themself. Conversely, it disincentivizes defendants from using delay tactics when they know they are likely to be found guilty.

Loser pays is the rule in only a minimal number of cases in California. The vast majority of civil litigation is not subject to this rule because special-interest groups put their finger on the scale to favor themselves. It is a perfect example of the undue influence of special-interest groups because the trial lawyers do anything and everything in their power to prevent any change in the civil litigation system. Certain states have been able to overcome that. Texas now has a form of loser pays. It has helped the business community prosper in Texas because frivolous lawsuits in Texas don't overrun businesses as they do in California.

Checks and balances are built into the loser-pays system. Nearly all countries that have instituted a loser pays system that employs a judicial review process which analyzes cases and limits the legal fees incurred by the losing side. Courts establish standards for the legal fees in loser pays: usually between 30 percent and 70 percent of the winner's costs. Jurisdictions that utilize a loser-pays system give judges and courts the power to penalize plaintiffs if they determine the lawsuit is without merit. In federal courts, a defendant served with a frivolous lawsuit can draft a motion for sanctions, which gives the plaintiff twenty-one days to withdraw their complaint and walk away without incurring any financial liability.

Let's stop treating Rick Roussin, Vincent Passanisi, and other small business owners like criminals, fining them and threatening them with jail time for simple mistakes that we could resolve quickly and inexpensively. California was once a business-friendly state, and the businesses came and prospered: agriculture, entertainment, aerospace, technology. Let's get back to the place when California welcomed companies with open arms and allowed them to flourish.

There's a reason why we have PAGA in California but not loser pays; it's the power of campaign money supplied by the trial lawyers. They're one of the biggest funders of the party in power in Sacramento. The need for their campaign cash is generated by the huge districts and sizable campaign war chests it takes to win in California. Enact Hear the People, shrink the districts so they can be won with personalized campaigning and not big money, and we will change this calculus to allow reform to happen.

CHAPTER 16

WHY CALIFORNIA'S EDUCATION RANK IS SINKING

Kayla Svedin, a mother of four who lives in Arizona, sat down and talked to me via video chat from her living room one Saturday morning in March 2021. She spoke about her involvement in Arizona's school choice program, for which she is an outspoken advocate. Arizona's school choice program uses publicly funded education savings accounts (ESAs) to fund private education. Svedin receives 90 percent of the cost to educate a student in Arizona, placed into an account for private education. Parents can use ESA funds to pay for private school tuition. The public education system typically provides special education services such as speech and physical and occupational therapy.

Arizona's ESA school choice program has been so popular that there is a proposal to expand the program to include every student living in an economically disadvantaged school district. That encompasses up to 65–70 percent of *all* Arizona students.

"I don't think education needs to be this 'one-size-fits-all' wholesale education as you'd get from Costco," Svedin said. "I think education needs to be more like a farmers market curated to individual tastes. Costco is great for certain things. You get big amounts for lower prices, but there's not a lot of variety. It's not very individualized. It works for some people. I would never say it needs to go away, but it doesn't work for our kids. Being able to customize their education has been so beneficial for them that I can't imagine going back and doing it another way."

Because of the students' long-term success, Svedin believes in a person-centered planning educational model. She thinks we need to move away from a system-centered approach to education that is not responsive to the individual student. "If we're focused on the students and what's best for them, we can improve education. Instead of pooling our resources at the [public education] district level where we have income segregation, racial segregation, and ability segregation based on residentially assigned public schools, we should pool our resources at the state level and disburse them equitably to the students," she said. "We can bring equity to education funding and level those playing fields where we see such disparity. But it requires centering on individual students and their needs. We should be centering on students, not this behemoth of a system that is not flexible, is not individualized, and cannot be all things to all people. It can't. No amount of money can make this gigantic education system work for every individual student."

School choice should be a fundamental right. Does the government have the power to tell you to shop for your food at Safeway or Trader Joe's? Can Sacramento choose where you live or work? Buy a car? Get insurance? Why is it OK for Sacramento politicians to dictate where your child goes to school? They do so presently only because they control the money. At the same time, teachers' unions control the politicians. That is unfair and disproportionally harms low-income students and families of color.

Parents should be able to choose the school their child attends. Parents, not bureaucrats, know the best educational fit for their children. Public funds can pay for private school choice in four ways: vouchers, education savings accounts, individual tuition tax credit programs, and tax credit scholarship programs. The payments the state makes for private education are called vouchers or scholarships.

Currently, twenty-two states and the District of Columbia offer some form of voucher or scholarship program. School choice voucher programs provide students with greater access to private schools. Families can use vouchers to pay for religious or nonreligious private schools. Voucher programs are typically need-based. The average voucher or scholarship award is $7,264 per school year. School choice programs provided $1.4 billion in vouchers nationwide to 218,007 students in the 2019–2020 school year.

The voucher and scholarship programs are popular. Survey after survey shows bipartisan support for vouchers, especially among parents with school-age children and people of color. A 2020 national Education Next Poll reported that 61 percent of parents supported vouchers, with 22 percent opposed. These percentages increased to 70 percent and 67 percent for black and Hispanic parents, respectively. A 2019 national Cato poll showed 58 percent of Americans support vouchers while only 40 percent oppose. Scholarships were favored by all racial and economic groups, especially socioeconomically disadvantaged students and African Americans, where the percentage skyrocketed to 73 percent and 69 percent, respectively. A February 2021 poll reported that 65 percent of people in Arkansas believe parents and students should choose their school, and 61 percent support school choice scholarships for lower-income families.

The facts are clear: parents want school choice for their children. Our leaders need to heed the call and break up the public education monopoly. The reason for these overwhelming numbers should be evident. Parents want what's best for their children. They know perfectly well that sending their child to the school best suited for their needs makes sense and is more likely to effectively educate their child and pave the way for future success.

California schools are underperforming when compared to states with school choice. As solutions, the California Teachers Association (CTA) promotes increased funding for public schools and higher teacher salaries. California pays its teachers the second-highest average salary in the nation—$20,500 above the national average. According to the Legislative Analyst's Office, school funding in California is at an all-time high. Yet, less than half of our fourth grade or eighth grade students are proficient in math or reading. It just goes to show: money doesn't solve every problem.

The real problem is the CTA. The idea of a teachers' union sounds great to many people. In public opinion surveys, teachers' unions usually received favorable ratings. That's because parents don't understand what a scam the unions perpetrate. One might assume the unions put children first. The opposite is true. Unions put their interests first. Unions have thwarted every attempt to institute school choice and vouchers to mollify teachers and, above all, to keep receiving $1,000 a year in dues they extract from teacher salaries.

How do *Californians* feel about vouchers and education savings accounts (ESAs) to fund school choice today? Well, 68 percent of Californians support ESAs , and 60 percent approve of vouchers.

I love teachers. As noted earlier, my mother was a dedicated teacher. Many teachers are excellent educators who go above and beyond to ensure that their students receive a high-quality education. Unfortunately, tenure protects too many poor teachers. Can your boss fire you if you are an unsatisfactory employee? Not if you are a teacher in California. It's almost impossible to fire a teacher here; the regulatory hurdles are just too high. Teachers have tenure. Tenure is a system whereby teacher hires are *permanent*, typically after only eighteen months. Tenure is a boon for teachers and their unions but terrible for children and parents.

We all know the difference between good and bad teachers. We have experienced both. A dedicated, dynamic teacher brings out the best in students. They inspire us to learn and realize our potential. Conversely, poor teachers can harm the academic and social-emotional well-being of students. A good teacher can change a child's life. A bad teacher can waste a year.

Tenure ensures that ineffective and harmful teachers remain in the classroom, regardless of their job performance. Tenure enforces the 'last in first out' principle. When districts cut teachers due to annual fluctuations in budgets and school enrollment, the last teacher hired is the first teacher fired, regardless of job performance.

The tenure system most hurts districts that serve lower-income students. These districts hire more new teachers, who are routinely let go. Tenure causes a high turnover rate for young, motivated teachers and insulates older teachers from any adverse effects of poor performance reviews. The students at most risk are those hurt the most.

Don't take my word for it. Listen to the experts: school superintendents who know the damage tenure causes firsthand. In *Vergara v. California*, a group of students sued California for protecting ineffective teachers and violating students' constitutional right to quality education. In one deposition excerpt from that trial, Tony Smith, former superintendent of the Oakland Unified School District, testified, "The current system is designed to support and protect adults at the expense of children. We're responsible for having the best, highest quality, most effective staff inside that school ready to teach kids every day. And if I'm limited and I can't do that, and I know what their life is like outside of school, it is immoral, unconscionable, and unfair that I'm not giving those kids every opportunity in the public system with public money."

School administrator staffing decisions are based on seniority only: "last in, first out." An ineffective teacher with greater seniority is retained, while a highly effective one is let go.

In another deposition, John Deasy, Los Angeles Unified School District superintendent, said, "The single most important issue for student learning is the effectiveness of the teacher." When asked about seniority, he stated, "I would argue that it had little or no effect on trying to determine effectiveness. Whether it be a Tuesday or a Thursday is immaterial to your effectiveness." Low-income communities bear the highest cost of tenure. As Deasy testified, "Schools that were disproportionately affected—meaning much higher numbers of the staff were laid off—were schools of the highest poverty."

Troy Christmas, the director of labor strategies for Oakland schools, supported Deasy's assertion in *his* deposition, stating: "The lack of seniority at a particular school meant that—I think it was—85 percent of that school who got layoff notices."

Tony Smith concurred: "The quality of the teacher in the classroom is the most significant factor in the child's academic progress," he said. "You have too often effective, engaged, quality professionals who are dismissed from service just because they're newer into the district."

Jane Robb gave testimony on behalf of the California Teachers Association and the California Federation of Teachers. She took a contrarian view. "I don't agree that the most important factor in students' learning is the quality of their teacher," she said. The unions will fight tooth and nail any attempt at the dismissal of a teacher. Vivian Ekchian, chief human resources director of the Los Angeles Unified School District, testified about the cost of dismissing a teacher. She observed: "It costs $350,000 on the average, and in exceptional cases, millions."

Troy Christmas stated, "If I know that my budget says I can take the four most egregious cases to hearing, and that's all my budget is going to allow—cases five through seven if they don't settle—they still work for us. There are a number of teachers we believe are ineffective with our students who we don't even seek to dismiss under the dismissal statutes." An average of 2.2 teachers per year are dismissed in California. That works out to 0.0007 percent of California's teachers. Tony Smith admitted, "The money, the time, the energy that should be invested in supporting children is disproportionately invested in trying to follow through on somebody who's been documented to not be effective."

What can a parent do when "the quality of their teacher" is not a top priority? The tenure system forces children to attend failing public schools. What choices do they have? In California, it's public charter schools or nothing. That needs to change. We need to bring school choice and vouchers to California. Why has California lagged behind the rest of the country? Vouchers and scholarships that support school choice programs have been the victims of a concentrated misinformation effort by public school teachers' unions. Their only objective is to prevent school choice at all costs. They're unwilling to relinquish their monopoly over California's six million public school students.

Let's examine some of the myths about school choice.

Myth #1: Private schools cost more money than public schools.

The National Education Association (NEA) is the national supervising union of the California Teachers Association. The NEA states, "Vouchers are expensive. Vouchers aren't good economics either. They essentially force taxpayers to support two school systems—one public, the other private."

Actually, private schools spend *less* to educate a student than public schools. The average scholarship awarded for private school choice was $5,059. The average cost to educate a student in a public school is $12,794. The math is compelling and straightforward. The cost to educate a public school student, minus the price of a voucher or scholarship, equals net savings per student.

Let's get back to Kayla Svedin, the Arizona school choice advocate. Svedin told me, "The ESA allowed us 90 percent of the amount the school was getting for her enrollment. That amount was about $3,600 for the year." That money will cover her daughter's tuition at a nearby private school and individual speech therapy once a week. "A lot of people think these elite private schools are so expensive," Svedin explains. "They don't realize that many private schools are reasonably priced. Private schools work with families by providing privately funded scholarships that bridge the gap or accept the [public ESA] scholarship as payment in full. These schools want to help kids, and if they're able to, they're going to accept those students."

Myth #2: Vouchers will only help wealthy, suburban white parents send their kids to expensive private schools.

The NEA declares, "Vouchers do not give parents real educational choice. Participating private schools may limit enrollment, and in many cases may maintain exclusive admissions policies and charge tuition and fees far above the amount provided by the voucher." Let's move past union propaganda and look at the facts. In 2018–19, the racial makeup of scholarship students in Indiana was 56 percent white (78.4 percent of the total population), 22 percent Hispanic (7.3 percent of the total population), 12 percent Black (9.9 percent of the total population), 6 percent mixed race (2.2 percent of the total population), and 2.5 percent Asian and Pacific Islander (2.7 percent of the total population). Most Indiana scholarship students come from metropolitan areas (61 percent). These figures demonstrate that minority students enroll in more significant percentages than their white peers. The data debunks claims that funding school choice with public money pays for wealthy suburban kids to go to private schools.

Florida's low-income scholarship students, predominantly students of color, who spent at least four years in the program, are 45 percent more likely to get a college degree than similarly disadvantaged public school students. School choice promotes racial equality and reduces poverty systemically. Vouchers break the connection between where a child lives and where they can go to school. Affluent families can move to neighborhoods with good schools, but low-income families do not have that luxury. School choice breaks the cycle of poverty by providing impoverished children with the same access to high-quality education as well-off students enjoy.

Education is the way out of poverty. Why are our leaders forsaking our next generation of low-income students? Democrats are happy to dole out checks that help people—until the money runs out at the end of the month, and the cycle of poverty resets and begins all over again. That is not a solution to the systemic racism and inequality that has caused our cities to erupt in flames. If politicians are serious about racial equality and believe that every child deserves the same chance to succeed, leaders must empower parents with school choice.

Vouchers help minority and lower-income students succeed in school and go on to college. People with college degrees live longer, earn more money, and escape the school-to-jail pipeline.

Myth #3: Private schools don't have to take special education students, so this vulnerable population is left behind by school choice.

The NEA insists, "Vouchers leave most children behind, especially those with special needs." That's propaganda. Here are the facts. Many private schools specialize in helping special education students that public schools have failed. Special education parents are among the strongest proponents of vouchers. In Florida, Step Up for Students strives to provide equal opportunity for lower-income students by connecting them with the Florida school choice program that best fits their needs. One child whom Florida's scholarships helped was six-year-old Elisabeth Edwards.

Elisabeth has a sensory disorder that prevents her from processing too much information at one time. She grew frustrated and angry when she could not understand her first-grade lessons. The kids and teachers made her feel stupid. She began banging her head against the wall at school and at home. Elisabeth came home one day and told her mother she wanted to die. She questioned why God had even made her. Elisabeth asked her mother if she could kill herself.

Consuelo and Max Edwards found a therapist for Elisabeth and started looking for private school options for their daughter. Elisabeth qualified for Florida's income-based scholarship program administered by Step Up for Students. The Edwardses visited Masters Training Academy, a private Christian school dedicated to students with behavior, learning, and health disabilities. They were immediately impressed. Elisabeth told Step Up for Students, "I felt like I was at home because I just saw everybody was happy."

Elisabeth did have an outburst during her initial visit. The school principal's reaction was not what Elisabeth or her mother expected. She told the six-year-old girl, "I'm sorry for your past hurt. We're not here to hurt you. We're here to help you." The principal hugged Elisabeth and told her she would see her tomorrow.

It took months before Elisabeth realized she could trust the teachers and students at her new school. Her academics and behavior improved. She still had her moments, but the staff deescalated her tantrums. "What they did for her in the beginning, when she had her blowouts and cried, the teacher would look at her and say, 'You know what? We still love you here. You can be mad at us, and you can cry, but we'll see you again tomorrow,'" Consuelo says.

Elisabeth is now a fourth grader at Masters Training Academy. She receives the extra time and help in areas where she struggles, but she no longer feels stupid. Elisabeth now says, "I feel like I'm the smartest kid in the world." Consuelo credits the scholarship program and the private school for saving her daughter's life. She says, "If it weren't for Masters, I'd probably be going to her gravesite grieving for her." The cost of saving a child's life? Nothing: the state of Florida saved money.

Myth #4: If students leave public school, the public school students who remain will suffer.

The California Teachers Association maintains, "There is no link between vouchers and student achievement. Studies continue to show there have been no significant improvements in student achievement in voucher schools. The most dramatic improvements in student achievement have occurred in places where vouchers do not exist." The research links provided to back up this claim date from 1995 to 2006. That's out of date. Let's look at the current research.

EdChoice looked at thirty different studies examining school choice's impact on nearby public schools in various states. Twenty-nine studies showed positive effects from vouchers and scholarships, and one was neutral.

In Louisiana, a study released in January 2021 looked at the achievement gains in math and language arts for low-income public school students after implementing the state's scholarship program. The students who remained at the failing public schools showed significantly improved math scores and positive improvements but not statistically significant gains in language arts. There was no negative impact on public education in the study.

A 2014 study of Florida's Tax-Credit Scholarship reported a positive correlation between implementing the program and improved language arts test scores for surrounding public schools. Those schools deemed the most impacted by competition showed the most significant improvement in their standardized test scores. Competition incentivizes public schools to improve so they can compete with private schools.

The California Teachers Association has blocked every attempt to bring school choice and vouchers to California. The CTA spent $26,366,491 to defeat Proposition 38 in the 2000 election. Had the measure passed, it would have created $4,000 vouchers to use for religious or nonreligious private schools. The CTA successfully lobbied for the prop to be renamed from "School Choice" to "School Vouchers." The ballot measure dropped 10 points in the polls the following day. Prop 38 was defeated 70.6 percent to 29.4 percent.

California teachers take home the second-highest salary in the nation, $82,000 per year. If a teacher works for thirty years, they can retire and sit back and collect 72 percent of their working salary for the rest of their lives. The pension obligation to the state is over $51,000 a year, more than many teachers currently working full-time in many other states make in salary. It costs the state of California over $1,000 per year per student to cover pension costs. At the same time, administrative costs in California eat up a large share of education costs. Isn't it time to make sure more money gets to the teacher and the classroom, not the bureaucrats?

Myth #5: Vouchers do not improve student achievement.

The NEA asserts: "Not only do vouchers divert public tax dollars to private schools that are not held accountable to the public, but they also do nothing to improve the education of the few children who receive a voucher."

Let's compare 2019 Smarter Balanced standardized test scores from the twenty-two states with vouchers or scholarships. In 2019, the last year standardized tests were administered, the national average fourth-grade grade math score was 240. California fourth graders scored 235. Mississippi fourth-graders scored 241. Five points below the national average might not sound too bad until you learn that five points are statistically significant. Of the twenty-two states with school choice, only Arkansas and Louisiana had lower math scores than California.

Things do not look any brighter when we examine eighth-grade math scores. The average score nationally on the standardized math assessment was 284. California eighth graders scored 276. Once again, only two states scored lower than California. Students in New Hampshire scored twenty points higher than California eighth graders.

The average nationwide standardized test fourth-grade reading score was 221 in 2019. California's score was 213: eight points below the mean. And yes, you guessed it: we were third from last again. Only Mississippi and Louisiana fared worse than California. When looking at eighth-grade test scores, California (262) again scored below the national average (266). Eighteen out of twenty-two school choice states performed better than California.

2015 was the last year students took the nationwide standardized science test. On the fifth-grade grade assessment, California students tied Mississippi with the lowest score (140). That is thirteen points below the average national score of 153. On the eighth-grade science test, California scored second to last.

Myth #6: Vouchers will take money away from public education.

The National Education Association alleges: "All voucher proposals reduce funding to neighborhood schools, meaning fewer textbooks, fewer teachers per student and more overcrowded classrooms. At the same time, these programs cost taxpayers millions of dollars and increase bureaucratic and administrative costs."

School choice not only benefits students and parents—it *saves* money. Vouchers will save California money by decreasing the cost of education. Since the cost to educate a child is greater than the scholarship or voucher, there is a net saving. The state funds school districts based on enrollment numbers, so fewer students means financial savings for the state.

The Florida Senate put out a fiscal impact report that stated for every scholarship dollar the state paid out, Florida saved $1.44. The University of Arkansas released a budgetary impact statement about Arkansas's proposed School Choice program. It found that tax-credit scholarships cost 35 percent of public school education: $4,444 instead of $12,800. The state will save $2,600 per student when all costs are factored into the equation. The school district from which the student disenrolls will save $900 per student. Scholarships will save taxpayer dollars.

The narrative spun by teachers' unions has always been that money is taken away from their public school when a student chooses a private school. That is false. Had Prop 38 passed in 2002, it would have provided $4,000 for any public school student in California to attend private schools. The State Legislative Analyst's Office projected the fiscal impact of Prop 38. The report claimed, "As children move from public schools to scholarship-redeeming schools, the state will save money that would have been spent on them in public schools. We estimate that the state initially would save almost $7,000 for each pupil leaving the system." When the $4,000 voucher cost was factored in, the net savings would be $3,000 per departing student.

If 15 percent of public school students chose a private school, California would save $700 million annually. If 25 percent of students shifted to private schools, the state would reap a *$3.4 billion windfall* annually. The report highlighted a projected savings of $100 million annually due to decreased costs to build and maintain schools and the debt those projects would incur through the issuance of bonds.

In a free market, increased competition brings down costs. Once we dismantle public education's monopoly, competition will restrain cost growth in public and private sectors. Competition is the key. Public school monopolies have no incentive to keep costs in check because consumers have no other options. Vouchers solve that problem, and the state reaps the financial reward.

The pandemic response from our political class should cement in people's minds the need to put the power of education back in the hands of the parents. All across California, public schools were shut down and children were forced to attend school on their home computers—if they had one. Thousands upon thousands of school-age children who didn't have access to the internet or a home computer were left with almost nothing for almost two years. Despite the entreaties of parents all over the state, the bureaucrats listened to the teachers' unions not the parents and kept schools closed. We won't know the full extent of this damage to our future for many years but believe me, progress for our children was slowed significantly by this action.

Most union leadership, especially in the larger districts such as Los Angeles, was more concerned about political matters than students' welfare. The head of the Los Angeles teachers' union went so far as to publish a "manifesto" demanding not only extensive protections to limit infections as well as massive school changes for air flow, but also included political demands such as government run healthcare and support for demands of groups like Black Lives Matters. The union leaders knew that the politicians wouldn't stand up to them and they took advantage of the situation to the detriment of our younger generation. We can't keep doing this to ourselves—we need parents back in charge.

School choice is the right choice for our students, parents, and the state. We need to limit the power of teachers' unions. It is no coincidence that all but three of the twenty-two states that allow publicly funded school choice programs are right-to-work states where teachers are not unionized.

Choice creates competition, and competition spurs innovation and improvement. Vouchers and scholarships work. Parents and children are clamoring for greater access to school choice programs. Teachers would also fare better under a voucher system. The competitive drive that would empower private schools would open the door to more money for teachers rather than administration. Too much money goes to bureaucracy in California. Vouchers would motivate schools to bid more for the best teachers, which would drive salaries higher overall.

Consumers must enjoy the same free-market choices in education as in the housing market. As a builder, I need to continually improve my product and services to compete in the housing market. If not, my competitors will drive me out of business. Remove the incentive, and you have the stagnation, inertia, and failure that characterize California's education system today.

School choice vouchers are an essential part of the answer to improving education in California. We need to focus on the student, not protecting the system. When we empower parents to choose which school their child attends, we all win. Why hasn't this been done? Again, it's because of the funding of campaigns by the teachers' unions and the need for that funding on the part of politicians. If we enact Hear the People, we'll make all campaigns so small they will have to be personal or door-to-door so you don't need money and we will empower the people not the organized forces like the unions that benefit from the status quo.

CHAPTER 17

FACING FACTS ABOUT SOCIALISM, COMMUNISM, AND GOD

One nation under God. These words are foundational to our republic. The Constitution acknowledged the existence of God while enshrining freedom of worship, affirming that the government shall impose no state religion. Our founding fathers based our Constitution and laws on Judeo-Christian values. But all major religions share the same moral tenets; all teach us tolerance, compassion, and love. These precepts guide our societal norms and expectations. Somewhere along the line, California's government abandoned God for socialism and traded trust in God for faith in the state.

Religion has been an integral part of my adult life, as it is for many Californians. Those who control our state's government have become antagonistic toward religion. Throughout history, Socialist and Communist governments have suppressed religious freedoms. The Soviet Union destroyed churches. Communist and Socialist governments rest on the principle of omnipotent state power. In the Communist and Socialist systems, you can have only one God—the state. In this way, these governments maintain control of their economy and create state-controlled monopolies such as public education.

During the pandemic, the state of California denied Californians their constitutionally protected right to worship. The COVID-19 government-imposed lockdowns caused many small businesses, schools, and churches to close. Tellingly, most big businesses were allowed to stay open as were cannabis shops and strip clubs—all deemed "essential" by the politicians who run the state. As the numbers improved, some small businesses were permitted to reopen, but not churches. Restaurants, liquor stores, and even massage parlors reopened. Yet all houses of worship remained shuttered. Two churches sued the state of California.

Pastor Jurgen Matthesius is an affable Australian with Southern California surfer good looks and a shock of blond hair. He explained his Awaken Church's response to COVID-19 and the lockdowns on their website. Awaken Church followed all county health guidelines and spared no expense in its reopening plans. The polar ionization units it installed kill 99.4 percent of viruses in the air. It offered three services for its congregation: stay-at-home, outdoor, and indoor. Pastor Matthesius defied the state edict to remain closed.

He explained, "We're standing alongside the Jews that meet on Shabbat every Saturday and the Muslims and the Catholics and the Christians and all the faiths because the faiths bring hope. America has the First Amendment, which affords us to have freedom of religion because our founding fathers knew that, in times of severe challenge, people need to run *to* God. People need to run *to* faith, not from faith. Right now in San Diego, and sadly California, and right around America, we are seeing unprecedented numbers of people who are suffering emotionally, mentally, physically, and spiritually. The suicide hotline, just in LA alone, had an over eight thousand spike in calls of people requesting urgent care and urgent help." All this while ICU units were below capacity, the government was doing nothing to aid Californians' mental health.

Pastor Matthesius criticized the state and county officials who refused to categorize houses of worship as essential. "They're calling strip clubs essential. They're calling the casinos and liquor stores and marijuana dispensaries—they're essential. The church is not essential?" he said. Not here in the Socialist state of California, no, it's not. Sacramento has taken up the mantle of communist oppression of religion.

Matthesius will continue to defy the ban because of "the mental health, the spiritual health, the emotional health, and the relational health" of his congregation. "We know we are saving lives. Therefore, we will continue to stay open because we love our neighbors and because we care about our community."

Besides Awaken Church of San Diego, other houses of worship defied the stay-at-home orders and safely opened their churches' doors following the CDC guidelines. It is a sad day in California when we criminalize pastors for asking for the same rights as casino and marijuana dispensary owners. What does that say about us as a society when worshipers are not afforded the same protections as restaurant patrons?

In February 2021, the Supreme Court of the United States in *South Bay United Pentecostal Church, et al. v. Gavin Newsom, Governor of California, et al.*, upheld religious liberty. The highest court in the land ruled California's shuttering of churches unconstitutional. Justice Neil Gorsuch wrote in his consenting opinion, "California has openly imposed more stringent regulations on religious institutions than on many businesses...California forbids any kind of indoor worship. Meanwhile, the state allows most retail operations to proceed indoors with 25 percent occupancy and other businesses to operate at 50 percent occupancy or more. California is the only state in the country that has gone so far as to ban all indoor religious services."

Gorsuch went on to criticize Gavin Newsom and California's reasoning. "The state presumes that worship inherently involves a large number of people. Never mind that scores might pack into train stations or wait in long checkout lines in the businesses the state allows to remain open. Never mind, too, that some worshippers may seek only to pray in solitude, go to confession, or study in small groups. Nor does California explain why the less restrictive option of limiting the number of people who may gather at one time is insufficient for houses of worship, even though it has found that answer adequate for so many stores and businesses," he said.

The judge continued his assault on the state's hypocrisy. "Next, the state tells us that worshippers are sure to seek close physical interactions…Yet, California is not as concerned with the close physical proximity of hairstylists or manicurists to their customers, whom they touch and remain near for extended periods. The state does not force them or retailers to do all their business in parking lots and parks. And California allows people to sit in relatively close proximity inside buses too," Gorsuch wrote.

The Supreme Court justice echoed the thoughts of many Californians. "Nor, again, does California explain why the narrower options it thinks adequate in many secular settings—such as social distancing requirements, masks, cleaning, plexiglass barriers, and the like—cannot [sic] suffice here. Especially when those measures are in routine use in religious services across the country today."

Gorsuch also wrote, "California worries that worship brings people together for too much time. Yet, California does not limit its citizens to running in and out of other establishments; no one is barred from lingering in shopping malls, salons, or bus terminals. Nor, yet again, has California explained why more narrowly tailored options, like a reasonable limit on the length of indoor religious gatherings, would fail to meet its concerns… Recently, this Court made it abundantly clear that edicts like California's fail strict scrutiny and violate the Constitution."

The arbitrary nature of Gavin Newsom's edicts was ruled unconstitutional. The Supreme Court ruled that churches may open with the same restrictions as other essential businesses. The ruling was a huge win for religious freedom.

The Socialist Republic of California

The Socialist state of California is not only taking away our religious liberties; it likewise continues to whittle away at our economic freedoms. In *The Wealth of Nations*, the famed economist Adam Smith claimed, "Institutions that protect the liberty of individuals to pursue their economic interests result in greater prosperity for the larger society." I couldn't agree more. Smith went on to warn of the dangers of unions exerting undue influence on politics to create regulations that favor special-interest groups over the common good. His view was prescient: California is indeed on its way to becoming a Socialist state. Central government planning is replacing the free market system, and public employee unions wield untold power.

Central planning of economies and cultures has been tried over and over again—failures every one. The U.S.S.R. Cuba. Venezuela. Would you want to live in any of those places? Neither would I. Mexico is now essentially a Socialist country, and the people of Mexico are so happy that thousands continue to flee to the U.S. every day in search of economic opportunity. Yet Sacramento believes it can engineer a green Socialist workers' utopia. The ruling political class has created a Socialist, union-dominated *dystopia* that works for the few but fails the many. The result is a mass exodus from California to states where capitalism and "In God We Trust" still mean something.

The United States is a capitalist nation. California was once the shining example of entrepreneurial capitalism. The private sector has brought innovation, jobs, and wealth to California. The private sector *always* outperforms the public sector. The free market is *always* more efficient than Socialist central government planning. Let's examine a few of the reasons why.

Government programs interfere with the private market. Government interference in markets creates inefficiencies and waste, while competition in the private sector promotes efficiency. The State Controller's Office has reported over $1 billion in public sector waste every year since 2015. The private sector can provide the same services for a fraction of the cost with a fraction of the waste.

Centralized government planning inhibits innovation and change. Capitalism rewards companies for disrupting the status quo. Netflix came up with a streaming service that completely changed the game. Companies like Blockbuster that couldn't compete were forced out of business.

When was the last time a government agency was forced out of business? Government bureaucracy is inflexible and inert. The status quo is protected and valued over innovation and change. On the contrary, private companies must continually upgrade their goods and services to survive. Been to the DMV lately? Not a huge focus on efficiency and service.

The state government cannot print money, so funding the public sector must come from taxes and borrowing. These funding sources come with huge costs that make the government less efficient than the private sector, right out of the gate. Taxes disincentivize productive behavior by reducing net earnings, savings, and investments. Public-sector borrowing consumes some of the capital that would otherwise be available for private investment.

For every dollar spent in the public sector, a dollar is taken out of the private sector. Free-market forces reward efficiency, production, and innovation. Political forces reward inefficiency, bureaucracy, and inertia. The government does not use resources as efficiently as private businesses. Inefficiencies and redundancies result in overall decreased economic output and gross domestic product (GDP). When you're complying with a government regulation or haggling with a government official, you're not producing or innovating. That hurts our economic growth.

Many government programs harm our economy. California's regulatory agencies increase the cost of doing business in California. Overregulation makes our businesses less competitive than other states and nations. Regulations add costs to goods and services, which are passed on to the consumer. California has the second-highest cost of living behind Hawaii, whose high prices are mainly due to the transportation costs required to get goods to the island.

Government programs adversely affect people's behavior. Government programs and subsidies forestall economically positive choices like saving for retirement or college when they provide public funds to finance private decisions. Economically negative options, like unemployment and welfare, are incentivized through government entitlement programs.

Government spending on certain things can have a positive effect on economies. The public sector *should* provide services typically ignored or unable to be provided by the private sector. Transportation infrastructure like roads, bridges, and mass transit improve productivity. Governments spend resources on law and order, providing safety and enhancing political and social stability. As discussed in the previous chapter, education is a government service that promotes economic development and growth. Limited public-sector spending, done carefully and intelligently, promotes a healthy economic and social environment and improves our quality of life.

Sacramento and the public employee unions love to emulate the European Union's Socialist policies. They often tout the benefits of the European model, with its worker benefits such as thirty-hour work weeks and government-mandated thirty days paid vacation a year. But at what cost? European Union governments devour 45 percent of their countries' GDP. The U.S. government spends 35 percent. The World Bank compared GDP growth for the European Union, primarily socialistic, and the capitalist United States. From 2010 to 2019, U.S. GDP grew from $14.99 trillion to $21.43 trillion, or about 43 percent. EU economic growth lagged far behind the U.S. European Union GDP rose from $14.54 trillion in 2010 to $15.63 trillion in 2019, or less than 1 percent.

The price tag for all that growth in socialistic countries? High taxes and high unemployment. The top tax rate for Sweden and Belgium is 60.2 percent. The list of countries with top tax rates of over 50 percent includes France, Finland, Denmark, Italy, Ireland, and Greece. Germany (47.5 percent) and the United Kingdom (47 percent) are not far behind. The 2019 EU unemployment rate was 6.7 percent. As of April 2019, our unemployment rate was at 3.6 percent, and the number of unemployed persons was 5.8 million. We have 328.2 million people in this country. For a good economy, the unemployment rate should be 3 percent. Compare our rate to the EU. Taxes, unemployment, and socialism go together like peas in a pod. I hate peas.

The Socialist republic of California. Think it couldn't happen here? Think again. The age demographics of California are changing. Millennials now outnumber baby boomers. A 2019 poll found some alarming differences between baby boomers (fifty-seven to seventy-five years old) and millennials (twenty-five to forty years old). There is a generation gap in how these two groups view socialism and communism. Fifty percent of millennials report they would vote for a Socialist candidate compared to 29 percent of the baby boomers. Thirty-six percent of millennials, but only 7 percent of boomers have a favorable opinion of communism. When asked if the government should provide a universal basic income whereby every citizen receives a government check, 36 percent of millennials agree. A 2020 CBS News poll showed 57 percent of likely Democratic voters viewed socialism positively compared to a 46 percent favorable rating for capitalism.

Reliance on the government and the programs it provides is growing, and this is precisely what the Democrats want. Theirs is a "divide and conquer" strategy based on special-interest groups and identity politics. Student debt loading you down? Bernie Sanders and the new Left will make it disappear like magic. And while we're at it, we'll make college accessible for everyone. Healthcare? Universal and free. Socialists vow to tax millionaires and billionaires to pay for it all. Sounds appealing, doesn't it? Especially if you are a thirty-year-old gig-economy worker with no 401(k) or health insurance, paying $2,000 a month for a one-bedroom apartment. It can't happen. Look around the world, countries that practice socialism not only can't pay their bills and provide decent benefits to their workers; they limit opportunities and suffer significant out migration.

We are raising a new generation of Americans who believe the government will solve their problems and take care of all their needs: cradle to grave socialism. These neo-Socialists may want to talk to a former East German factory worker to hear how that panned out or just look at historical photos. Their grim faces tell the real story—no joyful smiles on those faces. The Socialist government's central planning did very little for their standard of living or happy outlook.

The Democrats in Sacramento want to fix every California problem by regulating it into extinction. And their ambitions do not stop at the borders of California. Their goal is to turn the planet into a green workers utopia and have you and I pay for it. Our current energy policy is top-down government control—socialism at work in California.

A Carbon-Free Future and Rolling Blackouts

California has passed more laws on climate change than any state or nation in the world. California is making a political statement, but are we making a real impact? California does not exist in a vacuum. China and India continue to build coal-fired power plants at break-neck speed. Our climate change regulations' price tag is higher gasoline, utility bills, and food prices—with little real climate impact to show for it. With nearly four in ten Californians near or below the poverty line, we ask Californians to pay too much for too little. There is a limit to the affordability pain the Democrats can inflict.

Climate change is real. However, California's response to climate change is rooted in Socialist delusion. Gavin Newsom and the environmental lobby have decided the future of California's energy. They ignore market forces and the ratepayers who will finance it all. Newsom recently banned the sale of all gasoline vehicles in California by 2035. In California, lawmakers and special-interest groups think they are smarter than the market economy. The benevolent government's moral imperative is to protect the ignorant masses from themselves and the capitalist forces that would dare to give the people what they want at a fair price.

Capitalism keeps costs down due to free-market competition. Socialism is unconcerned with fiscal responsibility. The government can simply increase taxes to pay for its carbon-free future. California's public utilities are among the most expensive in the nation. Southern California Edison's rates are 45 percent above the national average. Pacific Gas and Electric customers pay 80 percent more than the national average per kilowatt-hour. San Diego Gas and Electric customers spend 100 percent more than the rest of the country.

Southern California Gas Company (SoCalGas) is the largest natural gas company globally. It services roughly half of all California homes and businesses. SoCalGas's March 2021 climate commitment announced that the company *and* its customers would achieve net-zero greenhouse gas emissions by 2045. The California Public Utilities Commission (CPUC), the public agency responsible for regulating utilities, has planned to phase out all natural gas. The governmental energy agency mandated 100 percent renewable, carbon-neutral energy by 2045.

This policy is incredibly shortsighted, especially in the context of global pollution. Let's face it: China is the largest polluter in the world, with India not far behind, according to some studies emitting more pollution than the rest of the world combined. One of the major contributors to carbon pollution is China's use of coal in power generation. California and the rest of America have vast reserves of natural gas. Wouldn't worldwide pollution be reduced if we developed, liquified, and shipped California's natural gas to China to compete economically with coal? At the same, California would benefit from the jobs, export earnings, and of course, less pollution coming east from China.

The consumer pays for the centralized planning of 100 percent carbon neutrality. California has not come up with a final price tag for its plans to go carbon free. Some estimates put the cost at $2,000 per year or $167 per month for every household for twenty years. At least we'll all have clean energy in our green Socialist paradise, right? Not so fast.

In the summer of 2020, California experienced its first rolling blackouts in twenty years. The blackouts were not the result of high demand. The demand for energy during the blackouts in August 2020 was not higher than usual. The pandemic and lockdown of 2020 closed movie theaters, businesses, restaurants, and schools. So, what was going on?

A report commissioned by Gavin Newsom enumerated the root causes for the rolling blackouts. They determined the main reason was climate change. Environmental extremists blame every problem on climate change because it furthers their radical green agenda. Secondarily, these extremists claimed that extreme heat led to increased demand, which overburdened the system. In other words, they had not planned for it to be hot in August in Southern California. The commission blamed climate change for the extreme heat.

The report blamed wildfires—again caused by global warming—for taking power plants offline and contributing to the power shortage. Governor Newsom took the time for a photo op with California burning in the background. He told the *Los Angeles Times*, "While we're leading the nation in low-carbon green growth, as we've led the nation in our efforts to decarbonize our economy, we're going to have to do more, and we're going to have to fast-track our efforts. While it's nice to have goals to get to 100 percent clean energy by 2045, that's inadequate. Across the entire spectrum, our goals are inadequate to the reality we're experiencing."

Did he say 100 percent clean energy is inadequate? What else can Californians do? We already pay exorbitant electricity rates for rolling blackouts. It sounds like Communist Eastern Europe in the '70s, doesn't it? Welcome to the Socialist state of California 2021.

What were the natural root causes of the blackouts? The transition from fossil fuels to wind and solar has left California without enough energy to meet its needs during peak hours. Sacramento has decommissioned natural gas and nuclear energy plants without thinking about the consequences. The brilliant minds in Sacramento have also taken down dams that supply totally renewable and clean hyrdroelectric power. The central planners and environmental extremists want Californians to use solar and wind only to generate energy. Well, there are times the wind doesn't blow, and every day the sun sets.

When the *Los Angeles Times* asked Stephen Berberich, the organization president who manages the state's power grid, about solar, he said, "Solar has virtually no value in the net peak hours in the evening." Why not? We don't have enough battery power technology to store electricity at night when the sun isn't shining. The Democrats have not planned for this, yet they have forced the decommissioning of natural gas and nuclear power plants that could provide necessary power when solar cannot meet peak demand.

California has pledged to use 100 percent renewable energy by 2045, but *not* with hydropower. Hydropower is a renewable and reliable way to generate power. It provides electricity 24/7 using clean, accessible water. Hydropower produced 19 percent of the electricity in California in 2019. Why is California phasing out hydropower if it is a clean, reliable energy source? It interrupts salmon reproduction and survival. Ignoring efforts such as fish ladders which allow salmon to swim upstream to spawn is convenient as is ignoring the fact that the salmon population has already rebounded quite significantly due to these ladders and other efforts. Despite this progress, hydropower is not one of the renewable energy sources permissible in the ever-tightening energy governmental control over our economy.

Mothers for Nuclear

Diablo Canyon is the last nuclear power plant operating in California. It supplies 8 percent of all the electrical power in California and 14.5 percent of the carbon-neutral energy produced. In 2018, a joint proposal was negotiated and issued by Pacific Gas and Electric, The Natural Resources Defense Council, Friends of the Earth, and other environmentalist groups. It recommended closing Diablo Canyon and replacing the clean energy—produced without incident since 1985—with renewable energy sources like solar and wind.

Mothers for Nuclear is a group of mothers who support the Diablo Canyon Nuclear Power Plant's continued operation in San Luis Obispo County, California. Mothers for Nuclear believes in a future that includes safe nuclear power. I spoke with Kristin Zaitz, one of the group's founders, over Zoom on a sunny afternoon in March of 2021. Zaitz is a civil engineer and project manager at Diablo Canyon. She is also a lifelong environmentalist who loves working at Diablo Canyon. The facility sits on a stretch of pristine coast near San Luis Obispo. Untouched tide pools line the shore. Employees take whale-watching breaks when humpback whales breach offshore.

Zaitz is a mother of three. Her two-year-old daughter Sasha sat on her lap as Zaitz spoke with me about her path to nuclear energy advocacy. She said, "I was raised with an environmental background and didn't know much about nuclear, but felt I should oppose it. It took me a long time working there and asking a lot more questions to change my mind and realize that working at a nuclear power plant was directly in line with my environmental values because it produces so much electricity on such a small footprint."

I asked Zaitz why nuclear energy should be a part of California's clean energy future. Zaitz replied, "Most people don't even know that nuclear is carbon-free; I certainly didn't." Nuclear is a carbon-free way to produce electricity 24/7! And there is another benefit," said Zaitz. "It's a reliable generator, so it's always on except when you plan to have it off. This contrasts with wind and solar, which essentially come on when they want to come on, which is not necessarily when you need electricity. California doesn't recognize this at all in their energy policy."

Another public health benefit of nuclear power is that we can safely store waste in concrete containment casks or cooling pools; there are no emissions. Other power plants spew their waste into the air, adversely impacting human health.

As Zaitz explained, "Its track record shows that it's the safest way to produce reliable electricity. If you look at the history of operations around the world, even including every major accident, it's the safest way to produce reliable electricity." Diablo Canyon has produced clean, reliable energy for over thirty-five years with zero emissions and zero carbon. Still, as I said, in 2024, the state plans to shut down Diablo Canyon, the last nuclear power plant left in California.

Why is California phasing out all nuclear and shutting down Diablo Canyon? Zaitz responded, "There is a long history of anti-nuclear activism, and a lot of it is focused on the state of California. If you look back at the history of Diablo Canyon, it almost didn't open because of opposition to the plant. We as a society have never really talked about nuclear being carbon-free or contributing to our climate action goals. It's so easy to say we're just going to build more solar and wind, and we will fight climate change. But it's just not that easy."

There is another reason California has chosen wind and solar as the winners and nuclear and hydropower as losers. "The policies that were put in place were lobbied for by certain industries, and those industries are benefiting from that. It's not strictly a moral purpose. There has to be a review of the tradeoffs for society. What's the benefit for Californians? Look at where our energy prices are going. We're paying a lot of money for very little progress on climate."

The government's role is to ensure nuclear power safety, not regulate it out of existence. Let free market forces decide if atomic power should be a part of our balanced energy plan. California needs a balanced energy policy that utilizes green renewables combined with clean hydropower, natural gas, and nuclear. We need to incentivize private research and development of emerging technologies such as hydrogen fuel cells and thorium, a cleaner nuclear fuel, to replace uranium. I am not advocating a return to the days of coal-fired plants. Let's create a diversified portfolio of energy sources that will provide us with the capability and flexibility to meet our energy needs.

Our energy policy needs to consider the needs of every Californian, not just the environmental Left. We cannot create a centralized energy plan in a vacuum. Sure, it would be wonderful if we could go carbon-neutral for free. But increased energy costs have the most significant impact on low-income families. Energy needs to be affordable to the average ratepayer. What good is it to build a zero-carbon energy system if it impoverishes a new generation of Californians? We need to make fiscally responsible decisions that are good for all Californians—not just environmentalist elitists and their cronies in Sacramento.

Most of all, we need to change the electoral system to lessen the power of the environmental lobby. We need to make choices based on sound judgment, not the amount of money lobbyists throw at politicians to fund their huge campaign war chests. Hear the People will help make sure we will get sound energy and climate policy dictated by good sense and not influence peddlers.

The California Rule

California's public-sector unions are calling the shots in Sacramento. Their lobbying efforts pour millions into campaign contributions for candidates and ballot measures. Their political clout, money from union dues, and "getting out the vote" prowess distort the will of the populace.

Public employee unions use their dues and activities to elect the very people who are supposed to supervise and manage them. You cannot have people supervising someone who is under their control. It doesn't work. California's public employee pension mess is a prime example.

CalPERS is the California Public Employees' Retirement System. CalSTRS is the California State Teachers' Retirement System. The average CalSTRS pension is $53,700 a year, or $4,475 a month. California's public pension systems are in big financial trouble. Only 70 percent of the pension debt is funded. That leaves a 30 percent hole that needs to be filled. Unfunded liabilities for CalPERS and CalSTRS were $246 billion in 2020. That is not sustainable. How did we get into this financial hole? Two reasons: the California Rule and public employee unions.

The California Rule states that pension benefits are guaranteed. The California Rule locks the state into pension agreements that can never be modified for contracted employees. Local school districts and municipalities bear the ever-increasing cost to fund pension obligations. That means less money for educating students and essential city services.

There have been attempts to fix California's broken public employee pension system. The city of San Diego was in dire financial straits due to its growing pension obligation. In 2004, USA Today called San Diego "Enron by the Sea." In 2012, over 66 percent of San Diego voters approved pension reform measure Proposition B. The law created 401(k) retirement plans instead of pensions for all newly hired employees except the police. Under intense public and political pressure from unions, a San Diego superior court judge declared the law null and void in 2018, invalidating the will of 154,000 San Diego voters.

As a CPA and an attorney who has drafted both defined benefit and 401(k) plans, I can tell you that most private businesses have gone to the latter type; most have also found that their employees benefited since the individual accounts in a 401(k) can grow in a significant way with the growth of the private markets with no limits. Not only that, but surviving children can inherit an employee's 401(k) balance, which doesn't happen in a typical pension plan.

Unfunded pension obligations have hit California cities hard. Budgets, already strained, were stressed to the breaking point. Due to unfunded pension debt, some cities like San Diego and San Jose reached the brink of insolvency. Other cities like Vallejo and San Bernardino were crushed under the weight of their debt and declared bankruptcy.

The public employee unions prevent any attempt to change the status quo, no matter the cost. It is socialism when employees of a business elect the leadership. Union bosses are controlling the politicians. We cannot have government agencies run for the employees. The government exists to serve the needs of its customers, the citizens.

In the private sector, the board of directors runs the corporation. The board of directors is accountable to the shareholders. It is not responsible to the employees. If the employees elected the board of directors with very little input from shareholders, we would have very different private companies. The quality of our goods and services would suffer. Name three products that Socialist countries have produced. The names don't roll off your tongue like Google, Coca-Cola, and Ford.

Remember the East German car, the Trabant? Of course you don't. It has been described as the worst car ever made. An automotive writer said the eighteen horsepower engine smoked like an Iraqi oilfield. Its zero-to-sixty miles per hour time? It didn't have one: the car couldn't reach sixty miles per hour. It lacked high-end options like turn signals and brake lights. The Trabant became obsolete the day the Berlin Wall came down, and communism was forced to compete with capitalism. *Time Magazine* called it "the car that gave communism a bad name."

Look at the bounty produced by capitalism. If you go into a store today, you can choose so many kinds of foods. Need gluten-free food? There's a whole section for that. There are over two dozen different kinds of juice in the supermarket near my home. The same exists with clothing, automobiles—you name it. If there is a market for a product, someone will fill that need. That is because of the capitalist system we have in America.

Perhaps the biggest indictment of communism came from Boris Yeltsin, the former president of Russia when he toured an American supermarket. Yeltsin commented, "When I saw those shelves crammed with hundreds, thousands of cans, cartons, and goods of every possible sort, for the first time, I felt quite frankly sick with despair for the Soviet people."

We have to continue to fight socialism and foster capitalism. Winston Churchill listed socialism's greatest virtue as "the equal sharing of miseries." We must reverse California's slide into a Socialist state. Capitalism has lifted more people out of poverty than any system in the world. The capitalism system incentivizes private citizens to create and innovate. Humans inherently strive to get ahead in the world, and competition breeds excellence.

Democrats and socialism incentivize reliance on the state. Socialism creates a permanent underclass that relies on public benefits and governmental solutions to their problems. That does not serve anyone well. Republicans believe in a capitalist system that incentivizes everyone to succeed and where society provides a safety net for those in need of assistance. Democrats want to hand out freebies in the form of entitlement programs that keep people dependent on the government and voting Democratic. This is the crux of the difference between Democrats and Republicans.

I believe in a level playing field that allows people to improve their station in life. Take education, the great equalizer. We can create a state in which all people, especially those marginalized and discriminated against, have a genuine opportunity to succeed. School choice is a moral imperative. It is immoral to consign a child to a future of low-wage jobs and poverty because of their assigned public school. Our free-market economic system has proven its superiority to socialism. Competition improves all products and services: it's time to allow free-market competition to improve education.

The Democrats don't want competition in education. They control education from the halls of Sacramento and prescribe a one-size-fits-all education policy. That is socialism. The legacy of the Democratic stranglehold on Sacramento is a substandard education for thousands of people who live in poverty. We need real change that gives low-income families a fighting chance to make it in California. As I emphasize again, school vouchers and school choice are the right choice for California.

We founded our country and our state on the pillars of God and capitalism. The founding fathers enshrined both in the Constitution. California has drifted dangerously away from the ideals upon which America was founded. Free enterprise is our heritage and must be our future. California must move forward on the path set out for us by the framers of the Constitution, who were men of great faith, courage, and conviction.

Socialist central planning has never worked, is not working now, and will never work. It flies in the face of human nature and is inefficient, unresponsive, and wasteful. Socialism perpetuates class divisions and traps people in an endless cycle of poverty. It also empowers some of the worst autocrats the world has ever known—when the government is in charge of everything, the people in charge of government are all the more powerful. History is littered with example after example of Socialist failures. In a famous 1948 speech Winston Churchill, the former prime minister of the U.K., echoed the words of Spanish philosopher George Santayana when he declared, "Those who fail to learn from history are condemned to repeat it."

California was built on the American Dream. "Go west" and make something of yourself through hard work and perseverance. Capitalism spurs us to greater heights. When we let people realize their dreams, everyone prospers. That is the future laid out for our country by our founding fathers: *One nation under God with liberty and justice for all.*

Nikita Khrushchev, the former general secretary of the Soviet Union, put it succinctly in 1959—"we don't have to have a war to institute communism in the rest of the world, they will become communist through their policies." He was pretty much on target. Even though politicians like Gavin Newsom will proclaim they are capitalists and declaim socialism, they are fostering socialist policies that tax producers and provide support to everyone else to make them more dependent on the government.

Our founding fathers created a government that had limited powers and reserved most to the states and the people. They created a Congress, a people's house that would reflect the will of the people. They would be horrified today to see large legislative districts that empower elites, big corporations and interest groups and the media at the expense of the people.

It doesn't have to be this way. Our system can be changed. We can do it intelligently, with people elected in small districts that are accountable and do not have to raise money or curry favor with the media to get elected or stay elected.

CHAPTER 18

FACILITATING LEGAL IMMIGRATION: THE LIFEBLOOD OF OUR NATION

The Southern Baptist Convention, a large Christian denomination that often weighs in on national issues, gives a succinct description of California's immigration woes on their website: "At the border, we have had two signs posted: NO TRESPASSING and HELP WANTED." This contradiction defines the heart of our state's immigration problem.

In a 2021 Gallup poll, 81 percent of Americans viewed illegal immigration as "important" or "critically important." If you ask those same Americans if current immigration levels should increase, decrease, or stay the same, their responses split fairly evenly among all three. Americans view immigration as a problem that needs to be solved—but we are divided on the solutions.

California is ground zero for the illegal immigration debate. Nearly 10 percent of California's workforce is undocumented. About 2.5 million illegal immigrants live in California, 6 percent of our population. While Californians diverge in their attitudes about immigration, they unite in their desire to see our immigration issues resolved. In fact, Californians view immigration as the state's most pressing issue, polling above the economy and jobs, according to a 2019 Public Policy Institute poll.

I spoke with a woman stuck in our current immigration quagmire over Zoom on a windy spring day in April 2021. She asked me not to use her real name for legal reasons. "Brigette" has curly red and blonde hair that shoots out in all directions at crazy angles. A grey hairband fails to control anything.

Brigette told me her story seated on a couch in her living room in Torrance, California. Her family emigrated from Germany in the 1870s, when her great-grandfather, an engineer, went to Mexico to build and oversee the first electrical power plant in Mexico. She was raised in Mexico City's German neighborhood and attended a private German school. When she was seven, she visited her uncle in Austin, Texas. She fell in love with America and began learning English immediately.

Brigette's family left Mexico and returned to Germany when she was nine years old. But she never felt at home in Berlin. After graduating high school, she studied ballet in London and improved her English. She got her big break and moved to Glasgow, Scotland, to dance with the Scottish Ballet. She met a dashing young Mexican airline pilot in Scotland and fell in love. The married couple returned to Mexico City and raised three children.

But trouble lay on the horizon. Brigette's husband became abusive, first verbally, then physically. The situation worsened, and Brigette and her children no longer felt safe. She decided to file for divorce. Brigette says her husband started stalking her and threatening to kill her. She decided to leave Mexico for her family's safety. Brigette remembered how much she loved Texas when she was a child. She resolved to take her family to America.

Crossing the border on a tourist visa on March 27, 2010, Brigette drove to a relative's house in Southern California. She enrolled her children in public school and began taking courses at Cal State Long Beach. She remained here legally on a student visa. Brigette was a strong mother with high expectations for her children. Her children thrived in American schools, earning top grades. Brigette earned her master's degree in psychology six years later.

Brigette loves Southern California. When I asked her why, she told me, "I cannot live without the ocean. I go daily to the ocean, and I walk and meditate, and when I can swim, I swim. I am like a fish; I dry out if I don't have the ocean." She loves living in the Los Angeles area because it combines a vibrant culture with opportunities to work and the beauty and serenity of nature.

She explains why she decided to make California her home. "This was perfect for me," she said. "When I came, I studied on a student visa as long as I could. The kids were in a good school. I was doing a lot of dance projects. L.A. is a great city, but you still have that beautiful environment and nature. I've never found this before. You can live in a beach city, and it's just a jump to L.A. You really have it all here. I've always felt like I belonged here. It feels like home. It's as if I was meant to be here."

Four years ago, Brigette's story took a troubling turn. Her legal status ended abruptly. She tried to apply for a green card, but her attorney told her that her application was not strong enough to be considered. Her options were running out. "I was thrown out of legal status, and there was no way to get back in. If we left, we would not ever be able to come back, so we just stayed. Where else would we go?"

Brigette's life changed drastically. She could no longer work. She stopped driving for fear of deportation. "Basically laying low," she said. "Not mentioning it to anybody else. I didn't know who I could trust anymore. I lost a lot of friends." The moral and economic anxiety was worse. "No possibility to work," she explained. "You cannot work unless you get a fake birth certificate and a fake social security number, and then you spiral down into being a criminal. I just refuse to do that. I was not raised to survive like an illegal. I was raised to do things by the book. The whole situation put me in a huge moral and ethical conflict. I decided to stay because it was best for my kids."

She told me why she left Mexico and won't return. "Nobody wants to leave their home. I had a nice house in Mexico. I had friends. I was established. I had to leave because of my husband. Our lives were threatened, and there was no other way out. Staying here under hard circumstances is still better than how it was before."

Various family members pitch in to help pay the rent. Her relationship with her family is now strained, and she feels like a burden. "I go to the food bank, to the churches to get food," she explained. "There were moments when we did not have a penny, nothing, no food. It's hell not being able to work. It broke my confidence."

Her eldest son tutored other high school students, sometimes riding his bike fifty minutes to Wilmington to earn fifteen dollars. His undocumented status prohibits him from being legally employed in California. "Basically, everything is hanging on a green card," Brigette said. Her oldest son attends Long Beach State. "My hope for my kids is that they can stay in California because this is their home. They don't know any other. My son had to learn Spanish in high school. So we're just waiting for some kind of opening to get papers."

Brigette's story illustrates the fundamental dichotomy in America's immigration policy. On the one hand, we are a nation of laws, and Brigette is breaking the law. On the other hand, we have a rich tradition of immigration that began with the *Mayflower* and has not slowed since. We appreciate the value immigrants like Brigette and her children have brought to our nation and our state. At the same time, we recognize the importance of immigration laws in maintaining order. Too many families are caught in the middle and see no way out.

Brigette broke the rules, but she is a good, hardworking person. We cannot blame immigrants that come here looking for a better life. Demonizing people can have disastrous consequences. We need to fix immigration, not blame immigrants. They are real people with real stories, and most are good and decent human beings. This nation has always welcomed immigration. And our economy needs it—just look at the vast unfilled jobs in the country in the wake of COVID. Immigrants deserve an immigration system that works.

Being a nation of immigrants and a nation of laws is a complex puzzle. Strict interpretation of immigration law can produce cruel and inhumane consequences. Conversely, allowing unchecked illegal immigration while turning a blind eye has brought undesired social and demographic changes that set us back. Estimates suggest that currently about twenty million undocumented immigrants live in the U.S. We publicly celebrate the positive impacts of immigration and privately worry over its unintended consequences.

The immigration debate sparked acrimony. Both sides lace their rhetoric with racism and personal accusations. Both the Trump and Biden presidencies have put our national immigration dilemma on display. We need to take back control of the narrative and enact comprehensive immigration reform.

America is the land of opportunity, a shining beacon on the hill. People come to the U.S. for a good education and a better life for their children. The history of California is the history of immigration. Manifest destiny and the great westward movement defined America's first hundred years. California was the geographical culmination of the great westward migration of the American Dream. When we sing "from sea to shining sea," we sing of California. The American Dream and manifest destiny had one final destination for millions of people from multiple generations: California.

California sang its siren song, and the people came—and they are still coming. They came across the Sierra Nevada Mountains from other parts of America. They crossed the deserts of Mexico and journeyed north from Central and South America. They sailed the Pacific Ocean from Asia. They fled their old worlds and ways to reinvent themselves in the new west. A man or woman could start fresh in the new world of California. They could, if they chose, reinvent themselves. No other nation in the world enables that sense of possibility—not one.

In 173 years, we have built California from an isolated wilderness into a modern, economic powerhouse. Ingenuity, risk-taking, and immigration have powered California's transformation from a sparsely populated outback into the world's fifth-largest economy. The Golden State has already represented the promised land of opportunity. California shows the American Dream at work.

But there is a cost. Illegal immigration costs California about $25 billion per year to provide education, healthcare, and government services. Fully 18.6 percent of California's schoolchildren are classified as English as a second language (ESL). Currently, ten languages are offered at various schools, from Arabic to American sign language. Most—85 percent—of California's ESL students speak Spanish at home. But at least fifty-nine other languages are spoken in California schools. The state of California requires specialized academic instruction in English and English language development lessons for all ESL students. This specialized instruction costs time and money, which are taken away from English-speaking students.

When the previous administration took a hard-line "law and order" approach to solve the problem, the other side pushed back. That has saddled us with sanctuary cities, sanctuary states, and other proimmigration measures across many states. California has led the response that many believe has swung the pendulum too far to the Left.

More immigrants come from Mexico than any other country. There has been a recent increase in immigrants from Central America. Central American governments like those in El Salvador, Guatemala, and Honduras cannot provide security and essential services. Drug cartels have corrupted their police. Indeed, experts estimate that cartels control over half of Guatemala. Unstable political situations create poor economic conditions and drive illegal immigration. We must provide actionable incentives to these countries to reform their political systems and law enforcement so their citizens feel no need to flee to the U.S. in search of a better life. None of that is easy. Doing it is essential.

Illegal immigration to the U.S. helps keep corrupt Central American governments in power. People who cannot find opportunities in their home country see fresh opportunities in California. If those citizens remained in their homeland, they could be agents of change. Salvadorans, Guatemalans, and Mexicans want their governments to provide essential services like adequate education and safe streets. It's not happening. Our faulty immigration policies shoulder part of the blame. We prop up dysfunctional, corrupt Central American governments when we fail to control our borders.

In 2018, undocumented immigrants sent home $528 *billion* in remittances. That money was taken out of the U.S. economy. Remittances finance and empower bad governments. Remittances are estimated to be 25 percent of GDP in impoverished Central American countries like Honduras. The money sent home tamps down the social unrest that might otherwise pressure governments to change.

Immigration is a global, regional, national, state, and local problem. No one state can fix it all, but there are some concrete measures that California *can* take.

California Values Act

Senate Bill 54 turned all of California into a sanctuary state. Ironically, SB 54 is known as the California Values Act. It does not reflect my values or those of most Californians. The California Values Act prohibits local law enforcement from cooperating with federal law enforcement when dealing with illegal aliens. If local law enforcement has a criminal illegal alien in custody, SB 54 prohibits the police from contacting Immigration and Customs Enforcement (ICE) to deport the criminal. Only certain felonies and violent offenses are exempt. This law ties the hands of local law enforcement and releases dangerous criminals into our communities.

Its name, the California Values Act, symbolizes what ails our immigration rhetoric and pushes the two sides farther apart. It implies that your values are suspect if you disagree with its provisions. Governor Jerry Brown admitted that to the National Press Club in April 2018. He called immigration an "inflammatory football that very low-life politicians like to exploit." The "low-life politicians" who opposed SB 54 include every Republican member of the state legislature.

Brown poured more fuel on the fire by framing the debate as a moral imperative. He continued, "I think it's shocking, it's despicable, and it's harmful to California, especially the people." He characterized ICE raids as "not human." Upholding the rule of law may not align with Brown's values, but it aligns with mine and those of many other Californians. Laws are what protect us from chaos and enable our society to function.

A 2018 poll from UC Berkeley found residents in Northern California counties and the central valley do not support SB 54. Only 11 percent of Republicans statewide support the sanctuary immigration law. Support declines to less than 50 percent for Californians over fifty years old. It is time for politicians to civilize the debate and repudiate the hate rhetoric.

Immigration enforcement agents risk their lives to arrest illegal alien criminals. These criminals entered our country illegally. They are gang members or other bad actors whom we should deport. SB 54 increases the risk of harm to police, which is unconscionable. Forty of fifty-eight California sheriffs opposed SB 54 because it releases criminals onto our streets. One county sheriff who opposed the law was Tulare County's Mike Boudreaux. In December 2018, Tulare County sheriff's deputies were forced to ignore an ICE detainer request and release a violent criminal convicted of armed robbery, was deported twice, and had spent twenty-seven months in federal prison.

Gustavo Garcia went on a rampage, killing one person and injuring six others. He began by shooting an undocumented farmworker standing on a ladder in an orchard. Garcia robbed a convenience store and shot up two gas stations, killing one man in Visalia. He shot at a woman in her car in a Motel 6 parking lot and fired at sheriff's deputies when they pursued him. The crime spree ended when Garcia stole a farm truck and fled the wrong way down a busy freeway at over one hundred miles per hour. The collisions Garcia caused sent four people to the hospital, including one critically injured motorist.

At his press conference after the deadly rampage, a visibly frustrated Sheriff Boudreaux said, "We did not recognize or honor that (ICE) detainer because the law (SB 54) says we cannot. That tool has been removed from our hands. And because of that, our county was shot up by a violent criminal. It could have easily been prevented." The sheriff urged common sense when he said, "I believe in DACA. I believe in Dreamers. I have two deputy sheriffs here who are Dreamers. That's not what I'm talking about. I'm talking about the criminal element." Sheriff's deputies could not hold Garcia for ICE agents even though he had committed armed robbery. Garcia committed the crime eleven months past the fifteen-year limitation. The sanctuary state law places illegal alien criminals above laws the rest of us must respect. Do you think that makes sense?

Orange County Sheriff Don Barnes explained why he opposes sanctuary states. He said SB 54 "has made our community less safe. The law has resulted in new crimes because my deputies were unable to communicate with their federal partners about individuals who committed serious offenses and present a threat to our community if released."

Barnes cited statistics that showed SB 54 had caused an increase in crime. Orange County law enforcement was required to release 2,031 undocumented inmates who had committed crimes and had ICE detainers. Four hundred and seven illegal immigrants were rearrested for committing crimes involving rape, robbery, assault, and battery.

Former Orange County supervisor chairwoman (now congresswoman) Michelle Steel backed Sheriff Barnes. In a February 2020 press release, she stated, "SB 54, California's Sanctuary State law, ties the hands of California local governments. This data confirms the board of supervisors' judgment in opposing SB 54. This law has increased crime and a decrease in the safety of our communities. Our first responsibility as local elected officials is to protect public safety. The state's dangerous sanctuary policy does exactly the opposite by allowing convicted criminals to be released onto the streets instead of being turned over to the proper federal authorities."

Releasing undocumented criminals onto our streets disproportionally affects communities of color. Low-income inner-city and poor rural areas pay the highest price for Sacramento's misguided radical policies. Victims are likely to be people of color, and often they are other immigrants.

We must ensure the rights of all Californians. The pendulum has swung too far in protecting those who enter our country illegally and break our laws for a second time. That has to stop.

Workplace Raid Law

Immigration is an antipoverty strategy. People flee to the U.S. to escape poverty. Any comprehensive solution must start with solving the problem of unemployment.

Assembly Bill 450 prohibits employers in California from cooperating with ICE. Employers must alert employees before immigration officials arrive at the workplace. California has no business protecting employers and employees who break federal immigration law. It is hypocritical to crack down on law-abiding employers for every minor workplace labor law infringement while condoning employers who hire illegal immigrants and pay them substandard wages.

There is a solution. Many states require employers to use E-Verify. E-Verify is a federal database that authorizes employment for legal aliens and U.S. citizens. Decreasing the participation of undocumented workers in the workforce helps those likely to compete for work with unauthorized immigrants. Wages have risen for legal immigrants in those states which use E-Verify.

Multiple studies show that E-Verify decreases illegal immigration by removing the economic incentive to migrate. Enforcement is essential for success. The threat of workplace raids and arrests increases the companies participating in E-Verify. In Arizona, for example, the implementation of E-Verify decreased the illegal immigrant population by 20 percent. Since businesses are the source of the economic incentive, it makes sense to dedicate more resources to employment verification.

Fixing the Broken System

Christian evangelical leaders have called for balanced and comprehensive immigration reform based on six principles:

1. Respect the dignity of every person.
2. Protect the unity of the family.
3. Respect the rule of law.
4. Secure national borders.
5. Ensure fairness for taxpayers.
6. Establish a path toward legal status and citizenship for those who qualify.

The Southern Baptist Convention combines the love of humankind with obedience to the law. The convention's statement on immigration offers a starting point. It honors the fact that we are a nation of immigrants and a nation of laws. It reconciles competing interests.

We need compromise to achieve immigration reform. The past administration's iron-fisted law and order approach and Gavin Newsom's open border response have both failed. Politicians fail to seek the middle ground because they don't want to solve the problem. They prefer to keep it alive to raise money. Alienating one side by declaring victory for the other creates more division, more fundraising—and more illegal immigration.

Immigration reform must be comprehensive. We cannot afford half measures. Immigration reform is a moral and economic imperative.

Secure the Border

Securing our southern border is essential to any successful immigration plan. Border enforcement must support and enforce the rule of law. Securing our borders is also a matter of national security, in line with drug enforcement goals and stopping human trafficking. We must use technology in concert with "boots on the ground" border patrol. A border fence has been built in most areas, but we must implement that across the board. The fence could be a physical or a "virtual" wall. Few people like the idea of fencing us off. Sadly, corruption and mismanagement in countries to our south mandate it.

Penalties for illegal immigration must be punitive: one strike and you're out for good, no second chances. Any new immigration legislation will be worthless without robust and consistent enforcement. We are a compassionate nation, but we are also a nation of laws.

The number of unaccompanied migrant children presently in U.S. custody has unfortunately increased, a sign of the growing crisis. Detention of illegals costs vast sums of money and does the incarcerated more harm than good, especially when separating families. We must work with Central American countries, especially Mexico, to stop the flow of migrants before they arrive at our doorstep.

Enforce Immigration Laws for Employers and Employees

Immigration has helped build California's economy into the fifth-largest economy globally, trailing only the U.S., China, Japan, and Germany. But our demographics are changing. Fewer workers in the economy mean decreased GDP and fewer workers to pay taxes. We are getting older, and our birth rate has declined to a point where we do not have enough young native workers. California needs new immigrants to generate income and pay the taxes that support baby boomers as they age into retirement.

Currently, many undocumented immigrants are paid under the table and therefore pay no payroll taxes. Immigration reform will increase the state's revenue and lessen the strain that immigration places on social services, education, and healthcare. Fixing our broken immigration system will turn legal immigrant workers into a vital and positive factor for our economy.

One major complaint you hear is that immigrants take jobs away from Americans. That's a canard. California citizens cannot fill all the open positions in low-skilled jobs like food service, janitorial, construction, and agriculture. The growth in low-wage occupations that do not require higher education or even a high school diploma will persist. Immigrants with lower education levels are filling these jobs, while a more significant percentage of U.S.-born Californians go on to college. Filling unskilled, low-wage positions with overqualified citizens would stifle the economy. We need high levels of immigration—legal immigration—to maintain or improve our standard of living.

Federal and state governments can support the sectors of the economy most dependent on low-wage low-skilled workers by creating qualification programs and quotas that are responsive to the ever-changing needs of these industries. We need to do this now.

Expand the Number of Foreign Students in Universities

We can streamline the visa process for international students going to college in California. U.S. universities attract the brightest and best students worldwide—over one million. The U.S. has more international students than number two, the United Kingdom, and number three, China combined. Other countries have caught on and are now actively recruiting more international students. California has 161,693 international students, more than any other state. USC has the most international students, followed by UCLA.

Allowing more international students to study in California offers many benefits. It draws a future talent pool here. California benefits economically from this brain gain. Many foreign tech students who attend Stanford will stay and become entrepreneurs in Silicon Valley. Foreign science students attending California universities will remain and fill critical roles in medicine and aerospace. Over half of all patent applications in the U.S. are filed by foreign nationals living in the United States, mainly Chinese and Indian. California once again leads the way in the number of patents filed by noncitizens. Let's expand the use of our universities to bring the most intelligent, most driven people to California and incentivize them to stay and create new and innovative companies in the Golden State.

The international students who choose to return to their homeland do so with affection for California and America. They have lived freely in a democracy and are likely to spread those ideas and promote democratic institutions in their homeland. Many future rulers and government officials of other countries were educated in the U.S. The list includes former U.N. secretary-general Ban Ki-moon, Taiwan's President Tsai Ing-wen, and Israel's Prime Minister Benjamin Netanyahu.

Students who return home build successful companies that do business with their friends in the United States. California is geographically positioned to benefit from international trade. For every 1 percent increase in legal immigration from a particular nation, exports from the U.S. to that nation increase by 0.5 percent. International students educated in California improve our economic and diplomatic ties with other countries.

Streamline the Immigration Process

The flow of talented individuals into our workforce allows us to innovate and maintain our competitive edge in the global marketplace. We foster innovation through cooperation among intelligent people with diverse backgrounds, varied knowledge bases, and unique perspectives on the world. Innovation allows us to compete against lower-wage countries in the global economy.

We need to streamline the immigration process. Any immigration overhaul must include technology upgrades that make the process more efficient. There should be a clearly defined process with time frames. An efficient and transparent process will alleviate some of the incentives to immigrate illegally and remove uncertainty and fear.

Partner with Religious Organizations

Many religious organizations are engaged in community outreach to immigrants. They know local resources and have their finger on the pulse of the local ethos. Religious institutions—Christian, Jewish, Muslim, Hindu, or other—can bridge connecting immigrants and the communities in which they live. Armies of volunteers stand ready to help. Religious institutions have the infrastructure to help newly arrived immigrants integrate into society.

In their immigration resolution, the Southern Baptist Convention pledged to "act receptively" and reach out to meet the physical, emotional, and spiritual needs of all immigrants, to start English classes on a massive scale, and to encourage them toward a path of legal status and/or citizenship." The Catholic Church is well-positioned to assist Catholic immigrants from Central America and already run effective outreach programs. Jewish, Chinese, and East Indian organizations are also helping.

The Canadian Model

How do we decide who gets to come and who doesn't? Canada's model is working. It includes a points system to identify workers whose skills are needed. There are six ways an applicant can earn points. Points accrue for reading, writing, listening, and speaking in the official languages of English and French. The point system incentivizes immigrants to learn the language before they apply to immigrate. Learning English has economic, social, cultural, and educational benefits for immigrants.

Immigrants can earn points for educational degrees and work experience in a chosen field. Age is another factor. Younger adults are more valuable to the economy and are given higher point values. Canada awards twelve points to eighteen- to thirty-five-year-olds. An applicant loses one point for every year of age above thirty-five. Under age eighteen and over age forty-six score no points.

People who already have the promise of employment score points based on how severe the labor shortage is in a segment of the economy. Adaptability is another factor. This category includes having relatives in the country and going to college in Canada. There are no fixed caps. The number of immigrants needed varies by year and by occupation. It is a flexible system that we can modify in times of boom or bust.

This point system is color-blind. It prioritizes what is best for Canada, not where the applicant is from, their religion, or the color of their skin. If we are serious about addressing racial inequalities in our society, such immigration reform tops the list.

Points-based systems can limit the number of legal entries each year. But the $64,000 question is: what happens to the 2.5 million illegal immigrants living in California in 2021? Amnesty is not the answer. If we did that, what would we say to the people who have patiently waited for years and have followed every rule? Illegal immigrants have broken the law and cut the line. They must follow the same rules as everyone else. It would be unfair to those who waited their turn and did it the right way.

California must find a way forward that acknowledges our heritage as a state of immigrants while respecting the rule of law and notions of fair play.

CHAPTER 19

FRANK TALK ABOUT MALE RESPONSIBILITY

To me, responsibility is one of the most important traits we humans possess. It elevates us beyond ourselves, and we become a part of something greater. It is a pillar of personal and societal character. Responsibility and love hold families together. I define life by my commitment: to my family, my fellow man, my community, my state, and my country.

In this age of instant gratification, responsibility may seem like an old-fashioned notion amid Americans' lust for individualism, freedom, and personal fulfillment. People who are not happy in their marriage are often too quick to get a divorce. People who don't want the responsibility of parenthood might get an abortion. It's in vogue to put you first and to trade everyday responsibilities for the excitement of personal autonomy and the pursuit of happiness.

I would argue that the opposite is where true happiness lies. Embracing responsibility gives our lives purpose and meaning. We find true satisfaction when we put others before ourselves and welcome our obligations. No parent who has ever watched their child graduate from high school or college would ever disagree. All the years of sacrifice, hard work, and dedication pay off. Being a responsible parent puts your children on the path to success. History is replete with examples of icons who put others before themselves: Jesus, the Good Samaritan, George Washington, Martin Luther King Jr., and Ronald Reagan, to name a few.

I am passionate about this issue. My natural father forced my mother into a sexual encounter, resulting in an unwanted pregnancy. She married my father, Albert Kaplan. They divorced soon after. Consequently, my natural father was never a part of my life. I know nothing about him.

From my history and what I see around me here in California and elsewhere, it is time for more men to step up to the plate. We need to be responsible for how we treat women and our families. Responsibility within the family means making decisions based on what is best for your spouse and children. Parents should always place the family's needs above their own. My father's irresponsible choices left my mother in a tight spot. Thankfully, my mother was an intelligent, resourceful, and strong-willed woman, as I said before. She graduated from the University of California Berkeley with two master's degrees, which was not as common back then. Her education allowed her to become the librarian at Calumet High School, a Chicago public school. In 1959, she married Thomas Cox, a postal employee, who was abusive to both of us.

As I also described it in an earlier chapter, my childhood was not idyllic, but it taught me responsibility. In recent years there has been a dramatic increase in extramarital births in the U.S. Forty percent of all children today are born out of wedlock, up 12 percent in twenty-five years or just one generation. Thirty-three percent of all California children live in single-parent homes. The breakdown of the two-parent family has deep-reaching personal, family, and community-wide effects.

Parental responsibility is a health issue. Those born into a home with no father present are at two times greater risk for infant mortality. Unmarried women have a significantly greater chance of low-birth-weight and preterm births than married mothers. Children raised in single-parent homes are two times more likely to be obese, get less physical activity, and watch more television than children of dual-parent households. Economic hardships brought about by single-parent households lead to poor nutrition and adverse health outcomes.

Parental responsibility is an economic issue. Single parenthood is a significant driver of poverty. Children who grow up in one-parent households are at four times greater risk of living in poverty. Only 8 percent of all children who live in poverty live in a home with a mother and a father. Conversely, 39 percent of all children who live in a household with no father live in poverty. Thirty-one percent of white children raised in homes with no father live in poverty, yet only 12 percent of all Black children live in poverty if both parents live in the house. This is not a racial issue—this is a responsibility issue.

Where we live is primarily dictated by economic opportunity and income. Insufficient financial resources make it difficult for families to live in safe neighborhoods with high-performing schools, green spaces, and clean air. Single mothers often need to work long hours or two jobs to make ends meet, which means more unsupervised children. It also leaves less time for things like homework, medical appointments, cultural activities, and sports. Women who raise children without a husband suffer economic consequences. They are more likely to be employed at low-wage, low-skill jobs. They face the challenge of balancing child care needs with the demands of their position or career. Irresponsible, too early fatherhood by boys and men has adverse effects on their educational attainment and economic well-being. The struggle to pay child support keeps many single fathers in poverty.

Parental responsibility is an educational issue. Absent fathers negatively impact the education of their children. Students from single-parent homes struggle academically compared to children from two-parent households. A national longitudinal study of adolescent health compared the combined GPA in English and math between dual and single-family homes. Kids from intact families had an average GPA of 2.9, while the GPA for students from disrupted families was 2.5. Families without a father present have lower educational expectations and higher suspension and dropout rates. The lowest-performing adolescents with the highest risk of failing to graduate high school are students who don't know their father's identity. Students from disrupted families are less likely to attend or graduate from college.

Men who grew up without a father are more likely to become absent fathers. Women who had no father figure are at greater risk of single parenthood. Boys without a father present have more behavioral problems, while girls experience more emotional issues. Girls with no father figure begin sexual activity sooner and engage in more risky sexual behavior. Daughters raised without a father are seven times more likely to become pregnant as a teenager. The cycle of single parenthood and poverty continues.

I submit, backed by statistical evidence, that the principal factor for the increase in crime in California is the lack of married parents. Recent studies that point out a standard narrative about the links between crime and economic status or race are wrong. The primary reason for the increase in crime is the breakdown of the two-parent family. Teens with no father figure are more likely to commit crimes and carry guns. They are more likely to get in trouble with the law and enter the criminal justice system. Teens with absent fathers are 249 percent more likely to deal drugs and have an 80 percent greater chance of being incarcerated.

Fatherlessness costs California money. When a father fails to support his family financially or emotionally, the state bears part of the cost. Fatherless families rely more on public assistance for healthcare, housing, and child care expenses. Seventy-five percent of single mothers receive government assistance like CalFresh (food stamps) or TANF (welfare).

Fathers play a critical role in the development and well-being of their children. A father is a foundation upon which a child builds their sense of self. Fathers help shape children into the person they will become. Fathers provide their children with physical and emotional security. They establish the structure and rules children need to thrive and become good citizens. They set expectations and boundaries. Males in the home nurture, teach, guide, and provide a positive role model.

As more women have entered the workforce, traditional roles have evolved. Males have taken on greater responsibility in raising children, partly out of necessity because the mother is at work. Men assuming more child-rearing responsibilities has multiple benefits for the family. The mother can pursue her career, thereby improving the family's financial stability. The father is more present to connect and build stronger bonds with their children.

Children raised in a home with an involved father have better social skills, exhibit more empathy, and get along better with their peers. They are better at impulse control and show less aggression. Fathers improve the self-confidence of their children when they are actively involved.

Fathers and mothers parent differently, and this benefits kids. Fathers encourage competition and independence more than mothers. Mothers are more adept at sympathy and creating a sense of security. Mothers protect their children, while dads encourage them to push their limits. The different parenting styles complement each other and facilitate more well-rounded kids who will be confident enough to expand their experiences and prudent enough to be safe.

Fathers and mothers discipline differently, which creates a healthy balance where children feel loved but held accountable for their actions. Fathers provide more consequences and enforce them more rigidly than mothers. Males stress fairness, justice, and duty. Females place greater importance on grace and sympathy. Dads tend to be more rule based, and moms are more relationship based when they discipline. Spouses will often modify their discipline styles and meet closer to the middle.

Fathers are more objective in their views about their kids than mothers. Dads are more honest and tell it like it is more than moms. Fathers are more likely to tell their offspring that they need to adapt to the world, while mothers believe the world should adapt to their children. Mothers protect their young from the cruelty and injustice of the world; fathers prepare them for it.

Fathers play differently than mothers. They engage in more active, rough-and-tumble activities that are more random than mothers play.

These capricious interactions prepare children for the unexpected experiences they will face growing up.

Students from two-parent homes get better grades in school. If the father actively participates in their child's schooling, children get more A's. One study showed that fathers' frequent involvement in literacy activities and play led to preschoolers' improved reading and math scores. Students living with both parents are 60 percent less likely to be suspended from school.

Involved fathers have a positive effect on the cognitive development of their children. Another study found a six point higher IQ at thirty-six months for children living in a two-parent home. Children who live with an involved dad are less prone to depression and other mental health issues. Children raised with a positive paternal presence are more likely to become good parents themselves. This positive cycle benefits our families, communities, and states today and in future generations.

In taking responsibility for myself and my family, I overcame the challenges I faced early in life. I am grateful that I had the drive and support when I needed it to succeed. Not everyone is so lucky. Many children have it much worse than I ever did. But some responsible adults are helping by becoming mentors. I spoke with Bob Goetsch, the founder of Be a Mentor, Inc., via Zoom call on the type of sunny spring day that reminds us why we love California. His nonprofit organization partners with schools, agencies, companies, and individuals to provide mentors for at-risk youth in California. The organization seeks to help children and youth from challenging circumstances make healthy life choices, set realistic goals, act with determination, and build successful lives through direct contact and relationships with caring and positive adult role models.

By providing management services and software on a large scale, Goetsch reduces the cost of mentorship. Be a Mentor recruits, performs background checks, and trains mentors. It provides education and coaching to their partners. It also brings money to the table through corporate funding and federal grants.

Goetsch told me, "We work with partners that already work with kids but do not have a mentoring component. We bring that mentoring component to them." Goetsch works with Bay Area Community Resources, which has over one hundred after-school programs in the San Francisco Bay Area. "They're mostly inner-city kids, mostly underserved, probably underperforming in school. They could very much use a mentor, an adult in their life to talk to, encourage, and review how they're doing in school to determine if they need tutors or some intervention," Goetsch said. Be a Mentor works in Los Angeles, helping organizations provide mentors for foster youth. "This is a perfect example of where kids need a mentor in their life. The outcomes for former foster youth are horrific when it comes to incarceration, substance abuse, and homelessness. Through no fault of their own, they are in situations where they need a lot of help." Mentors provide that help. They are the stable, reliable adult these kids crave.

Mentors are an adult that at-risk youth can trust. They can tell their mentor their problems without fear of retribution or punishment. Mentors provide critical support in a safe environment. Young people find an older, wiser person to rely on to have their best interests at heart. Mentors help connect kids and families to the appropriate services available to them.

Goetsch said, "Sometimes the mentors don't even see it. They don't feel like they're making a difference in that child's life. Sometimes it takes three or four years before the impact of having a role model makes a difference in the mentees' decisions. Other times it's seen very quickly. School performance improves, and the number of absences goes down. Sometimes it's just being accountable to someone who's looking after them and is genuinely interested in their well-being."

Mentees have decreased absences, discipline problems, and suspensions from school. They are less likely to do drugs and drop out of high school. When students interact with a mentor, their school grades and participation improve. Students who have a mentor are 55 percent more likely to attend college.

Goetsch told me about one particular mentee. "There was a young girl, a freshman in high school. She got paired with a city clerk in Fremont.

This girl wanted a mentor because she didn't want to follow her family members who had become gang members; she wanted to take a different path," Goetsch said. When the girl's grades were not improving, the mentor went to the girl's house. "It was a revolving door of people in and out, in and out. The girl had no place to study," Goetsch said. The mentor began bringing the girl into city hall every day after school, where she had a quiet and safe place to study in the company of supportive, caring adults. "She started going there every afternoon, and voila, her grades began to improve. This girl was a brilliant young woman. The workers at City Hall liked her so much they gave her a part-time job," Goetsch related. She became the first person in her family to go to college and graduated from San Francisco State University. Goetsch continued, "A number of years went by, and we didn't hear from her. A few years later, I got a letter from her that said she had started a program in New York City to provide mentors to underserved girls."

Mentors provide a positive and supportive adult in the lives of children who face challenges in their home life. Mentors assist with education, goal-setting, and life plans. They help young people make positive choices about their future. Mentoring programs provide structure and support in a safe setting, providing stability to kids living chaotic home lives. Excursions offer opportunities for new experiences and personal growth. Mentors help young people reach their full potential and become caring, responsible citizens.

The benefits to society are multifaceted. For every youth who turns away from a life of crime, California saves $1.7–$2.3 million. It costs $2,000 per year to mentor at-risk youth. Drug treatment costs ten times that much, and juvenile incarceration costs one hundred times more. Many young men who have no role model in their lives turn to gangs for a sense of belonging and acceptance. Mentorship provides an alternative to gangs. Mentorship reduces crime, which means fewer victims of crime and safer streets for us all. Having an adult who is responsible for at-risk girls reduces teen pregnancy and allows girls the opportunity to finish school and establish a career. Mentorship reduces the cycle of poverty and gives kids a fighting chance.

The government bears some responsibility to promote two-parent households. Public assistance regulations and tax policies should provide incentives for dual-parent homes. Study after study has shown that increasing public assistance leads to a growth in out-of-wedlock births. After the National Welfare Reform Act of 1996, single-parent households declined slightly across the U.S. The act was a comprehensive bipartisan welfare reform plan intended to transform the nation's welfare system by requiring work in exchange for assistance. This law includes a performance bonus that rewards states for moving welfare recipients into jobs. We need to give people a hand up, not a handout.

I believe California should partner with religious organizations to strengthen our families. Most faith-based organizations have deep roots in their communities. They have extensive, experienced organizations in place. Some people may view governmental institutions with distrust, but faith-based organizations have earned the trust of their communities. Religious organizations understand the mores and customs of their congregants. Their reach and influence are multigenerational.

California can partner with the private sector to improve the climate for dual-parent households. Financial security leads to more stable families and better outcomes for children. California can ensure people have access and pathways to good-paying jobs by providing job and technical training. Industry-driven and sector-based job training programs form a partnership between the public and private sectors. These programs successfully place trainees because they provide the skilled workers employers need.

Early intervention and childhood education give us the highest return on our investment. Early intervention is a cost-effective way to improve children's long-term health and educational outcomes. The word gap between higher socioeconomic children and poor children by the age of three is three million. Reach Out and Read is a nonprofit that gives books to pediatricians to promote literacy during office visits. Pediatricians educate parents about the benefits of reading aloud to children daily. Reach

Out and Read partnered with other nonprofits and private entities like Scholastic Books to put fifty thousand books in pediatric offices and medical clinics serving 4.5 million low-income children across the country.

Education increases responsible decision-making. Fifty-nine percent of high school–educated mothers gave birth out of wedlock. Only 10 percent of mothers with bachelor's degrees or higher had children out of wedlock. Increasing school choice leads to improved educational outcomes. Low-income families become trapped in low-performing schools in impoverished neighborhoods with long odds of making it out and breaking the cycle of poverty. School choice vouchers, which I discussed in an earlier chapter, give families a fighting chance.

We need to embrace our responsibilities, not run from them. The family unit is the bedrock of American society. Two-parent families lay a solid foundation for children to build a bright future. It is the solemn responsibility of the fathers, mothers, and political leaders to do everything in our power to protect and encourage two-parent families for the good of our children, our communities, our state, our nation, and our future. Reproductive responsibility for men and women is part of this picture. Prevention of unwanted pregnancies means making responsible decisions about sex. Currently, 23 percent of all pregnancies in California end in abortion. Abortion should never be considered a form of family planning.

I am unalterably opposed to abortion. It is morally wrong to take any life because all life is sacred and must be protected. Taking a human life is the most irresponsible decision someone can make. I believe there are better solutions to unwanted pregnancies than killing a defenseless fetus. In many ways, the Supreme Court decision in *Dobbs* is going to help start a national dialogue about this important issue, one that I hope emphasizes the responsibility of parenting and the life an unborn fetus rather than the "right" to dispose of an inconvenient burden on a woman. It could well be argued as well that with the advent and availability of birth control, abortion should be unneeded.

I spoke over the phone to Wynette Sills of Californians for Life one April afternoon in 2021. Californians for Life provides alternatives to abortion and supports mothers throughout the maternity process. The organization believes abortion is the most critical social justice issue of our generation. Its mission is to help women so that abortion becomes unthinkable in California.

Director Sills explained why she dedicates her life to the pro-life cause. "Our value is not dependent on the circumstances in which we were conceived, it's not dependent upon our size, or our level of development, or intellectual capacity, or location," Sills told me. I stand with those who believe in equality for everyone regardless of their circumstances.

One-fifth of all abortions in the U.S. takes place in California. Under Governor Newsom's liberal, pro-abortion agenda, California is fast becoming a popular abortion destination for women across the U.S. It has done nothing but accelerate after the *Dobbs* decision as Newsom sees a political advantage in making California the abortion capital of the country. Given that, Sills explains a way forward. "For any procedure, for any product in the marketplace, there is a supply and a demand. We can't do anything about the supply side here in California," she explained. "Our Democratic leaders have made them free and readily accessible, and every bit of legislation promotes more abortions. Where we have been successful is in decreasing demand. We can work together across party lines to do everything we can to decrease the demand side of abortion."

I spoke via Zoom to Susan Arnall, the director of outreach and engagement for the Right to Life League in April 2021. The Right to Life League is America's first pro-life education and service organization dedicated to preserving human life from conception to death. It provides various services for abortion alternatives, including the expertise to navigate the complex web of state regulations for women's reproductive health clinics and other pro-life entities. Its West Coast Maternity Home Association program connects a network of California residential maternity homes that support women who choose to keep their babies and need housing.

Pro-life groups believe advances in science, especially ultrasound and intrauterine videos, have led to a better understanding that life begins in the womb. Arnall told me, "Science is on our side. We're not science deniers. In fact, the pro-life industry embraces science. At ten weeks, you can hear the baby's heartbeat. It has fingernails, bones, an upper lip, a nose and ears, hair, and all of its major organs, including its sex organs. It has all of its teeth."

Wynette Sills agrees. As she maintains, "We are inherently human from the moment of conception, and science supports that premise. It's not based on faith—you don't need to be a Christian to arrive at that position. We are data and science-based in our opinions. We see that the trend of abortions going down is reflective of the science we all know to be true."

Sills is right. Abortions have been decreasing steadily in California since their high-water mark in 1990. It is estimated that 132,680 women received abortions in 2017, a 3 percent decrease from 2014. I say estimated because California does not require clinicians to report abortions, so there is no official count of the number of abortions performed in California each year.

This is just one more example of how the Democrats and Gavin Newsom use regulations to create an unequal playing field. Why aren't we keeping track of how many abortions are performed each year in a state that overregulates everything? This is a significant healthcare statistic. "Intentionally killing someone is never healthcare," Sills told me. "And we don't end poverty by killing poor children."

Sacramento selectively uses regulations to push its agenda and punish those who dare to oppose their views. California passed a law mandating that pro-life centers post abortion ads touting free, state-funded abortions. The Supreme Court of the United States struck down this law as unconstitutional in 2018.

California recently passed a law requiring the University of California and California State University campuses to provide abortion services free of charge at their student health clinics. Gavin Newsom signed it, even though Jerry Brown vetoed it in 2018. Sills told me, "It will turn each of our University of California and Cal State University health centers into abortion clinics." Sills explained the chemical abortion protocol. "The termination of a baby human life is achieved with a two-pill process, and that is now going to be provided at student health centers on campus with young women far from family, far from support." The first pill kills the baby, and the second induces contractions to expel the aborted fetus. The process is painful, physically and psychologically.

Pro-choice solutions should include real choices for women who need help. Californians for Life argued for funding for alternatives to abortion. "The legislature had no concern whatsoever about providing women with a full spectrum of choice, information, and resources," Sills explained. Pro-life groups want to empower women by providing them with choices and opportunities. "We were advocating for on-campus student housing for single parents or young families, or available on-campus subsidized child-care so that any young lady with aspirations of completing her education goals can get a college degree. She would feel like she had real choices in all this instead of abortion, abortion, and more abortion. Not only paid for at taxpayer expense but also tacked on to everyone's tuition."

Politicians in Sacramento use regulations to stack all the odds in favor of abortion. Sills spoke about "the exclusive one-sided abortion-only perspective that the dominant party in our state and our governor" promulgate. Pro-life groups just want a fair shake. Director Sills noted a new law that requires all insurance companies to waive all copays and deductibles for abortion services. Why can't the same deductible and copay waiver apply to women who wish to give their baby up for adoption? If you see your doctor because you plan to keep your child, why shouldn't you deserve the same breaks? Sills said, "It's such an imbalance towards the culture of death and ending a child's life rather than equipping and encouraging and empowering women to be all they can be while caring for the life of her child. We think that's something all Californians can agree about."

The most significant way Sacramento tips the scales in their favor is by controlling the flow of money. Arnall told me, "The abortion industry, including Planned Parenthood, doesn't have to fundraise. All of these little nonprofits and religious organizations have to go begging hat in hand for charity. Planned Parenthood and abortion providers don't have to do that. All they need is somebody on K Street lobbying for them." Medi-Cal and private insurance companies must pay for abortions; there are no out-of-pocket costs to the patient. The average first-trimester abortion costs about $700. That cost increases by about another $500 for a second-trimester abortion. Multiply that by 132,680 abortions a year, and the money involved is staggering.

At its core, abortion is a civil rights issue. Arnall explained, "Unborn people are still people. Unborn babies are human. I don't understand how people can deny the humanity of an unborn baby. We have to reverse that. We have to start respecting each other's rights. That comes from the top down, from leaders who believe that and want to ensure that the individual's rights are protected. Rights start with the individual. And the youngest and most vulnerable individual is the unborn child."

Arnall said, "What we're seeing is a harming of our culture, our American culture founded on the Judeo-Christian belief that our rights come from God, not government. That is because of the government policies that are being put in place. We have a secular government trying to replace God in our society."

I stand in solidarity with those who protect the rights of women and unborn children. We are all equally valuable in God's eyes. We need to return to the Judeo-Christian roots that made our country the envy of the world.

The nuclear family is the pillar upon which a stable and productive society rests. Men, we must step up to the plate and assume our responsibilities—a life of purpose is its own reward. Our responsibility is to cherish the family unit and work tirelessly to provide a loving, stable home environment. When there is peace and harmony in the family, individuals prosper, and society thrives.

CHAPTER 20

GAVIN NEWSOM'S PANDEMIC BLUNDERS

The COVID era has proven a time without precedent. In 2020, we had a contentious, divisive national election cycle. Many are still licking wounds from a hard-fought battle. COVID continues to present an international health and economic crisis.

The pandemic's impact, and the actions of those in power, have penetrated beyond our wallets into our psyches. The government's response has been appalling. The holidays are usually a time of cheer and gratitude when families can gather in their homes, sing the songs of their faith, break bread with their children, reflect, and look ahead. During the height of the COVID waves, the government had other ideas for American families.

No Singing, No Cheer, Just Government

In my home state of California, Governor Gavin Newsom and mayors told people they could not gather in their own homes for holiday events with "non-household members." For the first time in history, government banned private holiday gatherings—an astounding thing.

The elites in Sacramento proved out of touch with the challenges most Californians have faced during this pandemic. They extended their regulatory reach beyond Thanksgiving, beyond the classroom, and into our homes. The California Department of Health put out a chillingly titled, **"Mandatory Requirements for All Gatherings."** Below the bolded title is the warning: "All persons planning to host or participate in a private gathering, as defined above, must comply with the following requirements. Local health jurisdictions may be more restrictive than this guidance. Refer to your local guide for what is allowed in your area."

The mandates read like a wartime occupation poster:

1. Attendance
    - Gatherings that include more than three households are prohibited—including everyone present, including hosts and guests.
    - The host should collect the names of all attendees and contact information in case contact tracing is needed later.

2. Gather Outdoors
    - All gatherings must be held outside. Attendees may go inside to use restrooms as long as the restrooms are frequently sanitized.

3. Practice Physical Distancing and Hand Hygiene at Gatherings
    - For any gatherings permitted under this guidance, the space must be large enough so that everyone at a gathering can maintain at least a 6-foot physical distance from others (not including their own household) at all times.

4. Wear a Face Covering to Keep COVID-19 from Spreading
    - People at gatherings may remove their face coverings briefly to eat or drink as long as they stay at least 6 feet away from everyone outside their own household and put their face covering back on as soon as they are done with the activity.

5. Keep it Short
    - Gatherings should be two hours or less.

6. Rules for Singing, Chanting and Shouting at Outdoor Gatherings
    - Singing, chanting, and shouting are strongly discouraged. People who are singing or chanting are strongly encouraged to do so quietly (at or below the volume of a normal speaking voice).

The government said, quite literally, that you can't sing in your own home. Even the staunchest liberal would take issue with that, and the bans were widely mocked and criticized across the state. Some were able to find humor in the ridiculousness; comedian and actor Rob Schneider tweeted: "*Dear Emperor Gavin Newsom, during our allotted three family limits this Thanksgiving, if my Aunt comes over, can I throw her a slice of turkey from the window? We promise not to sing; we will all just whisper.*"

Actor James Woods pointed out the governor's hypocrisy when he tweeted: "*Just make a few signs protesting Trump. Then invite as many people as you want, and you'll have no problem.*"

The national news media went along for the ride. CNN published an article titled "How to Decline Thanksgiving in the Name of COVID" with a hectoring subheader reading: "Note the rules" as if they were in charge of your private life. The same day, Dr. Anthony Fauci, who was leading the COVID-19 task force in the federal government, commented to CNBC that the U.S. "has an independent spirit but now is the time to do what you're told." CNN's Jake Tapper looked into the camera and said, "Christmas is probably not going to be possible."

Thank you for canceling Christmas.

Three years ago, any one of these statements would have seemed ludicrous to the average American and would have resulted in the swift loss of the offender's job. Now they occur too frequently. What happened? Political overreach! And here's a little secret about giving the people in power more power: bureaucrats won't want to go back to the way things were before. We can't, as Americans, let that happen. One year they canceled Christmas and closed schools. Next year, it could be your ability to drive your car daily because of "environmental concerns." We must reverse course and restore our freedoms.

Rules for Thee, but Not for Me

If we trace the timeline of COVID-19's arrival into the United States and the government response, we can see how we got into such a mess. On January 21, 2020, the first confirmed coronavirus case in the United States was a man in his thirties who had recently traveled to Wuhan, China. A few weeks later, on January 26, 2020, the Centers for Disease Control confirmed California's first coronavirus case in Orange County. California got it early—this was only the third coronavirus case in the United States. In Southern California, as with major metropolitan areas across the nation, cases rose throughout February. In early March, Governor Newsom declared a statewide emergency, which still exists two years later at this writing, and announced that cities like Los Angeles would be going into a shutdown for "two weeks to flatten the curve." Remember that little white lie?

The time since then became a nonstop parade of business closures, governmental blunders, and power grabs by—who else?—special-interest groups. I'll give you a few examples of how corruption curbed freedom and competition in California. Early on in this pandemic, beginning in April, 2020, twenty-six states changed their laws to allow pharmacies to do COVID testing. California was not one of them. This inaction prevented many Californians from getting tested.

Why did that happen? The time-honored rule prevails: follow the money. Many healthcare providers fund politicians. For that, they receive insider status for government regulations and restrict access for competitors. Pharmacies are the competitors of big lab companies and big hospitals. The result was not good for the public but good for the special-interest groups making money off COVID tests. The government mandates

COVID tests for travel, work, and the like, while simultaneously deciding which companies are authorized to perform those tests. The money comes out of the public's bank accounts.

A similar thing happened with the schools. Even after it became scientifically evident that elementary and middle schools were not a significant vector point for COVID-19, the teachers' unions fought tooth and nail to keep schools shut down. They ran large social media campaigns that preyed on people's emotions.

The teachers' unions failed to consider that schools are essential to our society. Remaining out of school damages our children and negatively impacts their futures. Low-income children bear the brunt of the harm because they don't have the technology or parental support to learn from home effectively. The continual political squabbling, finger-pointing, and delays kept our children out of school for over an entire year.

As of April 2021, less than half of all California schoolchildren could return to school. Sixty-two percent of elementary school students have the option to return, while only 37 percent of middle schoolers and 39 percent of high school students receive in-person instruction, primarily in half-day hybrid models. While other states opened schools successfully, California fell behind. As of April 2021, 92 percent of Texas students and 100 percent of students in Florida were back in class five days a week. Thirty-four states had 80 percent or more of their students back in classrooms every day. The percentage of California students receiving in-person instruction was 41.8 percent: dead last in the nation.

Predictably, low-income students faced the most challenges in the distance learning model. Forty-three percent of students living in poverty in California had inconsistent internet and computer access. Sixteen percent reported having no internet at all. Many lower-income students came from single-parent homes where the primary caregiver was employed and could not help with distance learning.

Higher-income families reported more instructional time online with a teacher than lower-income families, further widening the divide. Higher-performing schools in more affluent districts required teachers to interact online with students for three or more hours daily. Many schools in low-income areas required no live interaction at all. There were multiple reports of entire schools just throwing in the towel, providing no instruction whatsoever .

The parents of low-income children were often preoccupied with adult problems like paying the rent and putting food on the table. One-third reported missing their current rent or mortgage payment. Four in ten African American parents with school-aged children said they did not have sufficient food. Reliance on schools for nutrition for students, as well as parents, skyrocketed.

Hospitals were open, and healthcare workers worked, and they didn't consider themselves martyrs. Grocery stores were open. Many restaurants offered outdoor seating. Many people working took the risk because they had to and because it was the right thing for the country. Yet the teachers' unions here shut down the schools and prevailed on Newsom to block private schools from opening. They did not want the competition because cheap alternatives would have popped up immediately. They knew that most people wanted to send their kids to school. They didn't want people escaping their system, so they held the welfare of our children hostage.

That is a pretty tough pill to swallow if you're a parent and yet another example of how the system needs to eliminate competition to feed itself and stay alive. We must demand the freedom to *choose* where and how our kids go to school. Parents should have that right. It shouldn't be up to a bureaucrat's whim.

The Los Angeles Unified School District's teachers' union, United Teachers Los Angeles (UTLA), fought every attempt to open schools until their litany of demands were satisfied. The delay happened even though most other districts around the country had already safely opened. A study of two thousand German schoolchildren who returned to school found no difference in COVID transmission rates for children attending in-person instruction and distance learners. Twenty-two European Union countries reported no increase in coronavirus cases after schools were open. This information was available in the summer before the traditional opening of schools in late August. Yet Gavin Newsom buckled to pressure from the UTLA and CTA, ignored science, and closed schools.

Since then, study after study has shown that opening the schools was safe. Governor Newsom has repeatedly stated that he would base his response on science, not politics. Newsom said in a statement, "As we contemplate reopening parts of our state, we must be guided by science and data…" The United States Centers for Disease Control recently published two studies that concluded: "there has been little evidence that schools have contributed meaningfully to increased community transmission." The CDC weighed in with this statement, that due to "the disproportionate impact that school closures can have on those with the least economic means kindergarten through grade 12 schools should be the last settings to close after all other mitigation measures have been employed and the first to reopen when they can do so safely." Later, CDC restated its strong opinion: "Given the crucial services schools offer and the benefits of in-person learning, it is critical for K–12 schools to open and remain open for in-person instruction, as safely and as soon as possible." Here is the grim reality: politics, not science, guided Gavin Newsom's pandemic response.

Parents had enough. They were stressed out trying to work or work from home *and* be the de facto teachers for their children. Many had to quit their jobs or pay out of pocket for childcare or tutors. Many dutifully stayed home to flatten the curve. That sense of duty turned to outrage as they watched their children suffer while the unions, the school districts, and the governor dither, negotiate, and ignore science.

Nine Los Angeles Unified School District parents filed a lawsuit against the local teachers' union to reopen schools. Shella Sadovnik, an attorney for Freedom First, represents the nine LAUSD parents who filed suit on April 1, 2021, against United Teachers Los Angeles, union president Cecily Myart-Cruz, the executive director of UTLA, and the Los Angeles Unified School District (LAUSD). The essence of the suit is that LAUSD schools have remained closed for over a year and children "continue to be harmed without scientific, legal, or moral justification." They contend that UTLA unlawfully denies children access to the type of education guaranteed by our state constitution. The UTLA even went as far as to say that defunding the police and Medicare for All were demands that needed to be met before they would return to school. These were clearly political demands unrelated to educating children and made clear that their actions were about political power, not children.

I spoke with Shella Sadovnik by video call. From her office, she told me, "Our lawsuit was really about trying to get parents to have a say in the negotiations between the union and the district because those negotiations are about the kids. No one is there to represent the students' rights in that labor negotiation." Sadovnik explained that students are third-party beneficiaries of the collective bargaining agreement and should be given a seat at the table because the outcome affects their constitutional right to an education.

Imagine that: caring about what kids and parents want when it comes to schooling! I wonder if that thought has crossed the minds of union leaders. "No one is listening to the parents," Sadovnik told me. "They've done everything they can, but their voices are not being heard. So, we had to file a lawsuit to make something happen." It's a travesty that the demands of a powerful, private labor union are obstructing the education of our children. It's symbolic of how special-interest groups have taken over Sacramento, that even our children are not safe from their influence.

Sadovnik and the suit lay the blame squarely at the foot of UTLA. "They are a private organization, and they held up the ability of students to go back to school," she said. "They are not an elected official; they're not even a public organization. They're a private organization that collects $46 million a year in dues, and they kept the kids hostage for over a year."

The fallout from all the missed in-person instruction is that two out of three students in Los Angeles are currently below grade level in literacy and math. This percentage increases for students of color. As our have-and-have-nots gap widens, California has devoted vast resources to closing the achievement gap for low-income students and students of color, erasing all the gains we have made have in one year. Those suffering the most significant learning loss are students of color, English language learners, socioeconomically disadvantaged children, students with disabilities, and kindergarteners.

All of the children in the lawsuit have suffered learning loss due to the lack of engagement inherent in Zoom distance learning. Special needs students included in the suit did not have their educational, emotional, or social needs met. The most vulnerable were those affected the most. Sadovnik said, "There's the emotional element of all this. The suffering the children have endured is just beyond belief." Many of the plaintiffs' school-aged children have experienced severe emotional problems, including depression. Two told their parents they wanted to commit suicide and are in counseling.

Mental health experts are concerned about the effects of isolating children for over a year. A child's peer interaction is critical for his or her socioemotional development. Children report higher degrees of loneliness, fear, and irritability. Doctors warn of increased rates of childhood depression, anxiety, and post-traumatic stress. The number of children counseled for suicidal thoughts has increased dramatically.

What was the response from the United Teachers Los Angeles? The union negotiated a two-hour decrease in the minimum workday requirement for the 2021–2022 school year after decreasing it by four hours, at full salary, at the end of 2021. Teachers will receive fifteen hours of extra payment to set up their rooms and thirty minutes extra pay every day for no particular reason. That is a cash grab of about $2.2 million a week by just teachers in Los Angeles. Schools cannot reopen until all teachers who want them have received both doses of the vaccine. Every student and teacher must be COVID-19 tested seven days before school begins and every two weeks after that.

The union did not stop there. They laid out their political demands: defunding the police, a single-payer public healthcare system, increased funding to cure the homeless problem, new programs to combat systemic racism, and elimination of charter schools. Of course, there will have to be new taxes levied to pay for their left-wing utopia.

The school district must provide students a solid education. Sadovnik explained, "Kids are required to attend school. If they are required to be in school and taxpayers pay $15,000 per child a year to go to public school, there is a duty owed to the students. It's not like, here's $15,000 a year in taxes, and here's my child, their body, their mental well-being—but you don't owe any duty to us. You can do whatever you want with them. The union has interfered with that duty because even if the district wanted to open, they can't open. The union is preventing them."

The plaintiffs' children returned to hybrid instruction in April 2021 after over a year of distance learning from home. The quality of teaching hardly improved. "The kids come to the classroom. They sit with noise-canceling headphones and watch the teacher teaching on their computer while a volunteer oversees all the kids sitting in the classroom," Savodnik said. There has been wide criticism of this "Zoom in a room" model.

A scathing report detailed the negative impacts on students. Forty percent of middle school and high school students in Los Angeles attended no classes from March to June at the end of last school year. Only 36 percent were actively engaged. The criterion for actively engaged? How is that defined? Signing in to the digital platform does not mean the student completed any school work. The percentage of Black and Latino middle school and high school students who signed in each day was less than 25 percent.

"We can't forget who the cause of this is," Savodnik said. "It is Governor Newsom in the sense that he didn't stand up to the unions that donate millions of dollars to him every year. They buy him out. If I were to say who's to blame, it's the unions pushing their own agendas, which is not good for the kids and the flimsy, pathetic politicians that kowtow to them because they are bought out by them."

At least Governor Newsom felt our pain. He was a self-described "Zoom school parent." On March 16, 2021, he told CNN, "I have four young kids myself. I've been living through Zoom school and all the challenges related to it." His children returned to their in-person private school in October 2020. The San Juan Unified School District, in which Newsom lives, reopened K–5 on March 22. The parents staged a virtual sit-in to protest the failure to reopen public schools.

The hypocrisy of lockdown restrictions left Californians angry and confused. Governor Newsom praised protestors who gathered in the thousands and ignored social distancing guidelines. Around the same time, he told Californians to skip the Fourth of July celebrations, "Please, avoid those crowds. We're going to do our best to try to mitigate people congregating." Really? That is not what it looked like on my TV. I watched from my house, dutifully following the pandemic regulations and recommendations as you probably did, while people broke lockdown rules and gathered by the thousands. Our leaders called it a civic duty to protest police brutality by looting and burning police cars. But they called it a crime to celebrate the birth of our nation with hot dogs and fireworks.

KCBS Radio's Doug Sovern interviewed Governor Newsom. He asked Newsom, "I've heard from several people who don't understand why they're being told you can't go see Grandpa this weekend, you can't see Uncle Joe, you can't have a barbecue with your neighbors, but then they turn on the TV and see hundreds or thousands of people protesting. So can you explain the selective enforcement or preferential treatment given based on political persuasion? Can you explain to people why they should listen to these messages when they do see that happening, and no one is getting tickets, no one is even being told to enforce the masks or social distancing?"

On November 6, a few days after Gavin Newsom told Californians not to gather for Thanksgiving in their own homes, he was spotted having dinner with at least twelve people at the French Laundry restaurant, where a dinner runs from $350 to $450 per person. The *San Francisco Chronicle* first reported the story. He was there to celebrate the birthday of Jason Kinney, a partner at the lobbying firm Axiom Advisors.

Dining with over ten people from multiple households was forbidden, as was any indoor dining. Newsom broke both rules, and falsely claimed the dinner was outside. Photographic evidence proved the lie. The wine bill was $12,000. A Californian making minimum wage would have to work for about half a year to pick up that tab. Dining indoors with wealthy political campaign contributors while average Californians were locked down, unemployed, and worried about how they would meet their rent or mortgage payments symbolized the disconnect between the liberal elite in Sacramento and the rest of us.

Drug manufacturers created vaccines in record time after the federal government's Operation Warp Speed reduced the usual approval process. California was unprepared for the vaccines shipped to the states. As of April 2021, California ranked twenty-fifth of all states in administering the vaccines delivered. The primary reason for the rollout delay was Governor Newsom's plan to vaccinate all healthcare workers and long-term care residents before anyone else, including those at the highest risk. Other states like Texas started giving vaccines to high-risk groups immediately and got a two-and-a-half-month head start. Governor Newsom came under attack because the healthcare workers and seniors who received vaccines were primarily white. At the same time, the high-risk groups, predominantly people of color, were forced to wait. Hispanics aged twenty to fifty-four were eight and a half times more likely to die of COVID than whites of the same age. There were no eligibility criteria that prioritized Black or Latino Californians, even though they composed most COVID cases, hospitalizations, and deaths.

The Republican governor of Texas, Greg Abbott, opened Texas up 100 percent and lifted the mask mandate on March 10. Governor Newsom finally relented to open California up on June 15, over three months after Texas, and, interestingly, only after the Gubernatorial recall became a reality. Texas has about 860,000 fewer cases of COVID and 11,000 fewer deaths than California. The unemployment rate is 1.7 percent lower in Texas than it is in California. That works out to about 300,000 Californians that could have been working if California had opened up sooner.

Californians were fed up. Other states opened without a problem while Californians sat and waited, losing patience and money by the hour. While Newsom dithered, people were losing their businesses and homes. His approval rating plummeted due to his inept handling of the pandemic and vaccine rollout. His hypocrisy and condescending manner haven't helped his cause either.

Every state across the union faced a health crisis. What differed was how they responded to the challenges presented by the novel coronavirus. Florida and California are diverse states with a large population of senior citizens and people of color—two groups at high risk for severe illness from COVID. Let's compare Florida's response to the pandemic with California's.

The Republican governor of Florida, Ron DeSantis, essentially allowed businesses to stay open with modified health guidelines like voluntary mask wearing and social distancing. He adopted the Swedish model of allowing society to remain open while protecting those at higher risk. DeSantis refused to issue a statewide mask mandate. Schools and restaurants remained open. Disneyworld, Florida, reopened in July 2020 and has reported no outbreaks. Disneyland, California, finally reopened at 25 percent capacity on April 30, 2021. The businesses that rely on the Disney theme park in Florida have been booming, while in California, these businesses continued to feel the pain of Gavin Newsom's misguided pandemic response.

The strategy paid off for Florida. Florida's death rate among seniors was 20 percent lower than California's. Their deaths per 100,000 residents were similar to California's. Florida's March 2021 unemployment rate was 4.7 percent, while California's was 8.3 percent. California lost over a million more jobs than Florida.

The differences in how Governor DeSantis and Gavin Newsom managed the crisis is stark. Good management comes from good leadership. Florida's example has proven that to Californians.

The Cost We Must Incur

The toll on the state's economy has been devastating. Future economists will earn PhDs analyzing just how much this pandemic has cost California. In 2020, California's unemployment rose higher than all but two states. At the end of 2020, California had 1.5 million fewer jobs than in February 2020 before the pandemic hit. Many were low-paying service sector jobs that hit Black and Latino families the hardest. Unemployment for those at or below the poverty line reached 26 percent. Low-skilled, low-paying jobs have been slow to return. The unemployment rate for Los Angeles County was still at 11.3 percent over one year after the shutdown began. As of this writing, it has dropped to 4 percent but many of those jobs are low wage restaurant positions.

***

California is home to 4.1 million small businesses. With small businesses making up 99.8 percent of all companies in California, employing 48.5 percent of all workers in the state, it's devastating that over half of all small businesses reported significant effects from the shutdown, including closure, layoffs, and missed payments. Consumer spending declined by 37 percent in April 2020, as opposed to 32 percent nationwide. In November, consumer spending in California still lagged behind the rest of the country by 6 percent.

PART 3

RESISTING CALIFORNICATION

CHAPTER 21

THE DANGER OF CALIFORNICATION

America's Coming Attractions

"As goes California, so goes the rest of the country." This maxim states a simple truth: what happens in California is a harbinger for the nation. Californication is the California ethos spreading across the rest of the country, a political and cultural imperialism emanating from California. The principal exporters of California politics and culture are Hollywood elites, Silicon Valley tech titans, and Democrats in Sacramento. The liberal Left sees California as the shining example for our less enlightened neighbors to emulate. We are the missionaries for the new age of equity, progressive ideals, open borders, vaccine mandates, environmental extremism, and the redistribution of wealth. We've never been short on hubris in the Golden State.

Our neighbors don't view it quite in the same light. Californication is a pejorative term used by other states to bemoan California's outsized influence on their state. "Keep Idaho beautiful...go back to California" and "Don't Californicate Colorado" read bumper stickers that sum up the frustration of the exportation of California's leftist norms into other states.

California's population and economy guarantee the rest of the country will pay attention. We are the most populous state in the union. California has accounted for 20 percent of America's economic growth in the last decade. Three of the ten biggest companies by market capitalization are located in Silicon Valley. With that kind of money comes power and influence. Hollywood and Silicon Valley use their influence to frame the conservative versus liberal debate and sell Californication to America.

The U.S. is beginning to look a lot more like California. Gavin Newsom recently tweeted, "California is America's coming attractions." Take it from me: that's a movie you don't want to see.

The United States of California

President Biden promised his administration would look more like America, but it looks a lot more like California. Kamala Harris is the vice president, thus proving the Peter Principle is alive and well in the Democratic Party. Californians are in charge of the Treasury, Homeland Security, Labor, Health and Human Services, and Energy. Several UC Berkeley graduates are part of Biden's team. Berkeley has been the country's ultra-liberal flagbearer since the '60s. Radical ideas that began in ivory towers on the Left Coast have made their way into the White House. Dubbed "The West Coast Avengers," these Californians are already shaping national policy.

President Biden's "Build Back Better" plan has been called "Making America California Again." Originally slated to cost $3.5 trillion, the bill's final version was trimmed to $1.2 trillion. It's now been implemented partially in the Orwellian titled "Inflation Reduction Act," which doesn't do anything about inflation but make it worse and hardly does anything about the world's pollution problem except lard on added costs to Americans while letting the Chinese and Indians off the hook. Biden's Build Back Better Plan/Inflation Reduction Act reads like a Left Coast wish list: implementing the Green New Deal, raising the minimum wage to fifteen dollars, and expanding family paid leave. It's no surprise that California was the big winner: the federal government will spend more money in California than in any other state. President Biden claimed that the plan would pay for itself. The Congressional Budget Office disagreed and found Biden's accounting was only $367 billion off.

California is shaping the national debate and influencing policy on myriad issues, including immigration, energy and climate change, public sector employee pensions, and the minimum wage. President Biden is following Governor Newsom's playbook of courting unions by attempting to give them the same privileges they enjoy in California. The Protect the Right to Organize (PRO) Act was the Democrats' effort at Californicating the entire country.

The PRO Act has many of the same provisions of California's disastrous Assembly Bill 5. AB 5 severely restricted the use of independent contractors by all businesses in the state. Wait a minute—not all companies. More than one hundred deep-pocketed corporations carved out exemptions for themselves. Uber, Lyft, and other ride-sharing apps used their money to fund and win Prop 22, exempting ride-sharing services from the law. Not exempted? Trucking companies, cleaning companies, yoga instructors, tutors, musicians, and freelancers of every kind. AB 5 is antibusiness and anti-independent contractor. The PRO Act has many of the same provisions as AB 5 and will hurt small businesses, which are the lifeblood of our economy.

President Biden again followed Governor Newsom's lead by stacking the deck in favor of unions. Biden encouraged union organizing and collective bargaining with the PRO Act. It would allow union bosses to collect dues from members even if they opt out of the union. Incredibly, it would give unions the right to seek arbitration if union organizing drives fail.

Richard Trumka was the president of the AFL-CIO, a confederation of fifty-seven unions. His remarks revealed the socialist underpinnings of this proposed legislation. Trumka stated, "If you really want to correct inequality in this country—wages and wealth inequality, opportunity and inequality of power—passing the PRO Act is absolutely essential to doing that." The U.S. Chamber of Commerce slammed the PRO Act, stating it would "undermine worker rights, ensnare employers in unrelated labor disputes, disrupt the economy, and force individual Americans to pay union dues regardless of their wishes." Thankfully, Republicans killed this thinly concealed union power grab.

Regrettably, the Californication of the national agenda continues. Nancy Pelosi, led the charge as Speaker of the House and the new minority leader, Hakeem Jeffries, was her top lieutenant and even more Left than she was. On the Democrats' agenda are socialist policies germinated on the Left Coast like guaranteed income, carbon neutrality, and universal healthcare. Gavin Newsom has turned California politics into a lifestyle brand to sell to woke America. Now positioning himself to run for president in 2024, Newsom is doubling down on abortion in light of the *Dobbs* decision and gun control in light of the recent rash of young men perpetrating mass murders. Never mind that California has memorialized a right to an abortion in its Constitution—an example of a state choosing its own rules rather than a court imposed federal "right." At the same time, California has some of the toughest gun control laws in the country but still has a surging crime problem. Newsom should instead call on the media to deny these mass killers what they want—publicity and fame.

California positioned itself as the moral, anti-Trump alternative, ready and willing to be the Left's standard-bearer in the political and cultural wars that have threatened to destabilize society. Big tech and the liberal media will broadcast their leftist agenda like it's a moral imperative based on irrefutable science. The front line of the culture and political wars will be fought in Sacramento and Silicon Valley. Newsom is going to try to get them to be national in a race for power as the next president. That cannot be allowed to happen; we cannot allow the whole country to be as mismanaged and unlivable for the middle class as is California.

Go East, Young Man

It's not just ideas that California exports; we export our people as well. California transplants are a significant factor driving the Californication of the nation. People have become more mobile, and many are leaving California and taking their political views with them. Democrats are redistributing themselves into red states and altering the political map. Younger people (who skew more liberal) are the most likely to leave California due to our high cost of living. They carry their political affiliation, turning red states either purple or blue.

Let's look at the effect California transplants are having on Republican states. In Texas, Republican governor Greg Abbott told the Texas Public Policy Foundation that Californication was "eroding the Texas model" and turning the "Texas miracle" into a "California nightmare." Governor Abbott is echoing concerns of conservatives across the country: the liberalization of urban centers due to an influx of Californians. For example, the Democratic advantage in the five counties containing the large metro areas of Dallas, Houston, Austin, and San Antonio increased by 670,000 votes from 2012 to 2018. The same thing happened in Atlanta, Georgia. Georgia voted for Joe Biden in 2020, reversing its 2016 support for Donald Trump. Progressive media darling Stacey Abrams (D-GA) announced she will run for governor again in 2022. In Arizona, Maricopa County, which contains Phoenix, has flipped from red to blue in recent years.

The Mountain West is becoming the new swing-state battleground due to Californication. As Californians stream into urban centers like Denver, Colorado; Phoenix, Arizona; and Boise, Idaho, they are bringing their liberal ideals with them. In Colorado, they have helped pass progressive initiatives like gun control, the legalization of marijuana, green energy, and gay civil unions. In neighboring Nevada, transplanted Californians are now more numerous than native-born Nevadans. "In the case of Nevada, the spillover effect is pretty clear," John Pitkin, a demographer from the University of Southern California, told NPR, "Nevada is almost a satellite of California." California transplants are helping to speed the Californication of the rest of the country.

Unholy Alliances

How did Democrats gain control of all three branches of government in California? And just as important: how will the rest of America use the California model to push the country ever farther to the Left? There was much talk of identity politics in the 2016 presidential election. That's because the Democrats came up with a winning strategy in California and have exported it to other states and Washington, D.C.

Democrats have skillfully knitted together a patchwork quilt of interest groups to form a powerful coalition. First and foremost are the public employee unions. The California Teachers Association is the most powerful player in California. They represent the most potent political force due to the millions in dues they extract from their members. Its 310,000 members vote, man phone banks, and donate millions of dollars to Gavin Newsom. The CTA influences elections at the local, county, and state levels. Next in this coalition are the myriad other unions whose interests align with teachers and the Democratic Party.

These union leaders have been very smart. They've entered into unwritten, and I would say unholy, alliances with other interest groups such as the trial lawyers, environmental lobbyists, LGBTQ groups, and marginalized and underrepresented people who want to influence the political process. What do the BLM movement, LGBTQ groups, tree-huggers, and trial lawyers have in common? They all want power. They all want to advance their agendas. So why compete? Why not band together and have it all? These groups support each other's candidates and liberal agendas. By and large, the candidates are on the Left end of the spectrum, so they can be counted on to support union politics, LGBTQ issues, environmental issues, or legislation that benefits trial lawyers. Democratic leaders and union bosses have created a powerful cooperative alliance In California out of formerly competing interests.

Education is a huge honeypot into which unions and other political actors dip their greedy little fingers. Spending on public education accounts for 40 percent of California's state budget. We spend over

$24,000 per student and now more than $100 billion every year. The CTA uses the power of its 310,000 dues-paying members to control California's public education system. Make no mistake: the teachers' union is calling the shots. They influence politicians through their voting and fundraising prowess. They have taken over control of school boards by electing their pro-union candidates.

The result is a state where students continuously underperform their peers in other states: California ranks forty-fourth in math scores, thirty-eighth in reading scores, and thirty-second in mean SAT score. Unions have the best interest of their members at heart, not the best interest of students. We saw a disturbing example of this during the pandemic. The United Teachers of Los Angeles (UTLA) refused to reopen schools until the demands in its socialist manifesto were met to rectify our country's "profoundly racist, intensely unequal society." The UTLA demanded free Medicare for all, a moratorium on charter schools, guaranteed housing, defunding the police, and a wealth tax, among others. I suggest the teachers' unions focus on improving California's low test scores and failing schools instead of pushing their socialist agenda and using our students as political hostages.

The CTA has joined forces with the BLM and LGBTQ community to decide on the curriculum taught in schools. As a result, Critical Race Theory and the repudiation of binary gender norms are indoctrinating young minds with the Democrats' liberal PC ideology. California became the first state to require LGBTQ history instruction in schools in 2011. Colorado, New Jersey, and Illinois followed. What's worse is that liberals demonize traditional and normative culture as perpetuating white privilege and devaluing minority voices. This is all part of the Left's plan to subvert our youth and solidify the Democratic Party as the sole protector of the rights of the underrepresented and underserved everywhere. We will Californicate our youth, and they will grow up to vote Democratic.

Liberal social ideas like Critical Race Theory have seeped out from California like a toxic oil spill and contaminated other states. Some governors are fighting back and protecting the traditional cultures that enrich their societies. Florida, Texas, Idaho, Tennessee, and others have banned the teaching of Critical Race Theory in public schools. Voters in the 2021 Virginia governor's race rejected critical race theory and Californication. Many states with strong Republican governors, including Texas, Arizona, Utah, and Oklahoma, have either restricted or banned LGBTQ instruction in schools. These governors have taken a stand against the Californication of public education. They refuse to let California's liberal ideas poison their youth.

The unholy alliance of unions and liberal groups has had far-reaching effects in California. This voting block is steadfastly Democratic and has helped the Democrats solidify their supermajority through their fundraising and get-out-the-vote prowess. Democrats have controlled every lever of power in Sacramento for the last decade. As a result, California has moved ever farther to the Left politically and socially.

Big tech and politicians beholden to their money champion the progressive liberal agenda of these groups. Guaranteed income projects have begun in several major cities in California, some funded by Silicon Valley titans. The state and social media encouraged BLM protesters to break COVID protocols and regulations in the name of social justice and police reform. Environmental issues are given priority over water, fire prevention, and jobs. Trial lawyers are making a killing due to government regulations like PAGA. And, most important of all, the unions are making a killing.

The Pension that Ate California

Public employee unions have grown into a monster. The expansion of public sector employment accelerated under former governor Jerry Brown. Today, our government employs about 2.1 million people at the state, county, and local levels. That is approximately 11 percent of California's nineteen-million-person workforce, meaning more than one in ten people in California work for the government. All of those employees cost money. Salaries and benefits for state workers have escalated well beyond what comparative occupations receive in the private sector. State workers draw salaries for twenty or thirty years, then they retire and receive generous health benefits and pensions for the rest of their days.

California's public employee pension system is in a financial crisis. California's unfunded pension liability in 2020 was $160 billion, the largest in the nation. California's pensions are only 70 percent funded. State governments are required by law to make pension payments, and our unfunded state pension liability eats larger portions of our state budget every year.

How did it get that way? In the 1990s, the stock market was booming. Tech stocks were making people lots of money. Lawmakers thought the good times would last forever. Democratic governor Gray Davis, perhaps the worst governor in the history of California and successfully recalled in 2003, signed Senate Bill 40 in 1999.

SB 40 substantially increased pensions for state employees. It increased the pension multiplier for defined benefits from 2 to 3 percent. Let me give you a numerical example of the magnitude of this benefit increase. If you started working for the State of California when you were twenty-two years old, you accrued 2 percent of your salary as a benefit every year you worked with a thirty-year cap. So if you worked to age fifty-two, you got 60 percent of your salary as a pension. But, you could not retire at fifty-two because there was a rule that said you had to still work until you were sixty-five.

Sacramento increased the accrual rate from 2 percent to 3 percent with a thirty-year cap. Now union workers could retire with 90 percent of their salary. SB 40 lowered the retirement age to fifty-five for most employees—and fifty for some. Sacramento handed out free medical coverage from retirement until Medicare kicks in at sixty-seven, further compounding the problem. As life expectancies increased, so too did ballooning obligations and debt.

Imagine retiring at fifty with free medical and 90 percent of your pay! That is precisely what many state employees have done. I know; I've spoken with many of them. I don't blame the union members; they are collecting what the state promised them. The problem lies with the outsized influence of unions in California politics.

Grey Davis's biggest campaign donors? You guessed it—public employee unions. The governor received $5 million, and we got a financial time bomb with a lit fuse. The politicians gave public employees gold-plated pensions with other people's money. Politicians didn't pay for those benefits; taxpayers did.

Sacramento promised there would be no financial liability to taxpayers: they lied. The dot.com bubble burst a year later, and California taxpayers were left holding the bag. The stock market posted negative returns for three consecutive years. We're still trying to dig ourselves out of that hole. The taxpayer bill to fund state employee pensions in 2020 was $5.4 billion. Our 2021 unfunded pension liability is approaching $1 trillion. That works out to about $80,000 per taxpayer.

Even former governor Davis admitted increasing pensions was a costly mistake. When asked by the *Los Angeles Times* if he regrets signing the legislation, he said, "If you're asking me, with everything I've learned in the last 17 years, would I have signed SB 40....no, I would not have signed it."

Pension obligations for public employees take money away from essential services like infrastructure and public safety. Politicians regularly push for tax increases to finance the debt for government pensions. Californians pay higher taxes and suffer reduced services to fund union pensions.

I live in the San Diego metro area. Let me tell you about San Diego's pension nightmare. In 2003, a City Employees' Retirement System Pension Board member, Diann Shipione, disclosed Enron-level accounting irregularities in the city pension system. San Diego's pension fund was bleeding money at an alarming and unsustainable rate.

The City Council and others on the retirement pension board ignored her warning. Instead of listening to her, they tried to remove her. The mayor and a city council majority voted to ban investment advisors from the retirement board. It just so happened that Shipione was the *only* investment advisor on the board. Later, they disbanded the entire pension board and appointed new members. The Securities and Exchange Commission began investigating improprieties in San Diego's pension obligations. Several city officials, including the mayor, resigned in disgrace soon after.

Sixty-five percent of San Diegans voted for Proposition B pension reform in the wake of the pension scandal. It replaced the current pension system for all new hires except police officers with a 401(k)-style plan. It was a common-sense approach to fixing an urgent problem. The reform measures were expected to save the city $1.6 billion through 2040. Labor unions immediately challenged Prop B in court. In 2019, six Democrats on the city council voted to nullify Prop B. The San Diego superior court invalidated Proposition B in January 2021.

A coalition of labor union bosses and city politicians vetoed the will of the voters. The power of the public employee unions silenced the voices of two-thirds of San Diegans and placed the city's financial future in doubt. The outsized influence of public employee unions on the politics of San Diego means city services will be cut and taxes will rise. The good citizens of San Diego will be left paying the bill for bloated public employee union pensions.

Here, There, and Everywhere

Democratic operatives in other states saw the successes in California. Democrats have controlled the California Senate since 1958 (except for 1968 and 1972 when Republicans split the seats evenly). They have held both houses of the legislature and the governor's office, known as the trifecta, for the last fourteen years.

Democrats exported the California model of bloated government, benefits, and pensions to other states. Places like New York, Illinois, New Jersey, and Pennsylvania have replicated the California paradigm. Public-sector unions now dominate state government in those states. Clearly, there has been minimal effort in California and other union-controlled states to make state government run more efficiently and leaner.

America's ballooning unfunded pension obligations illustrate the inefficiencies inherent in the public sector. Across the country, unfunded state pension liabilities total $5.82 trillion. That's $17,748 for every man, woman, and child in the United States. States like Illinois (39 percent funded with a $141 billion shortfall), New Jersey (38 percent funded with a $138 billion shortfall), and Pennsylvania (55 percent with a $15 billion shortfall) are leading the charge to fiscal insolvency.

Following the lead of California's pension boondoggle, Pennsylvania expanded its public employee pensions from 2001 to 2003. Pennsylvania's public employee retirement funds were 123 percent funded during the stock market boom of the 1990s. The Pennsylvania teachers' union lobbied Governor Tom Ridge and the state legislature to increase pension benefits in 2001.

Pennsylvania's Act 9 significantly increased pension benefits for public employee unions. It increased the accrual multiplier to 2.5 percent or 3 percent and added a host of other perks—all unfunded. Legislators saw their pensions increase by 50 percent. Teachers' pensions increased by 25 percent. The thinking was that investment gains, so reliable in the go-go '90s, would cover the increased costs. The governor signed ACT 9 on May 17, 2001. Four months later, the September 11 attacks changed everything.

The stock market downturns in 2002–2003 (post-9/11 and the dot-com bubble) and 2007–2009 (the subprime housing market crash) significantly increased the unfunded liability of Pennsylvania's pension system. Employing political group-think and accounting trickery that would make California legislators proud, Pennsylvania decided to wait until economic times improved to increase funding for pensions. The governor signed Act 38 in 2002. It provided cost-of-living increases to retirees. Incredibly, Pennsylvania simultaneously decreased state funding of pensions from around 7 percent to between 1 percent and 2 percent, with promised increases when the stock market rebounded. The Great Recession of 2007–2009 put an end to that fantasy.

How did Democratic governor Ed Rendell and the legislature solve this mess? In 2003, they kicked the can down the road—for thirty years! Act 40 changed the amortization of the debt from ten to thirty years.

Remember those 123 percent funded state pensions? The retirement fund is now 55 percent funded. Pennsylvania taxpayers currently pay between $4 billion and $5 billion per year to reduce the unfunded pension liability. Property taxes have risen to fund schools. Pennsylvania's $152 billion unfunded pension liability has been compared to a tapeworm that's eating billions of dollars each year.

The Californication of Pennsylvania has had disastrous consequences for the Keystone State. Pennsylvania is ranked forty-fifth out of fifty states in state pension health by the Pew Research Center. Pennsylvanians will need to make hard choices in the future to make up for their past mistakes. Taxpayers will have to pay the bill—we always do.

When unions and elected officials are in bed together, the people suffer. Unfunded pension liabilities are driving up taxes and reducing government services. Exorbitant pension and health benefits have delayed cost of living raises for state employees in many states because debt payments have gobbled up the money. The massive costs states must pay to finance their debt mortgages the future of hard-working Americans for political gain today.

Bloated public sectors take money away from the private sector. There is no incentive for the public sector to be efficient or produce more. More employees mean more power for unions and politicians. The system rewards inefficiency when bloated bureaucracies feed themselves by creating more regulations to justify their existence. No private sector business would survive if it were run like the government.

The private sector is always more efficient because capitalism rewards productivity and efficiency. The increased profits from improved productivity enable businesses to expand their markets, innovate, create new products, improve their services, and modernize their facilities. It is always in the best interest of business owners to be as efficient as possible. That is simply not the case with government workers because there is no incentive to be efficient.

The Democratic Party's experiment with cradle-to-grave socialism has failed California, and it will fail in every state that falls under

California's spell. Not everyone is foolish enough to follow California's lead. Governors in some states are pushing back against the power of public employee unions and their cozy relationship with the Democratic Party.

The Republican governors of Texas, Florida, Indiana, and Arizona are resisting Californication and have taken steps to fix their pension problems. These states require a combination of increased employee contributions and reduced member benefits to improve the financial health of their retirement programs. They are making the hard choices that every private business owner understands.

Texas and Indiana are going a step further. These states are transitioning from the defined benefits of traditional pension plans to the defined contributions of a 401(k) retirement plan. The beauty of 401(k)s is they are entirely funded; there will be no unfunded liability to taxpayers. These states will save billions by moving new employees into 401(k)-style retirement savings plans. This type of retirement savings aligns with the private sector, where 401(k)s are the norm and pensions are relics of a bygone era.

Energy Poverty

Californication means government-mandated green energy, rolling blackouts, higher electric and natural gas bills, and pain at the pump. Gavin Newsom has mandated that all vehicles in California be zero emission by 2035. On top of that, Sacramento's stated goal is to have a carbon-neutral power grid by 2045. Californians already pay 60 percent more than the rest of the country for electricity. Ours is not a model for the rest of the country to emulate.

California represents less than 1 percent of the world's pollution. The major polluters in the world are China and India, especially in the past ten years. They have been building dirty coal-fired power plants because they don't have our natural gas reserves and coal is the best alternative available to them. The U.S. has abundant natural gas reserves but climate extremists won't let them be developed. This then keeps the price higher than it should be, and causes China and India to burn more expensive coal. The extra costs imposed on California's consumers hardly makes a dent in overall world pollution at the same time California's limits on extraction of natural gas causes China and India to pollute more. It's absolutely nonsensical.

The rest of the country must not heed the siren call of a clean energy future liberals sing from California's rocky shores. Gavin Newsom plans to phase out *all* oil extraction by 2045. Governor Newsom stated, "As we move to swiftly decarbonize our transportation sector and create a healthier future for our children, I've made it clear I don't see a role for fracking in that future and, similarly, believe that California needs to move beyond oil." President Biden and his California Cabinet have picked up the mantle and have begun the transformation of our energy supply. "A Biden administration would mean everywhere would start to look like California in terms of investment in renewables," said Michael Wara, the director of Stanford's climate and energy policy program.

California's leaders know our market of forty million people is too large for national companies to ignore. When California bans gasoline-powered vehicles and promises a carbon-free future, their goal is for their initiatives to affect products everywhere.

Californication of the energy sector is meant as the first salvo in a war to determine the future of America's energy. Biden's special presidential envoy for climate change, John Kerry, chaired Joe Biden's environmental task force. The task force crafted Biden's national energy policy. The task force's report urged the nation to turn to California for inspiration and direction. It advised the president to "Immediately convene California, due to its unique authority..." We cannot permit liberal politicians in Washington to follow California's mistakes and implement the Green New Deal advocated by Biden, AOC, Nancy Pelosi, and the Bernie bros.

Political elites in California strive to be cutting edge on climate change. They want to build the California brand with liberal policies that enhance our standing as trailblazers yet harm our citizens. Millions of Californians cannot afford to drive new electric vehicles or install solar panels on their homes. Green energy policies have increased electricity and fuel prices to the point where millions are on the edge of energy poverty. Our environmentally driven energy plan is forcing energy industries out of the state. Our energy policies are failing Californians, and they will fail all Americans.

Federalism versus Californication

Californication is undermining the strength of our federalist system. The founding fathers established a system of governance based on the principles of self-determination spelled out in the Magna Carta. This seminal document set forth the principle that men were their own masters. People no longer served at the pleasure of a feudal lord. What has happened in California is threatening to reverse all that. The special-interest groups that have banded together with the Democratic Party have become the new power source, our new feudal lord. Democrats in other states see how this power grab has succeeded in California, and they crave that power for themselves. They want to make every state just like California.

The alliance among unions and progressive socialists has turned California from the land of opportunity into the land of forced equity. Democrats have abandoned free enterprise and self-determination and replaced them with government handouts and reliance on the state. We have traded in the risks of capitalism for the comforts of socialism. But that trade-off comes at a cost. When we look at Socialist and Communist governments over the ages, the government and its citizens struck a bargain. Citizens gave power to a small group of people and worked for the state in return. Individuals relinquished their rights to produce and keep their own goods. That is the bargain we make with socialism and communism. It's a deal with the devil, and it never works.

The problem with socialism is that it doesn't recognize that people are motivated by self-interest. When all of our hard work benefits the state and not the individual, it creates a disincentive to be efficient, innovative, and productive. Socialism and communism seek to erase inequities and replace them with two classes: the ruling elite and the proletarian workers.

That power centralized in the ruling elite more often than not turns into oppression and even violent subjugation. We've all seen the failure of communism and the limitations and pitfalls of socialism. Ronald Reagan warned that socialism only works in "heaven where they don't need it and hell where they already have it."

Liberals and Socialists decry capitalism because it creates winners and losers, which naturally results in inequities. But it is precisely this chance at winning, at creating your destiny, that propels capitalist countries to outperform Socialist and Communist countries. How many people were trying to climb the Berlin Wall to get *into* East Germany before President Reagan and the lure of improved living standards tore down the iron curtain? And that's the trade-off: a better quality of life versus inequality.

Our U.S. Constitution protects individual rights and freedoms from the power of a state that would take away our liberty for the benefit of a few. Federalism allows people and businesses to leave states with oppressive business climates, high taxes, high crime rates, failing schools, and high living costs. Where can people and businesses go if every state becomes a satellite of California? The Californication of America spells an end to the protections of federalism as enshrined in our Constitution.

What happens in California has always mattered beyond our borders. Our political, cultural, and technological influence has shaped America and the world. But there is a lesson here for the rest of America. If you imitate California, you may become California: a liberal, failed, one-party state. This begs the question: why would the rest of the country follow us on the road to ruin? To quote King Lear, "O, that way madness lies; let me shun that."

CHAPTER 22

HEAR THE PEOPLE!

Corruption and pay-to-play politics have eroded confidence in our democratic institutions. California's decade-long Democratic supermajority over all three branches of government has rendered impotent the checks and balances critical to a well-functioning democracy. Politicians are no longer accountable to the citizens they are sworn to represent. They are seduced by money and power, so corruption runs rampant in the halls of government. As of this writing, vast numbers of Californians report in polling that they don't trust either party or the media—with good reason.

The same is true of Congress. Polling in a 2022 Gallup poll found only 7 percent had trust in Congress, putting it at the bottom, below even Big Business and Television News for trustworthiness. The extremism, the pay-to-play politics, the nightly blathering on cable news—it all adds up to toxic stew that has all but erased the public's trust of our national leaders.

This lack of trust has also eroded voters' interest in voting and paying attention to the issues. Comedians regularly get laughs asking people on the street to name Supreme Court Justices or Senators with typically erroneous responses. Civics is rarely taught in our schools and the general public often has little interest in politics or learning about current events. Who can blame them? They know their vote matters much, much less than the campaign funders and media, who have an outsized control of our political arena.

An FBI sting operation in the mid-'80s, later dubbed "Shrimpscam," netted five state assemblymen who served prison time on racketeering charges for selling favorable legislation to a fictitious shrimp company *eighty miles* from the ocean for bribes. Corruption at the state capitol continued unabated through the 1990s. State Senator Alan Robbins served twenty months for accepting bribes. Congressman Duke Cunningham took $2.4 million from defense contractors and served eight years behind bars.

The granddaddy of them all was Artie Samish, the Sacramento uber-lobbyist who dominated Sacramento politics during the 1940s. "The secret boss of California" was sentenced to three years in prison following public outrage over a *Collier's* magazine picture showing Samish holding a Charlie McCarthy–like dummy. The caption read: "This is my legislature. And how are you today, Mr. Legislature?"

What we need today are statesmen, not politicians. We are suffering from a shortage of qualified leaders committed to analyzing, implementing, and explaining their policies to the voters. That's why we have budget deficits, immigration controversies, the lack of infrastructure, energy issues, and the inflation that now ravages our economy. Only 41 percent of Californians approve of the job the state legislature is doing. The approval rating for Congress has been below 50 percent for years; some polls show approval today under 20 percent. This country calls out for men and women who will serve their district, their state, and their country.

I am not just complaining about this set of affairs. I'm advocating for a solution—we call it Hear the People.

The basis of this reform is the creation of small—really, tiny districts that changes our current political calculus by taking away the power of money and media. This reform's tiny districts have the effect of making all campaigns for office about person-to-person campaigning and individual voter persuasion. By making each contested district super small, this systemic change shifts the power back to individual people in their local neighborhoods. People would have greater access to their local legislators on the issues that affect their lives. It's my solution to the corrupting influence of money, political donations, and mass-media control.

Let's explore how this works.

California has forty million people but its legislature only has eighty assemblymembers and forty senators. Thus, California's assembly districts have nearly half a million people, and the senate districts have almost one million. On the federal level, Congress by statute froze the number of congressional districts at 435 in 1911. That means that as the population of the country has grown, so has the size of congressional districts. There are now almost 750,000 people in each congressional district and the average competitive race involves raising and spending at least $5 million and often much more. Most congressional races aren't even competitive both due to the hurdles faced by such huge fundraising as well as the gerrymandering that the political class uses to pick its voters rather than the other way around.

Because of the enormous size of these legislative districts, all campaigns for Congress and large district state legislatures like California are massive and expensive. Television ads, mailers, and staffing a campaign require millions of dollars. That money corrupts the process. It favors the rich and powerful, empowers the media, and diminishes the influence of the individual voter. The people who run for Congress or the California legislature are either wealthy or political professionals who have the connections to raise enough money to run a successful campaign. Elites have expropriated our democracy and are running our government like an oligarchy. Good people don't want to spend their lives on the phone begging for money, so they disdain even entering the political arena. The result we usually get is candidates who are corrupt or ambitious or both and are using politics as a stepping stone to wealth and fame instead of true public service.

Hear the People is a simple plan to accomplish a huge goal—remove the power of money and media by making districts so small, they're not powerful. Under this plan, each Congressional district of about 750,000 people would be divided into 100 tiny Community Districts of about 7,500 people each. A Community Representative is then elected in each of those tiny districts; a couple of weeks after the election in November, those hundred Community Representatives meet to select one of their group to go to Washington as the Congressperson for the next two years. On the state level, it would work in a similar fashion; voters in the small neighborhood districts would elect a local Assemblyman or Senator, and the one hundred local reps in each large district would get together to choose that district's member of a Working Committee in SacramentoEach house, Assembly and Senate, would have a Working Committee in Sacramento to do all the legislative work. The Working Committee member would communicate with their local reps via technology. The local representative would thereupon also use technology to communicate with his or her constituents. A local representative can know and communicate with five thousand people, but they can't really know five hundred thousand constituents. On the congressional level, the congressperson in Washington would be similarly accountable to his or her tiny neighborhood district as well as the ninety-nine other Community Representativeswho voted to send him or her there.

This system also takes advantage of our wonderful technologies that enable instant communication. The congressperson in D.C. or the Working Committee member in Sacramento can communicate with the ninety-nine other neighborhood representatives back in the large district by text, email, or social media. They can in turn also use those communication technologies to keep in touch with the small number of voters in their tiny districts. Those voters will feel they can trust what information they are getting via social media and otherwise because they know their representative personally and can hold them accountable if they later find that they were misled.

The legislators sent to each capitol (Washington and Sacramento) would form committees as they do now to take on the daily work of the people with one huge difference; they won't have to spend time raising money or appearing on the media—they will spend their time researching and determining what policies will best address our state and country. Laws would still require passage by the majority of the 435 congresspeople on the federal level or the forty- and eighty-member working committees on the state level, subject to ratification by the local representatives back in the neighborhoods.

Voters would like it as well. They would get to know their representative and feel they had a voice. They would be able to get verified facts because they would know their local representative and hold the local representative accountable for any misstatements. The candidates would likely be much better than we currently have—local leaders such as small business owners, teachers, or religious leaders could run on their character and qualifications rather than their name recognition or fundraising abilities.

The beauty of this plan is that every member will have been elected in a local neighborhood and need very little money or time commitment for their election campaign—not the millions of dollars they have to raise and spend currently or the eighteen-hour days for two years it now often requires. Since election campaigns will be inexpensive, there will be no reason to spend countless hours raising millions from special-interest groups on the phone. The power currently wielded by special-interest groups will vanish. Legislators will not need their special-interest money and will have nothing to fear. Likewise, the media will not hold vast power over our elected representatives. Power will go back into the hands of the people, where it belongs.

You might ask: "Yes, but will it work?" I can tell you that small districtsalready work in New Hampshire and have since the state's founding. New Hampshire has a population of about 1.3 million people. There are four hundred members in its house of representatives and twenty-four members of its senate. Each member of the house represents about 3,500 voters. They are citizen volunteers and are paid the grand sum of one hundred dollars per year. Most people who run for the state legislature do not spend one penny of their own money and very little overall.

The idea is to bring campaigns and elections down to a granular level, to make campaign funding unnecessary, which all but eliminates the outsized power of the media and campaign funders. The beautiful thing is that we have a model—the New Hampshire house of representatives. It works there. Voters like their representatives there, and they get good people to run. Special-interest groups don't buy candidates, so they have nothing to fear. Candidates run on their merits and their platforms. No one runs negative ads. Campaigns aren't on television, the internet, or other forms of mass media. The mass media doesn't have the control it does in other states or in the federal system. That also has the effect of lessening the caustic nature of our media and politics in general.

In New Hampshire, voters expect candidates to speak with them individually, either by phone or in person. There are no vicious mailers, few lawn signs, and no robocalls. Candidates run on their policies, character, accomplishments, and personalities, not on general advertising funded by campaign contributions. Due to the small size of their districts, New Hampshire legislators are more responsive to their constituents.

Contrast that with the dire situation in California and Washington today. Our leaders do not bother to explain their policies or votes. They rail and lob confrontational salvos about the hot-button topic du jour like guns or abortion. Voters don't want to listen, either. They are more interested in sports or entertainment. They're detached because they don't believe they can have an impact on politics because they read about the vast sums contributed by the interest groups and know that their voice hardly makes a difference. They don't trust their leaders either; most polls put political leaders near the bottom in terms of trust and confidence. Politics has become a form of entertainment. The media consumer demands sensationalism over substance. In this age of social media and viral posts, a five-second sound bite can make or break a candidacy. Controversy and confrontation equal clicks. Negative ads are commonplace.Compromise and good policy are thrown out the window. The system we have today is patently stupid and distorted; we need this reform now.

Impact on Government

This reform—Hear the People—would have an immediate impact on nearly every issue described in this book. Big government is good business for politicians, bureaucrats, special-interest lobbyists, and public employee unions. Their main goals are to preserve the status quo and safeguard their source of power. I often say that conditions are the way they are because someone or some group likes them that way. Politicians are influenced by these groups to keep things the way they are so the groups benefit.

There is thus little to no incentive for the public sector to be efficient in our current system. Bureaucrats use their influence to grow their departments and create new ones. Public-sector unions seek more employees to increase dues—and thus political influence through contributions to candidates. The more regulations they create, the more their departments grow which means more dues and more ability to influence political leadership. Government employee groups with sizable bankrolls and an army of workers exert a big impact.

I'm not antiunion. My family's involvement with unions spans generations. My Great Uncle Perk—his real name was Hugh Perkins but he went by Perk—was a supervisor in the press room of the great historic newspaper, the *Chicago Tribune*, in 1948. It was published by the fiery Colonel Robert McCormick, as hard-edged a conservative as there was in the 1940s. My uncle was a staunch supporter of President Harry S. Truman, then locked in a tight battle for the presidency against Republican Thomas Dewey. McCormick insisted on printing a headline—over Perk's vehement objections—claiming victory for Dewey despite some evidence to the contrary and votes still being counted. As we all know from history, that headline, "Dewey Defeats Truman" went down in infamy as an incorrect headline President Truman reveled in, as we can see in this famous picture.

My mother was a teacher and a proud member of the Chicago Teachers Union, as was my Great Aunt Sylvia Perkins, Perk's wife. However, unions have now almost been erased from the private sector as around 10 percent of the private businesses are unionized in favor of public employees, who now dominate. President John F. Kennedy opened the door for federal unions and California Governor Jerry Brown did the same for state employees.

This has led to immense political power and, frankly, corruption of our election processes as public-sector unions have used their massive resources from dues to fund politicians and their employee base to support those same politicians that negotiate their salaries and benefits as well as work rules and other regulations. This is a major part of what has led to the dysfunction of many federal and state agencies. Hear the People reforms, I propose, would put an end to this thumb on the scale and result in an even playing field between taxpayers and unions.

Hear the People system is a free-market solution to our political problems. When people know their voice is heard and their vote matters, they will become more engaged. Constituents gain the opportunity to speak face-to-face with candidates and question them in small group, town hall–type forums. Voters will evaluate candidates based on their positions and values, not on thirty-second ads, Twitter posts, and mailers.

The entrenched powers will surely muster their forces to oppose this measure so that they maintain that power. Let's explore the possible arguments they will make against it.

1. It creates more politicians. This is the most common and likely argument they will use—we don't like the politicians we have now and you want to create one hundred times more? The response to this is that the Community Representatives are not politicians as we know them today; they are not professional fundraisers because they won't need money to run their campaigns. They will get elected because they met their voters and got their votes due to their competence and character, not massive spending and mere name recognition.
2. The proposal is way too expensive—all those extra politicians will want offices, staffs, and pensions. Again, the Community

Representatives will be local only; they will represent only a few thousand households which should not require a large staff or office. They won't be compensated as our current politicians are because they won't have to commit much time—their main role is merely to elect the congressperson who goes to Washington or the member of the working committee that goes to Sacramento.

3. These neighborhood people will raise money from special-interest groups and be subject to the same conflicts and corruption we have now. Some of them may in fact go that way and still collect campaign money and sell their votes to special-interest groups. The good news is that they can easily be voted out if they do so. Anyone can afford to run a campaign in a small district with little time commitment.The parties should be able to make sure any neighborhood legislator who goes off the rails is defeated in the next election.
4. Where are we going to get all these neighborhood people—many homeowners associations have trouble recruiting candidates and this sounds like that kind of position? The Community Representatives will have a vote of consequence—they will have duties to appoint and monitor the activities of the congressperson they send to D.C. as well as the working committee member they designate. The parties will assume the role of recruiter and trainer to make sure these positions are filled and function properly. These will be consequential positions—not because they control power or money but because they impact policy.
5. Won't special-interest groups use their money to control the appointment of the congressperson or working committee member? They could but again, all fundraising would be disclosed and any Community Representative can be defeated easily in the next election on this issue—there is accountability for corruption due to the small districts and the ease of running to replace a corrupt official.

The Community Representative will be people with an axe to grind or not representative of the local district. Here is where the parties need to be accountable for recruitment and training. If someone who is not representative of a district or has an axe to grind gets elected, an opposition campaign can easily be mounted in the next election to remove them. Again, the small districts create accountability that almost never exists today to remove failed or faulty representatives.

The bottom line is that those who make money from and have power in the current system will not want to see it change. We know the current system isn't working well and needs to change; there are no good arguments that they can muster to either defend the current system or reasonably attack Hear the People.

Striking a Blow to the Media

Campaigns for the Community Representatives would diminish media influence in political campaigns. Community Representatives will campaign person to person, not through the media. Currently, large campaign efforts give mass media an outsized influence. Media executives, anchors, and reporters wield power because they can pick and choose which leaders get exposure and "their story out." Their platforms magnify the voices so much they drown out competing viewpoints. We all know that each side has its own silo, where their voters pretty much just listen to opinions that validate their own. Not much critical thinking going on there. Reducing the power of the media would open up more opportunity for leaders from these neighborhood districts to foster honest and open debate and reconciliation, something sorely lacking in our politics today.

Vast sums are spent on political consultants, media purchases, mailers, staff—the list goes on. The high cost deters many looking to become public servants. Large campaigns require major funding. Candidates must focus on fundraising and currying favor with special-interest groups. Tiny districts minimize this challenge.

Small districts elevate ideas over name recognition. Sensationalism or news value becomes less important when campaigns are door-to-door and small group–oriented. Issues and policies would take center stage, replacing confrontation, fearmongering, and personal attacks.

Increased Accountability and Election Integrity

Community Representatives would be accountable to the voters in their neighborhood districts. If you don't like what they're doing, you can remove them. You can organize your neighbors to win an election and change your representative. Every voter would have an opportunity to weigh in and make their voice heard.

Election integrity is a hot-button issue. The Left fired the first salvo when it accused Donald Trump of colluding with Russia to interfere in the 2016 presidential election. In 2020, Trump fomented the idea that the vote was rigged. In response, the Right has attempted to restrict voter access in states like Georgia and Arizona. The Left pushed back for unlimited mail-in balloting, which is an invitation to fraud.

Now, voters are losing faith in election results. Candidates who lose agitate their supporters to contest elections. Phrases like "Not My President" and "The Great Steal" undermine the legitimacy of our elected leaders. When this happens, confidence in our government and the system's integrity erodes. The peaceful transition of power is a cornerstone of our representative government. Without it, our democracy is a house of cards, ready to be toppled by the slightest provocation.

Hear the People is the antidote. When we create districts of only a few thousand voters, small numbers of votes will decide contests. Thus, those neighborhood candidates will have a direct interest in ensuring that every single vote is cast legally and counted securely. Given the small numbers, dozens or hundreds of votes may decide elections in each of those tiny districts. Those candidates running in those tiny districts, whose election depends on an honest and fair count, will ensure the procedures used are valid and that every vote is counted and reported accurately.

Tackling Gerrymandering

One culprit in the lack of trust and engagement is gerrymandering. Gerrymandering allows powerful political leaders to draw lines and choose their voters. Primaries devolve into de facto elections when gerrymandering turns districts into one-party strongholds. Hear the People and its small districts make gerrymandering a thing of the past; there will be little picking and choosing of voters when districts only have a few thousand voters to begin with.

Noncompetitive voting districts favor extreme candidates who cater to the Far Left or Far Right. Railing against a problem makes for better press than coming up with a plan to solve it. It is a symptom of our disengaged electorate that often less than about 20 percent of registered voters turn out for primaries. Hear the People system engages the electorate on their doorstep; they will have to be informed of issues because someone will be coming to their door; their vote matters due to the small number of total voters—people will have to become more engaged and that is good for our democracy.

Reform is always challenging to achieve. The naysayers will give you a thousand reasons why we can't pass an idea like Hear the People. What they cannot do is defend the current system. The current system erodes trust and confidence. It prevents good policy and compromise. It encourages fraud and influence peddling. It makes the media and rich funders all important, not the people. This isn't a choice; we have to change a system that is indefensible and failing to deal with the myriad challenges our country faces. Hear the People system would render gerrymandering worthless. Tiny districts of a few thousand voters would hardly allow any gamesmanship in selecting voters or drawing district lines. Districts would be based on valid criteria, be mostly a contiguous neighborhood, and would foster true competition.

Actually, we can do it. We can change the way government works. We can change the election system to provide accountable and responsible leaders. Success requires work, but anytime you do any historically important, work is required. The payoff is that success will enable us to take back our country's and state's future and provide a government that serves the people, not the special-interest groups. What are we waiting for?

CONCLUSION

I began working on this book over two years ago. My first day at my desk at my home in San Diego, I told myself that I wanted to write a big book about a big state that would make entrenched elites angry and the average taxpayer feel like someone was not just speaking to them, but *through* them. Anyone can transcribe their political ideas to paper. My goal was to uncover deeper truths about how California's power structure really functioned, and how that system influenced national politics. I also wanted to learn more about myself as a citizen and what role I could play in spearheading change beyond running for public office. At the time, I was in the middle of a campaign for governor of California, but I wanted to create a body of work that rose above partisan politics and had legs beyond that political race. Ideas needed to be tested against history to see how well they hold up.

I needed the whole story, not the cherry-picked talking points you see on the nightly news. I dove headfirst into research. I rooted through historical data, media archives, and the public records of corrupt government departments. All the dirty laundry is there, for anyone to find, but those in power bank on no one looking. I went looking. It was a painstaking, difficult and long process. Every time I uncovered some abuse of power, often a headline worthy scandal buried in boring paperwork, it made my skin prick. Each day spent slogging through mountains of figures on state budgets and hair-raising quotes from Gavin Newsom added a little more to a story of government mismanagement, wasted tax dollars, and squandered opportunity. One thing is for certain: the incompetence and pure political power seeking and division that characterizes Gavin Newsom must never find its way into the halls of the White House and the levers of power of this great nation. His feckless politicization of and grandstanding on social issues, his hypocrisy exhibited before, during, and after the pandemic, his continued catering to narrow interests at the expense of the vast majority of his citizens suffering from high taxes, cost of living, lack of housing, lack of water, lack of energy, fear of wildfires, fear of crime, and myriad other issues argue strenuously for him not to be our nation's chief executive. We don't need to have done to the rest of the country what he has done to California.

As I got deeper, two ideas stood out:

1. California has the ability to solve its difficulties if it gets a change in its election system, without which it will wither on the vine.
2. That systemic change on the federal level as well as in California must transfer power from elites in government, media, big unions, and big business back into the hands of the people.

My second realization kicked off a new phase. I picked up the phone and started calling *real people* whom bad government impacted. The small-business owners. The long-haul truckers. The restaurant proprietors shuttered by COVID lockdowns. The victims of drive-by shootings. They had a lot to say. Farmers worried about losing their crops because of state-imposed water quotas. Teachers like my mother wanted meritocracy back in the classroom. Fathers with three kids lamented moving out of California because they could only afford a one-bedroom apartment.

My conversations touched a deep part of my conscience. These people are the lifeblood of our state and our country. My heart cried out to them. They are men and women our founding fathers would be proud to call Americans, people who continue the legacy of the Constitution through hard work and deeply held values. Everyone I spoke to was the kind of citizen that will make America again what Ronald Reagan called that shining city on a hill. Standing in their way: political leadership that is bought and paid for and a government that doesn't give a damn about their interests, their families, their homes.

The more people I spoke to, the more I realized that citizens out here are on their own. They've been abandoned. They are in desperate need of leadership. The kind of leadership that empowers them to live independent lives full of meaning.

Ronald Reagan remains, after all these years, a poster child for executive leadership. I was twenty-six years old when Reagan took his first oath of office in 1981. The first time I read about Reagan in the newspaper—I must have been in my early twenties—I related to him. He had a drunk for a father. My old man wasn't around. But Reagan's mother, like my mom and so many other single mothers in our country where fatherhood is devalued, picked up the slack. She instilled faith and values. I wouldn't be alive, much less where I am today, if it hadn't been for my mother doing the same thing. And Reagan weathered rejections early in life, like the disappointment of his first marriage. But he eventually found Nancy, the love of his life. As my life progressed, this too I shared with him.

In the early 1980s, Reagan inherited a situation that eerily mirrors the one we see today in California and across America. Under the Carter administration, America faced an energy crisis. Carter walked around the White House in a beige cardigan and appeared on TV less than two weeks after becoming president during a cold winter to tell the nation to "make modest sacrifices and live thriftily." The fireplace next to him remained unlit throughout the speech, a symbol of his own sacrifice. Uninspiring, to put it kindly. His policies fared no better than his no-fireside chat.

Under the well-meaning but hapless Carter, oil prices zoomed from three dollars a barrel to twenty dollars a barrel. As I write this, oil has gone from forty dollars a barrel to almost $80 a barrel. The price of gas has soared along with the price of oil, and California is facing energy blackouts again in the summer of 2023. Carter cut defense budgets when America faced threats from communism. In 1979, our students were taken hostage by Iran. Now China threatens us the same way the Soviet Union once did. We are fighting communism's weaker cousin, socialism, abroad in Russia and China and in our own country as well as dealing with an invasion of a sovereign Ukraine by its aggressive neighbor. This was invited by a weak leader in the Presidency fulfilling Reagan's prediction that no nation got war by being too strong; it got war by being too weak.

I was there in the late '70s and early '80s. I saw an America that was flat on its back, accepting mediocrity and limits on energy, freedom. and education. Today, Joe Biden and Gavin Newsom preach that we must accept limits and scarcity. Under their leadership, we are repeating the errors of the '70s.

California and our nation face tough challenges. But as I hope this book has shown, practical solutions for them exist. They are neither liberal nor conservative, Republican nor Democratic solutions. They don't aim to invest any politician or political party with power. We can properly educate our children. We can make housing affordable for families. We can deal effectively and humanely with the problems of the homeless. We can make our communities and families safe. If Israel can solve its water problems, California can. We can have abundance not scarcity. All through history, so-called leaders have told us we would not have enough food or energy or water—yet we now have over eight billion souls on this wonderful earth and we produce more than enough food, water and energy—for the moment but not in the future unless we make needed changes to our electoral system.

What is required is the right leadership and a change in our elections to bring it to us.

Many people don't appreciate how the world changed under Reagan. The thinking of the time was that the government had to be there to give us what we need to live. Reagan said this was nonsense: government wasn't the solution; it was the problem. It was too involved in the economy, but was failing at its most important job: defense. I saw this economic mismanagement firsthand. At the time, I did tax returns for people paying

70 percent marginal rates who didn't invest for that reason—most of their profit would be taxed away by government. Reagan dropped rates to 28 percent. That had a bigger impact than anyone could imagine. Money flowed into venture capital when you could keep 72 percent of what you earned. The technology boom of the '80s and '90s started with that one major change.

Reagan's foreign policy turned America back to battling to preserve democracy. The fall of the Soviet Union freed millions and the tech boom enabled many to find opportunities and improve our standard of living. We no longer had a shortage of energy. We didn't have a food shortage. The private economy unleashed both. And in running for president, Reagan stood out as an underdog who no one thought could win. He wasn't the conventional favorite. That was George Bush. Reagan was considered a Neanderthal and warmonger, both of which turned out to be remarkably off base.

But more than that, Reagan's sunny disposition and strong commitment to his faith and values overrode politics. Today, we are in that predicament again. The bitter partisanship is tearing us apart under Biden, as it did in the Trump era. But Reagan, unlike Trump, showed us that you can be conservative and not vengeful or caustic. You can inspire people. When Reagan gave speeches to the evangelical community, he connected to people rather than inciting them. He emphasized our shared values rather than denigrating others' motives. During the 1986 Reykjavík Summit, Reagan's steadfast negotiations with Gorbachev show his commitment to defending our values. His work and genuine friendship with Democrat house speaker Tip O'Neill showed you can work with the other side to do big things.

Reagan wasn't a god, and I'm no acolyte to the Church of Reagan. His story is also a story of mistakes, notably Iran–Contra and not tackling AIDS quickly enough. But Reagan's narrative was about turning hardship into victory on what *matters*. He didn't start out as the son of a wealthy person who turned millions into billions. He came from humble beginnings, like me, and understood what it's like to work hard and struggle with a difficult family situation. To me, he still symbolizes a return to values and away from the manipulation and corruption of big government.

Reagan's story ought to inspire young people and those who have grown cynical about our country to believe again in the American Dream. People *want* to believe in that dream. They just feel disconnected from it. They want to believe in their leaders. They have had so much nonsense crammed down their throats, had their pocketbooks picked and their intelligence insulted for so long, that they are loath to trust new leaders. America doesn't need another Ronald Reagan. We need to follow Reagan's example so that we can become leaders ourselves. The leaders are *us—all of us*. It's time to unshackle ourselves from government overreach and put power back in our communities, back in our families. We certainly do not need a slicked-back shape-shifter seeking to divide us like Gavin Newsom, who has so mismanaged this wonderful Golden State that millions would leave in an instant if they could.

The best way we can engineer reform in a short period of time is making Hear the People a reality both in Congress and our state. I think Reagan would have loved the idea. It's a powerful tool for putting decision-making back in the hands of people. It's a simple change, radical in its effect but simple to implement. It's a new way of electing representation that turns on personal contact at the grassroots, technology, and instant communication between representatives and their voters. No more celebrities. No more media influence from Fox News or MSNBC. Voter involvement at a microscopic level. Individuals electing their representatives. Knowing them. Electing people based upon their qualifications, leadership ability, and commitment to public service, not just making a buck off of politics.

I believe that if this idea takes hold, it will help break the deadlock of the two-party system. When I dream big, I see a new political party forming around Hear the People. Maybe it'll be called the Citizens Party. Who knows? I'll leave that up to the people. This party would take back representative government from the media and special-interest funders—unions and corporate. The calls for a new party have been coming for a long time. Chicago billionaire Ken Griffin recently called for a new party to be formed solely around education. That's thinking too small. The real issue in education is the influence of special-interest groups who want union control of education and power over the billions of dollars we spend on it. It's the same with the environment, business regulation, and social issues. All of this legislation is based upon the funding of politicians by special-interest groups who vote the way their donors tell them. And the media props up the whole dirty system.

Hear the People and its adjacent political party would cut the knees out from under that system. Over the last two years I've spent writing this book, I believe it's the best solution to putting power back in your hands.

You are smart enough, industrious enough, and wise enough to make decisions about your own life. You certainly can't do worse than our government is doing right now. You can return prosperity to your communities. You can clean up your own streets. You can. You are the one for the job, not some faceless bureaucrat. You can save this country. You *will* save this country. You just need to band together with your fellow citizens, get moving, and never stop once you do.

Now let's get moving. Together.

With deepest respect,
John Cox

BIBLIOGRAPHY

Chapter 3

"15-Day Registration by Political Party." https://elections.cdn.sos.ca.gov/ror/15day-gen-2020/historical-reg-stats.pdf.

"As California Fully Reopens, Governor Newsom Announces Plans to Lift Pandemic Executive Orders." Office of Governor Gavin Newsom. June 11, 2021. https://www.gov.ca.gov/2021/06/11/as-california-fully-reopens-governor-newsom-announces-plans-to-lift-pandemic-executive-orders/.

Bacher, Dan. "Big Ag Billionaires Donate $250,000 to Newsom's Campaign Against Recall." CounterPunch. March 26, 2021. https://www.counterpunch.org/2021/03/26/big-ag-billionaires-donate-250000-to-newsoms-campaign-against-recall/.

Barmann, Jay. "NorCal Woman Has Allegedly Been Collecting Unemployment Benefits in Dianne Feinstein's Name." SFIst. December 18, 2020. https://sfist.com/2020/12/18/norcal-woman-has-allegedly-been-collecting-unemployment-benefits-in-dianne-feinsteins-name/.

Blake, Mike. "The California Recall's Lesson for Republicans." *National Review*. September 15, 2021. https://www.nationalreview.com/2021/09/the-california-recalls-lesson-for-republicans/.

Bond, Paul. "Larry Elder Speaks to Newsweek on Why He Lost to Gavin Newsom and What He May Do Next." Newsweek. September 16, 2021. https://www.newsweek.com/larry-elder-speaks-newsweek-why-he-lost-gavin-newsom-what-he-may-do-next-1630009.

"CA EDD Admits Paying as Much as $31 Billion in Unemployment Funds to Criminals." ABC7 News. January 25, 2021. https://abc7news.com/california-edd-unemployment-fraud-ca-scam-insurance/10011810/.

Cabrera, Tony. "Youth Sports Advocates Rally at High Schools across California, Calling for Resumption of Competition." ABC7. January 16, 2021. https://abc7.com/sports-high-school-covid-coronavirus/9697601/.

"California Roars Back: Governor Newsom Signs $100 Billion California Comeback Plan to Accelerate State's Recovery and Tackle Persistent Challenges." Office of Governor Gavin Newsom. July 12, 2021. https://www.gov.ca.gov/2021/07/12/california-roars-back-governor-newsom-signs-100-billion-california-comeback-plan-to-accelerate-states-recovery-and-tackle-persistent-challenges/.

"Cash for COVID Shots: California Unveils $116 Million Giveaway to People Getting or Already Vaccinated." CBS News Bay Area. May 27, 2021. https://sanfrancisco.cbslocal.com/2021/05/27/covid-vaccine-incentive-plan-california-newsom/.

"Chamath for California Governor." https://www.chamathforca.com/.

Chasmer, Jessica. "Newsom Rally Speaker Calls Larry Elder 'a Black Face on White Supremacy.'" Fox News. September 6, 2021. https://www.foxnews.com/politics/newsom-speaker-larry-elder-black-face-white-supremacy.

Christopher, Ben. "Who's Bankrolling the Newsom Recall Campaigns?" Cal Matters. May 28, 2021. https://calmatters.org/politics/2021/05/newsom-recall-campaigns-funding/.

—"Recall Money Wars: What Do Newsom's Million-Dollar Donors Want?" Cal Matters. August 2, 2021. https://calmatters.org/politics/2021/07/newsom-recall-million-dollar-donors/.

Di Camillo, Mark. "Gubernatorial Recall Election Much Closer Among Voters Considered Most Likely to Participate Than Among the Overall Electorate." Berkeley Institute of Government Studies. July 27, 2021. https://escholarship.org/uc/item/27x9k5qt.

Hanson, Ethan. "Youth Sports Guidelines Updated after 'Let Them Play' Lawsuit Reaches Settlement with State." Redding Record Searchlight. March 4, 2021. https://www.redding.com/story/sports/2021/03/05/cif-schools-follow-guidelines-despite-let-them-play-settlement/4586201001/.

Harkinson, Josh. "Meet the California Couple Who Uses More Water Than Every Home in Los Angeles Combined." *Mother Jones*. August 9, 2016. https://www.motherjones.com/environment/2016/08/lynda-stewart-resnick-california-water/.

Hepler, Lauren, and Stephen Council. "Who Will Pay for All of California's Unemployment Fraud?" *North Coast Journal of Politics, People & Art*. February 23, 2021. https://www.northcoastjournal.com/NewsBlog/archives/2021/02/23/who-will-pay-for-all-of-californias-unemployment-fraud.

Hoeven, Emily. "How Much Will California's EDD Scandal Cost Newsom in the Recall Election?" Palo Alto Online. September 7, 2021. https://www.paloaltoonline.com/news/2021/09/07/how-much-will-californias-edd-scandal-cost-newsom-in-the-recall-election.

"How Does Recalling a California Governor Actually Work? Here's the Process." ABC7 News. May 6, 2021. https://abc7news.com/gavin-newsom-recall-status-petition-sign-online-how-do-you-a-california-governor/10345112/.

Kestenbaum, Sam. "Since This California Church Began Flouting Pandemic Restrictions, Attendance Has Surged." *Washington Post*. February 26, 2021. https://www.washingtonpost.com/religion/2021/02/26/godspeak-calvary-covid-rob-mccoy/.

Kimelman, Jeremia. "Follow the Money: Gavin Newsom Recall Edition." July 28, 2021. https://calmatters.org/politics/2021/05/gavin-newsom-recall-money/.

"Latest Polls of the California Recall Election." FiveThirtyEight. September 14, 2021. https://projects.fivethirtyeight.com/california-recall-polls/.

"Let Them Play: Growing California Coalition Urges Gov. Newsom to Resume Sports." Climate Online. January 29, 2021. https://climaterwc.com/2021/01/29/let-them-play-growing-california-coalition-urges-gov-newsom-to-resume-sports/.

Luna, Taryn. "Photos Raise Doubts About Newsom's Claim That Dinner with Lobbyist Was Outdoors amid COVID-19 Surge." *Los Angeles Times*. November 18, 2020. https://www.latimes.com/california/story/2020-11-18/newsom-french-laundry-dinner-explanation-photos-jason-kinney-california-medical-association-covid-19.

Manoucheri, David. "EDD Backlog and Fraud Timeline: How We Got Here. KCRA. June 23, 2021. https://www.kcra.com/article/edd-backlog-and-fraud-timeline-how-we-got-here-california-unemployment-jobless-covid-19/35312619.

Marinucci, Carla. "Silicon Valley Exec Pumps $100K into Newsom Recall Push." Politico. February 2, 2021. https://www.politico.com/states/california/story/2021/02/02/silicon-valley-exec-pumps-100k-into-newsom-recall-push-1361606.

McGreevy, Patrick. "California Officials Say Unemployment Fraud Now Totals More Than $11 Billion." *Los Angeles Times*. January 25, 2021. https://www.latimes.com/california/story/2021-01-25/california-unemployment-fraud-11-billion-investigations.

McIntyre, Doug. "I Guess I Missed Out on Newsom's Cash Giveaway." *Orange County Register*. June 26, 2021. https://www.ocregister.com/2021/06/26/i-guess-i-missed-out-on-newsoms-cash-giveaway/.

Medina, Jennifer. "California Election Recall Results." *New York Times* September 15, 2021. https://www.nytimes.com/interactive/2021/09/14/us/elections/results-california-recall.html.

Melugin, Bill, and Shelly Insheiwat. "Fox 11 Obtains Exclusive Photos of Gov. Newsom at French Restaurant Allegedly Not Following COVID-19 Protocols." Fox 11 Los Angeles. November 18, 2020. https://www.foxla.com/news/fox-11-obtains-exclusive-photos-of-gov-newsom-at-french-restaurant-allegedly-not-following-covid-19-protocols.

Myers, John. "Essential Politics: Newsom's $100-Billion Budget Plan." *Los Angeles Times*. May 10, 2021. https://www.latimes.com/politics/newsletter/2021-05-10/gavin-newsom-budget-recovery-plan-essential-politics.

"New Study Gives Insight into How Often COVID-19 Spreads Through Households." UNC Gillings School of Global Public Health. August 30, 2021. https://sph.unc.edu/sph-news/new-study-gives-insight-into-how-often-covid-19-spreads-through-households/.

Nixon, Nicole. "California Unemployment Agency Fraud During Pandemic Now Estimated at $20 Billion." CapRadio. October 26, 2021. https://www.capradio.org/articles/2021/10/26/california-unemployment-agency-fraud-during-pandemic-now-estimated-at-20-billion/.

Padilla, Alex. "Recall of Governor Gavin Newsom, Filed by Orrin E. Heatlie: Extension of Time to Circulate Petitions and Revised Calendar of Events." State of California Elections Division. November 17, 2020. https://elections.cdn.sos.ca.gov/ccrov/pdf/2020/november/20251ra.pdf.

Procter, Richard. "Remember When? Timeline Marks Key Events in California's Year-Long Pandemic Grind." Cal Matters. March 4, 2021. https://calmatters.org/health/coronavirus/2021/03/timeline-california-pandemic-year-key-points/.

Rebuild California. "Five Pillars: 4. Self Governance." 2022. https://www.rebuildcalifornia.com/pillars/#pillar-four.

Rescue California. "It's Time to Rescue California." https://rescuecalifornia.org/.

Romo, Vanessa. "California Gov. Newsom Lashes Out at 'Extremist' Republicans, Pledges to Fight Recall." NPR. March 16, 2021. https://www.npr.org/2021/03/15/977648661/california-gov-newsom-lashes-out-at-extremist-republicans-pledges-to-fight-recal.

Ronayne, Kathleen. "Meet Orrin Heatlie, the Ex-Cop Leading the Push to Recall California Gov. Gavin Newsom," *The Desert Sun*. April 1, 2021. https://www.desertsun.com/story/news/politics/elections/2021/04/01/who-orrin-heatlie-ex-cop-leading-recall-gov-gavin-newsom/4836932001/.

Roos, Meghan. "Gavin Newsom Under Renewed Fire Over French Laundry Lobbyist as Recall Bid Gains Strength." Newsweek. December 31, 2020. https://www.newsweek.com/gavin-newsom-under-renewed-fire-over-french-laundry-lobbyist-recall-bid-gains-steam-1558396.

— "What the French Laundry Has to Do with Gavin Newsom's Recall Election." Newsweek. September 9, 2021. https://www.newsweek.com/what-french-laundry-has-do-gavin-newsoms-recall-election-1627282.

Roosevelt, Margot. "Despite Gradual Reopening, California's Unemployment Rate Remains Stagnant." June 19, 2020. https://www.latimes.com/business/story/2020-06-19/coronavirus-unemployment-california-jobs-may.

Rosenhall, Laura, and Sameea Kamal. "Newsom Overwhelmingly Defeats California Recall Attempt." Cal Matters. October 22, 2021. https://calmatters.org/politics/2021/09/california-recall-election-newsom/.

Rott, Nathan. "California Issues 1st Rolling Blackouts Since 2001 as Heat Wave Bakes Western U.S." NPR. August 15, 2020. https://www.npr.org/2020/08/15/902781690/california-issues-first-rolling-blackouts-since-2001-as-heat-wave-bakes-western-.

San Diego Union-Tribune Editorial Board. "Criminals Got Billions in Jobless Benefits They Didn't Deserve as Hundreds of Thousands of Needy Californians Were Stuck in Backlogs. *San Diego Union-Tribune*. October 28, 2021. https://www.sandiegouniontribune.com/opinion/editorials/story/2021-10-28/newsom-indelibly-stained-by-double-barreled-fiasco-at-employment-development-department.

Shannon, Chelsea. "A Timeline of California in the Coronavirus Pandemic." ABC10. March 19, 2021. https://www.abc10.com/article/news/health/coronavirus/covid-19-timeline-pandemic/103-03046184-ed02-498b-b6d0-795a60646c6b.

Siders, David, and Carla Marinucci. "How Gavin Newsom Beat the Recall." Politico. September 15, 2021. https://www.politico.com/states/california/story/2021/09/15/how-gavin-newsom-beat-the-recall-1391015.

Siders, David. "The Three Men Who Could Take Down Gavin Newsom." Politico. March 19, 2021. https://www.politico.com/news/magazine/2021/03/19/gavin-newsom-recall-476746.

Smith, Erika D. "Larry Elder Is the Black Face of White Supremacy. You've Been Warned." *Los Angeles Times*. August 20, 2021. https://www.latimes.com/california/story/2021-08-20/recall-candidate-larry-elder-is-a-threat-to-black-californians.

Thompson, Don. "Court Upholds California Governor's Use of Emergency Powers." Associated Press. May 5, 2021. https://apnews.com/article/california-coronavirus-pandemic-health-fb75c1e0906e8867ac16fa84460e8473.

White, Jeremy B. "Opponent of Newsom Church Restrictions Identified as California Recall Donor." Politico. January 5, 2021. https://www.politico.com/states/california/story/2021/01/05/opponent-of-newsom-church-restrictions-identified-as-california-recall-donor-1352561.

Willon, Phil. "Gavin Newsom Recall Effort Faces 'Dark Money' Complaint Over Alleged Hidden Donors." *Los Angeles Times*. January 4, 2021. https://www.latimes.com/california/story/2021-01-04/california-campaign-watchdog-complaint-newsom-recall.

Chapter 5

Ayres, Sabra. "Californians Moving to Texas to Find Cheaper Homes, More Space." Spectrum News 1. October 21, 2021. https://spectrumlocalnews.com/tx/south-texas-el-paso/news/2021/10/20/californians-moving-to-texas-to-find-cheaper-homes--more-space.

Bazelon, Emily, and Jennifer Medina. "He's Remaking Criminal Justice in L.A. But How Far Is Too Far?" *New York Times Magazine*. November 17, 2021. https://www.nytimes.com/2021/11/17/magazine/george-gascon-los-angeles.html.

Caporal, Jack, and Lyle Daly. "Average House Price by State in 2023." The Ascent. May 11, 2023. https://www.fool.com/the-ascent/research/average-house-price-state/.

El Dorado County District Attorney's Office. "Guest Column: New California Epidemic—Mass Looting." *Mountain Democrat*. December 8, 2021. https://www.mtdemocrat.com/opinion/guest-column-new-california-epidemic-mass-looting/.

Fulton, William. "It Seems Like All of California Is Moving to Texas. Is That True?" Rice University Kinder Institute for Urban Research. March 2, 2021. https://kinder.rice.edu/urbanedge/it-seems-all-california-moving-texas-true.

"Gov. Gavin Newsom on Looting, Smash-and-Grab Robberies: 'We Want People Prosecuted.'" CBS News. November 22, 2021. https://sanfrancisco.cbslocal.com/2021/11/22/crime-victim-gov-gavin-newson-smash-and-grabs-we-prosecution/.

Gutierrez, Melody. "Bay Area Hit with Spate of Large-Scale Smash-and-Grab Robberies." *Los Angeles Times*. November 21, 2021. https://www.latimes.com/california/story/2021-11-21/bay-area-hit-with-spate-of-large-scale-smash-and-grab-robberies.

Jankowicz, Mia. "Timeline Shows the Spree of Smash-and-Grab Robberies—Mostly in California—Stripping Stores and Terrifying Staff." *Business Insider*. November 24, 2021. https://www.

businessinsider.com/timeline-stores-raided-thieves-macys-nordstrom-california-2021-11.

"Judge Rules Mostly in Favor of LA County Prosecutors' Union in Lawsuit against DA Gascon over Reforms." ABC7. February 8, 2021. https://abc7.com/george-gascon-lawsuit-prosecutors-los-angeles-county/10322037/.

Karimi, Faith. "Why Some US Cities Are Facing a Spree of 'Smash-and-Grab' Crimes." CNN. November 24, 2021. https://www.cnn.com/2021/11/23/us/smash-and-grab-thefts-explainer-cec/index.html.

Kiszla, Cameron, and Jennifer McGraw. "'We Will...Do Everything We Can to Put You in Jail': Beverly Hills Police Chief Continues to Push Back on Crime Spree." KTLA5 News. December 12, 2021. https://ktla.com/news/local-news/we-will-do-everything-we-can-to-put-you-in-jail-beverly-hills-police-chief-continues-to-push-back-on-crime-spree/.

Kurzweil, Tony, and Eric Spillman. "'When You Wrestle with a Pig, You Both Get Muddy,' L.A. County DA Says amid Feud with Sheriff Villanueva." KTLA 5 News. December 9, 2021. https://ktla.com/news/when-you-wrestle-with-a-pig-you-both-get-muddy-l-a-county-da-says-amid-feud-with-sheriff-villanueva/.

Mooney, Michael. "Why People Are Moving to Texas from California." Axios Dallas. October 7, 2021. https://www.axios.com/local/dallas/2021/10/07/texas-california-economics-moving-census.

Chapter 8

Fritts, Janelle. "State Corporate Income Tax Rates and Brackets for 2023." Tax Foundation. January 23, 2023. https://taxfoundation.org/publications/state-corporate-income-tax-rates-and-brackets/.

Lopez, Julianna. "The 10 Best (and Worst) States for Small Business Taxes." Business News Daily. February 21, 2023. https://www.businessnewsdaily.com/9898-best-states-business-taxes.html.

Chapter 10

Ward, Ethan. "Understanding LA's Homelessness Issues." LAist. September 9, 2021. https://laist.com/news/housing-homelessness/understanding-homelessness-city-los-angeles.

Chapter 21

Bernick, Michael. "The Tech Aristocracy's 'Guaranteed Income,' and a Jobs-Based Alternative." *Forbes*. June 2, 2021. https://www.forbes.com/sites/michaelbernick/2021/06/02/the-tech-aristocracys-guaranteed-income-and-a-jobs-based-alternative/?sh=6634507358c0.

Bishop III, Barney. "Barney Bishop: Joe Biden and the Left's Energy Policy Would Lead to the Californication of America." *Florida Daily*. October 29, 2020. https://www.floridadaily.com/barney-bishop-joe-biden-and-the-lefts-energy-policy-would-lead-to-the-californication-of-america/.

Brannon, Ike. "California's Pension Woes Are Made Worse by Moving Emergency Services in House." *Forbes*. February 28, 2021. https://www.forbes.com/sites/ikebrannon/2021/02/28/californias-pension-woes-are-made-worse-by-moving-emergency-services-in-house/?sh=7867ec723629.

Brocious, Ariana. "Looking Back at SB 1070 a Decade Later." AZPM. August 7, 2020. https://news.azpm.org/p/news-articles/2020/8/7/178119-looking-back-at-sb-1070-a-decade-later/.

Brode, Noah. "The Makings of Pennsylvania's Pension Funding Crisis." WESA. May 15, 2013. https://www.wesa.fm/politics-government/2013-05-15/the-makings-of-pennsylvanias-pension-funding-crisis.

"California State Legislature." Ballotpedia. https://ballotpedia.org/California_State_Legislature.

Cowan, Jill. "Why California Is Planning to Ban Fracking." *New York Times*. May 4, 2021. https://www.nytimes.com/2021/05/04/us/california-ban-fracking.html.

"Economy at a Glance." U.S. Bureau of Labor Statistics. https://www.bls.gov/eag/eag.ca.htm.

"Florida's Racist Anti-Immigrant Bill Overturned in Federal Court." Southern Poverty Law Center. September 22, 2021. https://www.splcenter.org/presscenter/floridas-racist-anti-immigrant-bill-overturned-federal-court.

Frey, William H. "Less than Half of US Children under 15 Are White, Census Shows." Brookings. June 24, 2019. https://www.brookings.edu/articles/less-than-half-of-us-children-under-15-are-white-census-shows/.

Gilroy, Leonard, Zachary Christensen, and Steven Gassenberger. "Analysis of Texas Senate Bill 321." Reason Foundation. May 5, 2021. https://reason.org/policy-study/texas-senate-bill-321-analysis/.

Gonyea, Don. "House Democrats Pass Bill that Would Protect Worker Organizing Efforts." NPR. March 9, 2021. https://www.npr.org/2021/03/09/975259434/house-democrats-pass-bill-that-would-protect-worker-organizing-efforts.

"Governor Newsom Signs Suite of Legislation to Support California's Immigrant Communities and Remove Outdated Term "Alien" from State Codes." Office of Governor Gavin Newsom. September 24, 2021. https://www.gov.ca.gov/2021/09/24/governor-newsom-signs-suite-of-legislation-to-support-californias-immigrant-communities-and-remove-outdated-term-alien-from-state-codes/.

"Governor Ron DeSantis Signs SB 168: Federal Immigration Enforcement." Office of Governor Ron DeSantis. June 14, 2019. https://www.flgov.com/2019/06/14/governor-ron-desantis-signs-sb-168-federal-immigration-enforcement/.

"Governor Ron DeSantis Takes Action to Protect Floridians from the Dangerous Impacts of the Biden Border Crisis." Office of Governor Ron DeSantis. September 28, 2021. https://www.flgov.

com/2021/09/28/governor-ron-desantis-takes-action-to-protect-floridians-from-the-dangerous-impacts-of-the-biden-border-crisis/.

Greenblatt, Alan. "How California Is Turning the Rest of the West Blue." NPR. August 29, 2013. https://www.npr.org/sections/itsallpolitics/2013/08/29/216150644/how-california-is-turning-the-rest-of-the-west-blue.

Greenhut, Steven. "The PRO Act: California Is Coming for You." R Street. March 18, 2021. https://www.rstreet.org/commentary/the-pro-act-california-is-coming-for-you/.

Halper, Evan, and Anna M. Phillips. "California Officials See Boon in Biden's Climate Plan." *Los Angeles Times*. October 19, 2020. https://www.latimes.com/politics/story/2020-10-19/bidens-climate-agenda-would-be-a-boon-for-california.

Halper, Evan. "Make America California Again? That's Biden's Plan." *Los Angeles Times*. January 17, 2021. https://www.latimes.com/politics/story/2021-01-17/make-america-california-again-how-biden-will-try.

Herrington, Eldrid. "What Happened?: Arizona Turned Blue in the 2020 Presidential Election, but the Republicans Still Control the State." Phelan US Centre. January 21, 2021. https://blogs.lse.ac.uk/usappblog/2021/01/21/what-happened-arizona-turned-blue-in-the-2020-presidential-election-but-the-republicans-still-control-the-state/.

Hill, Bryce. "Hidden Pension 'Tax' Costs Each Illinoisan More Than $1,400 per Year." Illinois Policy. March 2, 2021. https://www.illinoispolicy.org/hidden-pension-tax-costs-each-illinoisan-more-than-1400-per-year/.

Hooks, Christopher. "Californians Could Ruin Texas—But Not the Way You Might Think." *Texas Monthly* (March 2021). https://www.texasmonthly.com/news-politics/californians-could-ruin-texas-but-not-the-way-you-might-think/.

I&I Editorial Board, "Don't 'Californicate' the Rest of America." *Issues & Insights*. November 19, 2020. https://issuesinsights.com/2020/11/19/dont-californicate-the-rest-of-america/.

—"Get Ready for the Californication of America." *Issues & Insights*. January 7, 2021. https://issuesinsights.com/2021/01/07/get-ready-for-the-californication-of-america/.

Ivanova, Irina. "California's Gig Worker Law Will Mostly Affect Non-Gig Workers." CBS News. September 13, 2019. https://www.cbsnews.com/news/california-ab5-will-affect-much-more-than-uber/.

Kettmann, Steve. "The Californization of America." *New York Times*. June 2, 2018. https://www.nytimes.com/2018/06/02/opinion/sunday/california-progressive-politics.html.

Kim, Young. "The PRO Act Nationalizes the Worst of California's Policies." The Hill. March 17, 2021. https://thehill.com/blogs/congress-blog/economy-budget/543556-the-pro-act-nationalizes-the-worst-of-californias-policies/.

Kotkin, Joel. "Fully Oligarchic Luxury Californication." The American Mind. June 28, 2021. https://americanmind.org/salvo/fully-oligarchic-luxury-californication/.

Larma, Jacqueline. "Pennsylvanians Pay Extra for Public Pensions." *Philadelphia Inquirer*. April 24, 2021. https://www.inquirer.com/business/psers-teachers-cost-deficit-shared-risk-sers-pension-20210424.html.

Leins, Casey. "These States Require Schools to Teach LGBT History." U.S. News and World Report. August 14, 2019. https://www.usnews.com/news/best-states/articles/2019-08-14/states-that-require-schools-to-teach-lgbt-history.

Lucas, Scott. "How California Gave Us Trumpism." Politico. April 18, 2017. https://www.politico.com/magazine/story/2017/04/how-california-gave-us-trumpism-215038/.

Marcus, Samantha. "N.J.'s Public Worker Pension Shortfall Got Even Bigger Last Year. Here's Why." New Jersey. May 14, 2021. https://

www.nj.com/politics/2021/05/njs-public-worker-pension-shortfall-got-even-bigger-last-year-heres-why.html.

Montanaro, Domenico. "How the Browning of America Is Upending Both Political Parties." NPR. October 12, 2016. https://www.npr.org/2016/10/12/497529936/how-the-browning-of-america-is-upending-both-political-parties.

Moritz, John C. "Gov. Greg Abbott, 10 GOP Governors to Talk in South Texas about Immigration Policies." *Austin American-Statesman*. October 5, 2021. https://www.statesman.com/story/news/2021/10/05/gov-abbott-gop-governors-talk-south-texas-immigration-policies/6011065001/.

Mulcahy, Shawn. "Overhaul to Texas State Government Employees' Retirement Accounts Advanced out of Legislature." *The Texas Tribune*. May 26, 2021. https://www.texastribune.org/2021/05/26/texas-government-employee-retirement-system/.

Murphy, Katy, and Eleanor Mueller. "California Labor Secretary in Serious Contention for Biden Cabinet." Politico. December 10, 2020. https://www.politico.com/states/california/story/2020/12/10/california-labor-secretary-in-serious-contention-for-biden-cabinet-1345100.

Petrucelli, Dennis. "Ronald Reagan Tried to Warn Us about Danger of Socialism." *Villages-News*. December 19, 2019. https://www.villages-news.com/2019/12/19/ronald-reagan-tried-to-warn-us-about-danger-of-socialism/.

Pollack, Lynn. "Here Are the States that Will Gain the Most under Biden's Infrastructure Bill." Globest. November 29, 2021. https://www.globest.com/2021/11/29/here-are-the-states-that-will-gain-the-most-under-bidens-infrastructure-bill/?slreturn=20230605023548.

Probasco, Jim. "Understanding Infrastructure Legislation." Investopedia. May 27, 2023. https://www.investopedia.com/here-s-what-s-in-the-usd1-trillion-infrastructure-bill-passed-by-the-senate-5196817.

Ring, Edward. "Newsom's Public Education Spending Binge." *California Globe*. May 18, 2021. https://californiaglobe.com/articles/newsoms-public-education-spending-binge/.

"San Diego, California, Proposition B, Changes to Retirement Plans for City Employees Initiative (June 2012)." Ballotpedia. https://ballotpedia.org/San_Diego,_California,_Proposition_B,_Changes_to_Retirement_Plans_for_City_Employees_Initiative_(June_2012).

Schwartz, Sarah. "Map: Where Critical Race Theory Is under Attack." Education Week. June 11, 2021. https://www.edweek.org/policy-politics/map-where-critical-race-theory-is-under-attack/2021/06.

Sherman, Natalie. "How California Is Changing the US." BBC News. October 16, 2018. https://www.bbc.com/news/business-45767736.

Soneshein, Raphael J. "California's Political Standing among Democrats a Big Winner in Gavin Newsom's Recall Victory." The Conversation. September 15, 2021. https://theconversation.com/californias-political-standing-among-democrats-a-big-winner-in-gavin-newsoms-recall-victory-167947.

"Stop the PRO Act." U.S. Chamber of Commerce. https://www.uschamber.com/major-initiative/stop-the-pro-act.

"Summary of Cost Estimate for H.R. 5376, the Build Back Better Act." Congressional Budget Office. November 18, 2021. https://www.cbo.gov/publication/57627.

Suneson, Grant. "Every State's Pension Crisis Ranked." 24/7 Wall Street. December 4, 2020. https://247wallst.com/special-report/2020/12/04/every-states-pension-crisis-ranked-3/10/.

Thompson, Derek. "American Migration Patterns Should Terrify the GOP." *The Atlantic*. September 17, 2019. https://www.theatlantic.com/ideas/archive/2019/09/american-migration-patterns-should-terrify-gop/598153/.

Walters, Dan. "California's Immense Pension Dilemma." CalMatters. August 10, 2020. https://calmatters.org/commentary/dan-walters/2020/08/california-court-pension-debt-unfunded/.

Wong, Peter. "Good and Bad News for Oregon's Public Pension System." *Hillsboro NewsTimes*. January 14, 2020. https://www.hillsboronewstimes.

com/news/good-and-bad-news-for-oregons-public-pension-system/article_6cab97c4-2321-5ec0-aeae-3442eda23570.html.

Zickgraf, Ryan. "The Biden Administration Is the Californication of the Democratic Party." *Jacobin*. January 28, 2021. https://jacobin.com/2021/01/california-democrats-corporate-liberalism-biden.

Chapter 22

Baldassare, Mark, Dean Bonner, Rachel Lawler, and Deja Thomas. "PPIC Statewide Survey: Californians and Their Government." Public Policy Institute of California. February 2022. https://www.ppic.org/publication/ppic-statewide-survey-californians-and-their-government-february-2022/.

— "PPIC Statewide Survey: Californians and Their Government." Public Policy Institute of California. March 2022. https://www.ppic.org/publication/ppic-statewide-survey-californians-and-their-government-march-2022/.

"California Residential Rent and Rental Statistics." Department of Numbers. https://www.deptofnumbers.com/rent/california/.

"California Sales Tax Rates." Avalara. https://www.avalara.com/taxrates/en/state-rates/california.html#:~:text=California%20sales%20tax%20details,be%20as%20high%20as%2010.25%25.

"California State Legislature." Ballotpedia. https://ballotpedia.org/California_State_Legislature.

"Census Bureau Releases New Data on Minority-Owned, Veteran-Owned, and Women-Owned Businesses." United States Census Bureau. October 28, 2021. https://www.census.gov/newsroom/press-releases/2021/characteristics-of-employer-businesses.html#:~:text=According%20to%20the%202020%20Annual,(331%2C151)%20of%20all%20businesses.

Daigneau, Elizabeth. "What We Can Learn from New Hampshire Politics." Governing. October 3, 2013. https://www.governing.

com/archive/gov-what-we-can-learn-new-hampshire-politics.html.

Dennison, Sean. "How Rich Is Bernie Sanders?" GOBankingRates. July 23, 2021. https://www.gobankingrates.com/net-worth/politicians/bernie-sanders-money/.

Gill, Dee. "As Home Prices Soar Elsewhere, California Starts to Seem Almost Reasonable." *UCLA Anderson Review*. December 15, 2021. https://anderson-review.ucla.edu/as-home-prices-soar-elsewhere-california-starts-to-seem-almost-reasonable/#:~:text=The%20researchers%20note%20that%20a,including%20a%20%24160%2C000%20down%20payment.

"Immigrants in New Hampshire." American Immigration Council. August 6, 2020. https://www.americanimmigrationcouncil.org/research/immigrants-in-new-hampshire.

Lee, Iris, and Christina Bellatoni. "California's Members of Congress Are Worth at Least $439 Million." *Los Angeles Times*. March 5, 2018. https://www.latimes.com/politics/la-pol-ca-richest-california-lawmakers-20180305-story.html.

Lee, Iris, and Los Angeles Times Staff. "California Sends 20 Millionaires to Congress. Here's What We Know about Their Fortunes. *Los Angeles Times*. March 5, 2018. https://www.latimes.com/projects/how-much-are-they-worth/.

"New Hampshire Crime." Neighborhood Scout. https://www.neighborhoodscout.com/nh/crime.

"New Hampshire Rent as a Fraction of Income." Department of Numbers. https://www.deptofnumbers.com/rent/new-hampshire/#:~:text=For%20New%20Hampshire%2C%20median%20monthly,2019%20according%20to%20the%20ACS.

"QuickFacts California." United States Census Bureau. July 1, 2022. https://www.census.gov/quickfacts/CA.

Schrag, Peter. "Political Corruption Nothing New in California." *San Diego Union-Tribune*. April 12, 2014. https://www.sandiegouniontribune.

com/opinion/commentary/sdut-political-corruption-california-2014apr12-story.html.

Stebbins, Samuel. "This Is the Average Cost of a Home in New Hampshire." 24/7 Wall Street. https://247wallst.com/state/this-is-the-average-cost-of-a-home-in-new-hampshire-2/.

"Taxes in New Hampshire." Tax Foundation. https://taxfoundation.org/state/new-hampshire/#:~:text=New%20Hampshire%20has%20a%20flat,not%20levy%20local%20sales%20taxes.

"The Citizen Legislature." *Civics 101*. New Hampshire Public Radio. May 2, 2019. https://beta.prx.org/stories/302156.

"The General Court of New Hampshire." State of New Hampshire. https://www.gencourt.state.nh.us/.

Tindera, Michela. "How Elizabeth Warren Built a $12 Million Fortune." *Forbes*. August 20, 2019. https://www.forbes.com/sites/michelatindera/2019/08/20/how-elizabeth-warren-built-a-12-million-fortune/?sh=20bb8d14ab57.

"Topics of Interest in New Hampshire." CitizensCount. https://www.citizenscount.org/topic.

Zarzycki, Nicholas. "The Small Business Owner's Guide to California State Taxes." *Bench*. August 12, 2022. https://bench.co/blog/tax-tips/california-state-taxes/#v5mi-b.

ACKNOWLEDGMENTS

I want to acknowledge all those who have helped me along the way—my family of course, my work associates, my clients and investors and of course, those who have been directly involved in this book, including Kai Flanders, Mark Halperin, Fred Davis, Dan Schnur and those wonderful folks that participated in my many efforts to change the politics of Illinois and California, two grossly mismanaged and wonderful states who will benefit mightily from leadership that is not compromised by the lure of money or the siren song of media fame.

ABOUT THE AUTHOR

John H. Cox is an attorney, CPA and investment adviser who has started five successful small businesses but has also devoted a major part of his life to both charitable and political endeavors. A devoted father of four wonderful daughters and husband of Sarah Hall Cox, he has run unsuccessfully for several offices, taking on difficult efforts in states and locales that desperately needed better leadership but due to corruption and media influence have entrenched difficulties that made his efforts uphill to say the least. Raised by a single mother who was a librarian and teacher in the Chicago Public School system, Cox never forgot his roots or his mother's admonition to make a difference in this great country. Cox is an honors graduate of the University of Illinois (BA Political Science and Accounting, 1976) as well as a graduate with high honors from IIT/Chicago Kent College of Law. He is the author of law review articles as well as a book, Politics, Inc, which argues for electing statesmen rather than career politicians.

Made in the USA
Monee, IL
21 November 2023

47063918R00184